William Patten

Eyes of Molluscs and Arthropods

William Patten

Eyes of Molluscs and Arthropods

ISBN/EAN: 9783337890247

Printed in Europe, USA, Canada, Australia, Japan

Cover: Foto ©ninafisch / pixelio.de

More available books at **www.hansebooks.com**

Eyes of Molluscs and Arthropods.

By

William Patten,
from Boston, U. S. America.

With Plate 28—32.

Introduction.

The following studies were begun at the Zoological Station in Naples late in the Spring of 1885, and were continued with several interruptions until the following January.

It is difficult to express my gratitude to the Director and Assistants of the Zoological Station for the personal kindness shown towards me; to do it in words would sound extravagant to those who did not understand the peculiar circumstances. It is with mingled feelings of humiliation and admiration, that I contrast the uncertain and hesitating support given by Americans to such a purely scientific undertaking, with the frank and generous manner in which Americans have been invariably treated by the Director of this institution. Whatever may be the reasons, or apologies that could be offered for such a condition, I sincerely hope and trust it will not remain so long.

It was my intention, originally, to study the anatomy and development of the eye of *Pecten*, hoping to find some explanation for the presence of such a large number of highly developed eyes — if indeed they were such — in an animal which, apparently, could make no special use of them.

Accepting the modern theories of evolution, we are brought to a stand-still in attempting to apply this method of reasoning to the origin of the eyes of *Pecten*. There can be no doubt that structurally, they are as perfectly adapted for seeing as those of the Cephalopods. But while two eyes are sufficient for the latter animals, *Pecten*, whose complex of activities is far less intricate, is provided with nearly fifty times as many! It is absurd to suppose that these inactive creatures, with hardly a trace of the higher animal functions, should n e e d a hundred eyes. But if they are not necessary, how could they have been developed by natural selection? Even supposing them once developed, they must be an enormous vital expense for which the animal gets no return. It is contrary to all our conceptions of evolution, to suppose that these expensive organs can be long sustained without some beneficial return to the animal. But they must have developed once, and we may be sure they did not spring into existence, Minerva-like, armed with all the functional powers their complicated structures would indicate. What factors, then, could force the development of these organs to their present height, and sustain them there? That was the question which first induced me to study these eyes more closely; the facts related in the following pages furnish, I believe, a partial solution to the problem.

I desire to say a word in justification of certain statements, to be made in the following paper, which may appear too dogmatical, or without sufficient foundation in fact. I am, I believe, perfectly conscious of the uncertain ground upon which I tread. That my statements concerning the original function of the ommatidia, of the eye, and of animal pigment, are positive, is just what I desired. Facts must be tested in two ways: first, by observation, and second, by their »touch-stone« properties. An observation that explains nothing is no more a fact, than an explanation founded upon nothing. In this paper, I have attempted to apply the same principle. I consider my observations as worthless without their »better halves«, the deductions. My observations have been tested by their ability to support reasonable deductions. It is not a theory that I have tried to make, nor observations, but to marry theory to observation, to obtain facts.

Positive statements have been made for several reasons: first, for the benefit of the reader, that he may understand what I consider to be the signification of the observations; he may then reject, or accept them as he sees fit; secondly, because, I believe, to weigh an observation with this and with that, and after a long discussion come to the conclusion that we know nothing at all about it, only burdens to no purpose the already overladen literature, and might better have been left undone.

I hope the reader will treat my deductions in the same spirit that they were given. not as dogmatic statements, but as tests of observations.

From the unsatisfactory results obtained by the study of *Pecten* alone, I was led into other fields where I should have been working still, if circumstances had not obliged me to bring this paper to a close.

The arrangement of these pages does not follow the order in which the observations were made, nor any system, except that which appeared to lead up to a better understanding of the more complicated eyes.

My studies upon the Arthropods have led me to conclusions as widely different from those of GRENACHER as could possibly be the case, even in such complicated structures as the Arthropod eyes. I have the more faith in the observations, since they lead to the reduction of the essential parts of all visual organs to one structural plan, which can be followed through the whole animal kingdom, from the lowest to the highest.

I have endeavored, first of all, to obtain as accurate a histological knowledge as possible of any one eye: upon this knowledge I have based my conclusions concerning those of other groups or genera.

GRENACHER's ideas have received such universal acceptance, that it is almost entirely with him I have to deal. But my own observations, and the interpretation I put upon them, differ so widely from his, that it is impossible to accept his terminology without great confusion. Whenever it was possible, I used old names rather than invent new ones: but in many cases, I was obliged to adopt the latter course. In the following, the meaning of the new terms, and the added or modified signification attached to the old, will be explained.

In many places upon the Molluscan hypodermis, especially those parts exposed to the light, the cuticula is divided into two layers, an outer structureless one, the corneal cuticula, and an inner layer, the retinidial cuticula, filled with the retia terminalia, or ultimate ramifications of the hypodermic nerves.

The ommatidia (Pl. 32, figs. 128, 132 etc.), or structural elements of all eyes, consist of from 2 to 4 colorless cells, the retinophorae (*n. rf.*), surrounded by a circle of pigmented ones, or retinulae (*pg.*).

The cuticular secretion of each cell forms a rod, containing a specialized part of the retia terminalia, or retinidium.

In the more specialized ommatidia, the rods of the retinulae disappear, leaving the double (Molluscs, Worms etc.) and quadruple (crystalline cone of Arthropods) rods of the retinophorae.

The apposed walls of the retinophorae disappear to a greater or less extent, so that the nerve fibres between the cells come to lie in the centre of the group, and constitute the axial nerve (Pl. 32, *ax. n*).

The retinulae become modified at certain levels into pigmented swellings for the protection of corresponding parts of the retinophorae: the remaining parts are reduced to colorless and hyaline rods, the bacilli *bc*.

The retinophorae in the Arthropods are expanded at their outer ends to form the calyx (fig. 128, *c. c.*) containing the crystalline cone. The attenuated inner ends are united to form a hollow tube, the style, (fig. 128 *st.*); the expansion of the inner end of the style, the rhabdom of GRENACHER, is called the pedicel (*pd*).

The fused, membranous, outer continuations of the inner row of retinulae constitute the sheath of the calyx (fig. 128 rt^2).

The compound Arthropod eye consists of a double layer: a thin outer one, the corneal hypodermis, secreting the corneal facets (fig. 128 *c. hy.*); and a thick inner, or ommateal layer, consisting of the united ommatidia.

A retineum (fig. 132) is a collection of ommatidia in which the retinidia of both retinulae and retinophorae, or of the latter alone, form a continuous layer, the retinulae retaining their pigment and primitive arrangement around the retinophorae: e. g. invaginate eyes of all Molluscs (except *Pecten*).

An ommateum (figs. 133 and 138) is a group of ommatidia in which the retinidia, produced by the retinophorae alone, are completely isolated: e. g. the compound eyes of Arthropods and Molluscs. A retina (fig. 140) is composed of a group of ommatidia in which the retinulae have lost their rods and are transformed into pigmentless ganglionic cells; e. g. *Pecten* and Vertebrates.

The term ommerythrine, I have applied to the red pigment in all eyes, whether confined to the rods alone, to the retinulae, or to the underlying tapetum.

Chapter I. Mollusca.

Arca.

Arca Noae, and in fact all the species of this genus which I have examined, are extremely timid animals, the slightest disturbance being sufficient to cause them to close their shells for two or three hours. One unconsciously associates with nearly all Molluscs great stupidity and sluggishness; I was, therefore, surprised to see how quickly specimens of *Arca Noae* closed their shells whenever a slight shadow was cast upon them. If, for instance, an aquarium containing one of these animals is placed in a room well lighted from both sides, and a hand put in front of the glass (care being taken to avoid any jar or shock to the water), a faint shadow will be cast on the animal, sufficient, in spite of its indistinctness, to cause it to close its shell with remarkable quickness, but always one or two seconds afterward, the promptitude depending upon the depth of the shadow. The sensitiveness and rapidity of reaction depend also upon the vitality of the animals, always being less in those which have been for some time in confinement, yet still so great, that those kept two or three months in small aquaria, with no special provision for food, n e v e r failed to close the shell when a shadow was thrown upon them. Still other simple experiments show that it is not necessary to cast a shadow upon them, in order to prove that they have organs specially sensitive to light. If, for instance, an ordinary, black lead pencil, or any other equally small object, is approached with extreme caution within two and a half or three inches of the anterior end of the open shell, and in such a position that no p e r c e p t i b l e shadow falls upon the animal, it at once closes its shell, and with the same energy as when a deep shadow is cast upon it. If, on the other hand, a glass rod is brought within the same distance of, or even much nearer to, the anterior end of the open shell, and moved quite rapidly to and fro, n o e f f e c t is p r o d u c e d u p o n t h e m u s s e l. The last experiment shows that, in the trial with the pencil, the closing of the shell was not produced by the disturbance of the water, since in the former experiment care was used to avoid that effect, while in the latter, even a decided agitation produced no result. All three experiments — with the shadow, a small dark object, and a small transparent one, — were repeated at least twenty-five or thirty times with different animals, and under different circumstances, and invariably gave the results related above. Moreover, I have watched the animals many times for extended periods, but have never seen them close the shell, unless startled by some sudden change in the intensity of light, or by shocks or disturbance of the water in which they were.

I have not made any experiments upon *Arca barbata* or *A. tetragona*.

It is only reasonable to suppose that the organs of vision, which by the foregoing experiments we have proved to exist in *Arca*, must be situated upon that portion most exposed to the light: and, indeed, such is really the case, for on examining the exposed part of the mantle edge, one readily sees, with an ordinary hand lens, innumerable, small pigment spots, which, upon closer inspection, prove to be highly organized eyes. But before we describe more minutely these interesting organs, it will be well to give a general idea of that portion of the mantle upon which they are located.

In all the species examined, the same division of the mantle edge into **shell**, **ophthalmic**, and **velar fold** was found (Pl. 30, figs. 55 and 56), all three extending along the entire edge of the mantle. In sections, one sees that the shell, or outer fold[1], whose inner wall is slightly thickened, is thin and deep (*s. h. f.*). The ophthalmic fold (*o. f.*) is somewhat thicker and taller than the former; its free end is thickened and bears the eyes. It is usually covered with dense, dark brown or black pigment, most abundant on the branchial side. The velar fold is the largest, (*v.*) although very insignificant when compared with that of *Pecten*, and is covered with dark brown pigment, specially abundant at the anterior, and posterior portion of the mantle.

The velum of *Arca barbata* is well developed and forms a thin, narrow and colorless band in the middle of the mantle, while towards the anterior end it becomes deeply pigmented on both sides, and more than twice as broad as before.

In all three species, the anterior portion is especially thickened and completely covered with a coat of dark brown, or black pigment, the intensity of which seems to depend upon the health of the individual animal, and always diminishes with prolonged confinement. If the edge of the mantle be now examined with a pocket lens, a nearly regular row of dark brown spots will be seen, arranged along the summit of the ophthalmic fold, larger near the pigmented anterior and posterior thickenings, but smaller and much more numerous in the median portions. None are to be found near the hinge, on the last centimetre of the anterior and posterior edge of the mantle. These eyes may be divided into three kinds, the **faceted**, the **invaginate**, and the **pseudo-lenticulate** eyes, the first named being the most highly developed. They form slightly flattened, hemispherical elevations of the epidermis, confined to the anterior and posterior thickenings of the mantle.

The surface of the elevations appears to consist of a varying number (10—80) of perfectly transparent and refractive lenticular projections of the cuticula, which, when viewed from above, appear like

---

[1] In speaking of the mantle, the inner surface means towards the branchial cavity, and the outer toward the adjacent shell.

perfectly round, black holes, separated from each other by chocolate brown pigment. The statement of WILL is perfectly justifiable. that »one might name them aggregate eyes, for they have all the characteristics of those compound eyes, which we are accustomed to designate by that name.«

In one example of *Arca Noae*, 8,5 cm long, I have counted 133 faceted eyes in the left mantle edge. and 102 in the other. In the upper edge, I have counted 30 in the first centimetre, and 37, 18 and 10 successively in the three following. Then comes a wide space without faceted eyes, succeeded by three centimetres, each containing 14. 20 and 4 eyes respectively.

I have said that these eyes were arranged at perfectly regular intervals, this is, however, not strictly true, although, when observed with a hand lens, such is the general effect produced. One often sees two eyes so close together that they form one large, oval and double eye spot (fig. 41). This occurs so frequently that, in one individual. I have counted four or five such double eyes in various stages of union; from one in which they form two eyes, so near together as to touch each other, to those in which the double origin is only indicated by a slight departure from the usual circular outline, and by a shallow, hardly perceptible furrow in the middle. Now, since the single eyes vary considerably in size, it is difficult to determine in all cases whether some of the larger are formed by the fusion of two smaller, — the traces of union having entirely disappeared — or whether some of the latter were originally formed by the concrescence of two still smaller eyes. On the branchial side of the ophthalmic fold, that is on the side towards the light, the hypodermis with its cuticula is especially thickened and contains numerous isolated, or scattered ommatidia in a high stage of development (figs. 46 and 47).

In *Arca barbata*, I have found. in a specimen measuring 5 dm in length, 91 faceted eyes on one side of the mantle. and 83 on the other, making in all 174, about the average number.

In *Arca tetragona*, 10 to 15 mm long, there are from 25 to 30 faceted eyes in each mantle edge.

Each eye is situated in a triangular, pigmented area; in the thickest part of the mantle, the areas fuse with each other to form a continuous, pigmented layer. The isolated areas differ in the intensity of their coloring; they are usually Vandyke brown, and contain a number of darker, irregular, pigment spots, largest and most numerous in the immediate vicinity of the eye. In some cases these spots are absent.

The pigmented areas culminate in a slight elevation, on the summit of which the eyes are usually situated; they either project some distance above the surface, or occupy shallow depressions, where they hardly more than attain the level of the surrounding epithelium. In all cases, they are surrounded by a narrow and less deeply colored furrow (figs. 44 and 45).

The invaginated eyes are smaller, and more easily overlooked, than the faceted ones. They form a narrow band along the summit of that portion of the ophthalmic fold, beneath the ventral opening in the shell through which the byssus projects. A certain amount of light can always penetrate this opening, which cannot be closed, and is only protected by a brush-like outgrowth of the cuticular covering of the shell. These eyes are perfectly black, round or oval, pigmented cups varying in size from .014 to .07 mm in diameter. Sometimes they form the floor of shallow, saucer-like depressions of the epidermis, or, as in the more perfected forms, lie at the bottom of deep pits, whose openings have often become constricted into narrow slits, extending at right angles to the edge of the mantle. In the oldest examples, the pits are less numerous, or often absent, on the anterior portion of the mantle, where the faceted eyes are most abundant: in the middle, where the faceted eyes are absent, they reach their highest development. In the posterior portion there are a few faceted eyes and numerous invaginated ones of all sizes and degrees of development, so that in many cases it is difficult to tell whether they belong to one type, or the other. The arrangement described above is that generally met with, and although there is a wide individual variation, one is always sure to find certain areas occupied by both faceted and invaginated eyes, together with numerous, intermediate forms (figs. 46 and 47). The larger, and more highly developed, invaginated eyes are arranged in a single row along the summit of the ophthalmic fold, often so near together as to touch each other: while, on each side, but more especially on that next the velum, are innumerable, smaller eyes showing all gradations. from simple pigmented spots, or even clusters of two or three pigment cells, to the fully formed eyes.

The mantle edge in this region is colorless, with the exception of pigmented areas similar in size and shape to those in which the faceted eyes are situated. The number of these pigmented areas is much smaller than that of the eyes, several of which are often situated in one of these spots. A network of shallow canals, formed by simple folds of the skin, is distributed over the edge of the mantle. The invaginated eyes are usually situated in cross canals so that, in most cases, the smaller ones appear like simple, pigmented pits in the floors of the canals. It often happens that, when these eyes are examined from above, in surface preparations, they appear like very black, round, pigment spots, and it is difficult to believe they are really sunken below the surface. But on the other hand, if the openings of the pits be closed, as is often the case, one sees a black, narrow, and slit-like opening with the fainter outline of the retina beneath (Pl. 30, fig. 47). In the latter instance, it is hardly necessary to prove by means of sections that they are pigmented pits sunken below the surface; in fact they are exactly the same as those simple, invaginated eyes in the tentacles of *Patella*. The number of these eyes is something extraordinary, when we consider that these retiring animals are already provided with about 250 very perfect eyes. I have counted in *Arca barbata*, $5^1/_2$ cm long, as many as 420 or 430 eyes on one side, and 440 or 450 on the other, not including a number of very small ones, difficult to distinguish from ordinary pigment spots.

There is still a third form of eye, the pseudo-lenticulate, resembling the last type, but not invaginated, and consisting of a few retinal cells (to be soon more accurately described), covered with a lenticular and refractive body like a cornea, or lens. These forms, difficult to recognize except in sections, are distributed irregularly among the invaginated eyes, with which they are brought into close relationship by a number of intermediate forms. I estimate that there are about a hundred such eyes in each mantle edge (fig. 54).

Here then we have a genus of almost motionless and helpless animals whose complex of activities consists in hardly more than closing the shell to avoid an enemy, or opening it to obtain nourishment, and yet each of these lowly organized animals has 250 compound eyes, each of which (as we shall see later) is apparently as complicated an organ as the eye of such active and carnivorous Amphipods, as *Gammarus* or *Orchestia*. It has 800 or 900 eyes like those of *Patella*, and then about 200 simple and minute ocelli, making a sum total of about 1300 eyes for each individual, not including numerous, small groups of ommatidia, too minute to be easily counted by means of an ordinary pocket lens.

Historical.

When we consider that these remarkable eyes, which even a casual observer could not fail to see, have since 1844 been known to exist, it seems hardly credible that they should have so long escaped that thorough examination, which many less conspicuous and deserving organs received long ago.

As early as 1844. WILL (5) furnished us with the first notice of these eyes. He recorded a number of fairly accurate statements of their general appearance and distribution, and, moreover, fully recognized the compound nature of the faceted eyes, the only ones he appears to have seen. His mind seems to have been strongly impregnated with terms applied to the various parts of the Vertebrate eyes, and, apparently on the supposition that, either physiologically or morphologically, equivalent parts were to be found in all eyes, he has applied to the Mollusca, terms from Vertebrate anatomy, when a better knowledge of the facts shows that the parts, thus designated with the same names, are widely different structures, and can neither morphologically nor physiologically have any characteristics in common. A certain »a priori« bias is produced, which tends to confusion, and from which it is difficult to rid the mind. For instance, a simple fold formed by abnormal contractions, he has, in *Pinna,* called an iris, and has applied the same name to the circle of pigment cells surrounding the retinophorae. An ommatidium, he called a simple eye, which, indeed, could hardly have been nearer the truth, even if he had had a much more extended knowledge of the matter than he really did. The terms tapetum, choroidea, vitreous body, and iris, appear at all times, and in places where it is difficult, but in fact hardly necessary, to determine to just what structures these terms were applied. His imagination carried him so far that he has described minutely eyes of certain genera of Mollusca, that it has required nearly forty years to prove do not exist, unless indeed he examined other species than those at the command of subsequent workers. I repeat it is a remarkable thing that this description, as accurate in observation as it was fantastic in conception, should not have drawn the attention to this subject that its importance deserved, or provided us with a more detailed description of one of the most remarkable systems of eyes — if I may use the term — at present known to exist in the whole animal kingdom.

Subsequent authors seem to have been satisfied with WILL's description, and deemed further knowledge on the subject unnecessary. This was the case with SIEBOLD (7), SCHMIDT (17), SHARP (18) and GEGENBAUR (14). The latter erroneously speaks of the eyes of *Arca* and *Pectunculus* as being borne upon special eye stalks. He also says, referring to the eyes of *Pecten, Spondylus,* and other Lamellibranchiata,

p. 367, »Obgleich in dem Baue dieser Augen manches Eigenthümliche besteht, so stimmen sie doch im Wesentlichen mit den Sehorganen anderer Mollusken überein«. This statement indicates more faith in the uniformity of structure of Molluscan eyes, than actual observation.

These are the only remarks upon the eyes of *Arca*, to my knowledge, up to 1883, when CARRIÈRE published an imperfect and inaccurate description of the eyes of *Arca* and *Pectunculus*, in which he fails to add anything new to the subject. At the same time, he exposes himself to the charge of plagiarism, for he lays special stress on the fact that the eyes of *Arca* are compound, or »fan eyes« as he calls them, and passes over in silence the fact, that WILL had long ago fully recognized the same — which has not been mentioned by any recent author, — in an article no longer easily accessible. He has, moreover, produced drawings of sections, cut with a modern microtome and prepared with all the help modern histological technique can give, in which he has represented, and also described in the text, the eyes as being formed simply of cone-shaped cells coated with pigment, each one being provided with a lens-like thickening of the cuticula. A reference to my own drawings will give an idea of how accurate I consider his descriptions to be. Such observations are of double harm, for they not only introduce false notions into science, but disarm suspicion, coming, as they do, from one who has made a specialty of the subject, and who is, presumably, equipped with a technique, which should enable him to keep pace with the progress of modern histological research.

The compound eyes, as we have already said, consist of from 10 to 80 ommatidia, and measure from .07, to .14 mm in diameter. Each ommatidium consists of a central, colorless core, formed of two fused cells, whose bases are directed outward and support a double, highly refractive, and transparent rod. The central cells, or retinophorae as we shall call them, are surrounded by eight pigmented cover cells, or retinulae, arranged in two rows of four each, one above the other (Pl. 30, fig. 59). The whole ommatidium, which is about .04 mm long, is wedge-shaped, the apex being directed inward. In order to obtain a good idea of the structure of these compound eyes, it is necessary to resort to some macerating fluid in order to separate the different cells; if the maceration is stopped at different stages of completion, preparations can be made of the isolated ommatidia in all stages of disintegration. The maceration must be complete, in order to isolate the retinophorae from their investing pigment cells. When this is successfully done, these cells, on account of their characteristic shape and general appearance, can at once be distinguished from all others. They vary considerably in size, probably due to the fact that they come from eyes in different stages of development, or from different parts of the same eye. This variation, however, does not affect their characteristic form, since they are in all cases wedge-shaped, with a blunt outer end, and a pointed, inner extremity prolonged into a long, varicose nerve fibre (figs. 52 and 59). The transformation of the inner extremity of these cells into nerve fibre is so gradual, that it is impossible to say where the one ends or the other begins. This is characteristic of the retinophorae in all Mollusca, and is in marked contrast with the nerve endings on the surrounding pigmented cover cells, or, indeed, on the indifferent cells of the epithelium. If the maceration has been carried so far as to separate the rods from the retinophorae, it will be seen that the broad end is abruptly rounded, and that, at the very outer limits of the cell, but always on one side, a nearly spherical nucleus is situated. It is filled with many fine and deeply stained granules, while, in the centre, is a small but distinct nucleolus. The nucleus is placed so close to the cell wall, that it is often difficult to distinguish their respective boundaries. On the side of the cell opposite to that on which is situated the nucleus, is an irregular, roundish and refractive body, absorbing little coloring matter, but sufficient to distinguish it as the abortive nucleus of the second of the two cells composing the retinophora. It is not always easy, and in many cases I have found it impossible, to satisfy myself of the presence of this body, but the shape of the cell, and the lateral position of the other nucleus, indicated that the retinophorae were, in all cases, formed by the fusion of two cells, although it was not always possible to distinguish both nuclei. The broad, outer end of the retinophorae, — in the broadest part about .005 mm wide, — is filled with a clear, finely granular protoplasm, a narrow area of structureless and refractive fluid surrounding the larger nucleus. The remaining portion of the cell is occupied by closely packed, transparent and refractive globules, divided into two groups, an outer one composed of larger globules, and an inner one of smaller ones. They are easily destroyed by too much maceration, but, since a prolonged treatment is necessary to separate these cells, it is difficult to observe this structure, although I have seen it often enough, and with sufficient clearness, to be confident that it must be the normal condition. This globular structure is found in the colorless cells of *Haliotis* and *Patella*, and is probably characteristic of these elements. When macerated either in osmic and acetic acid (according to HERTWIG's formula), or in dilute sulphuric acid, the globular contents of the cell shrink into a small and refractive body situated in the middle of the cell; the remainder of the cell then appears to be filled with a clear fluid, while, just back of the nucleus, a partition is formed, dividing the cell into an external part containing the nucleus, and a large internal portion once filled with refractive globules.

In sections, and in partly macerated specimens, it is seen that the retinophorae are capped by an oblong, transparent and refractive body, which at once suggests that it is a corneal facet, or cuticular lens. This, however, I am convinced is not its true nature, but, on the contrary, its structure, and abundant supply of nerve fibres, shows that it is the light perceiving element of the eye, or the rod. This rod is brilliantly refractive and perfectly colorless. The inner surface has the same curvature as the outer wall of the underlying cell. The somewhat broader, distal end is well curved in *Arca Noae*, but is somewhat flatter in *Arca barbata*; in cross sections it is perfectly spherical. The same fact may be observed in the living eye by looking directly into the ommatidium, when one sees through the perfectly transparent rod the black pigment beneath, producing the effect of a deep and round, black spot surrounded by light chocolate-colored pigment cells. In longitudinal sections, one sees an extremely thin, cuticular-like outer layer, covering the outer surface of the rods, and continuous with the cuticular of the pigmented cover cells. Toward the edge of the rods. it is more distinct, and there passes over to form the very much thicker, cuticular layer of the cover cells. It is in specimens macerated in sulphuric acid, that one is best able to demonstrate this membrane, for by this method, large pieces with several rods attached may be easily separated. I have spoken of these structures as the rods, while, in reality, they are formed by the fusion of two pieces, but so closely and intimately applied that it is not always easy to demonstrate their dual origin. To do this with fresh and but little macerated specimens is well nigh impossible, except in abnormal cases. I have found two such cases, in which the freshly macerated rod was formed of imperfectly joined halves, the configuration of each half being as distinct, as though they belonged to two separate cells (fig. 52). Such cases are, however, rare. On the other hand, if the cells were thoroughly macerated, in every rod could be seen a median division, with a corresponding indentation on the outer surface. This dividing line could be distinguished from the longitudinal pores of the rod in two ways, first, by its greater distinctness, and, second, by the fact that, during a revolution of the rod on its axis through an angle of $90°$, it disappeared, reappearing by a further revolution. This shows that the median line is an optical section of the plane between the component halves of the rod. Each half of the inner surface of the latter is convex, a cross section of the lower end of the rod always giving a more or less circular outline, containing two ovals, — varying in size with the niveau of the section, — separated by a central band. On the other hand, a longitudinal section of the rod may be doubly concave on its inner surface, while, if the plane of the section is turned through an angle of $90°$, the result is a simple, concave outline. The rods never become turbid by the action of any of the usual histological reagents. In sulphuric acid, they expand somewhat at the outer end, thus slightly exaggerating their normal shape. By a prolonged action of chromic acid, they become constricted in the middle, while the outer and inner ends assume about the same width. After a long treatment with haematoxylin, they stain an intense blue. When studied with an immersion lens, a series of fine, cross lines, whose curvature corresponds with that of the outer surface of the rod, can be seen. These lines, which appear to be composed of minute dots, or dashes, decrease in distinctness and frequency towards the inner ends of the rods. Other lines which, in this case, seem more like pores in the substance of the rod, begin at the base, where they are quite broad and well defined, and extend nearly parallel with each other toward the outer surface, where they finally disappear (fig. 59).

Each retinophora, with its double rod, is completely surrounded by eight pigmented cells, four forming an inner, and four an outer row. Each one of the four outer cells is laterally flattened, the inner two thirds being reduced to very thin colorless bands, consisting of hardly more than the cell walls, while the outer ends are wide and thick, and filled with a dark brown pigment. The centre of each thickened end is thinner than the sides, and is closely applied to, and conforms with, the surface of the retinophorae. In sections, therefore, the inner contour of the four pigment cells forms a circular space filled by the retinophorae, while the outer contour is more or less pentagonal, or hexagonal.

In the centre of the pigmented ends of these cells, is situated the oval nucleus, which usually causes a protuberance upon that surface of the cell turned away from the retinophora. The outer end of the cell is capped by a thick layer of transparent, and perfectly homogeneous cuticula. The inner, membranous prolongations consist of flattened, and longitudinally striated bacilli, which end abruptly in three or four short, root-like fibres. The expanded pigmented ends, as far as the base of the nucleus, form a broad collar for the retinophorae (fig. 59).

The inner circle of cover cells consists of four wedge-shaped, and deeply pigmented cells, covering the two inner thirds of the retinophorae: they are widest and thickest at the outer limit of the pigment. There, the outer edges are bevelled, and rapidly decrease in thickness to a very thin, structureless membrane, continued as far as the outer extremity of the rods. The membranous prolongations of these four cells unite to form a delicate sheath surrounding the outer portion of the retinophorae, between them and the external cover cells, thus indicating that the cells, to which these membranes belong, are more intimately connected with the retinophorae than the outer row of pigment cells (fig. 59 $rt. s.$). The proximal ends of the four inner cells are narrowed nearly to a point. The outer cells are so arranged that their narrow, basal portions cover the line of contact of the adjacent, inner cells. The oval nuclei of the latter are situated in the middle of the cells, and thickly surrounded with pigment, so that they are seldom seen, except on cross sections. They stain deeply, and with a dullness which is in marked contract with the lighter, but clear and sharp stain characteristic of the nuclei of the retinophorae.

Since the whole ommatidium is simply a highly specialized portion of the hypodermis, we should expect to find the same method of nerve endings there, as in the less modified portions. On sections of the eye, it is hardly possible to observe more than the passage of nerve fibres through the basal membrane, and along the cells towards the surface. Isolation of the cells by maceration, according to the methods described below, furnishes the best results. Unfortunately I was not able to obtain perfect control of the process, and the results often varied, especially as far as a complete and rapid isolation of the cells was concerned; for sometimes only 24 hours maceration in bichromate of potassium, 2%, disassociated the cells completely, and, at the same time, in a remarkably perfect and normal condition, a result which, at other times, was only imperfectly effected after prolonged maceration, and after many important characteristics of the cells had been destroyed. I am inclined to believe that it depends on the physical condition of the animals experimented with: perfectly healthy and fresh ones being more difficult to treat than those which have become weakened by prolonged confinement. It is, however, not at all difficult to obtain excellent preparations, in which the nerves now to be described may be easily studied.

Among the isolated cells of such preparations, one can easily distinguish the retinophorae — either with or without the rods — sometimes with the pigmented cover cells attached to them. It is very seldom that one can trace the nerve fibres, or find their broken ends upon the outer row of cover cells, but I have succeeded in doing so several times. In such cases, one sees extremely fine fibres, either running along the stalk of the cell, or projecting considerably beyond its base. The fibre is often free everywhere, except at the outer, or pigmented, end of the cell, to which it is attached so firmly, that considerable rapping upon the cover glass is necessary before it can be entirely isolated; and, indeed, even with the roughest treatment, it is sometimes impossible to separate it from the cell. This is due to the fact that lateral nerve fibrillae, applied to, or penetrating, the cell wall, are only formed at the pigmented portion of the cell, in which the nucleus is situated.

The nerve fibres of the inner row of pigment cells are larger and more numerous than those of the outer row. To study these nerve fibres, the cells must first be isolated, to do which requires a more prolonged maceration than is necessary for those of the outer row. Very instructive preparations are obtained by a slight maceration, which not only separates the ommatidia from each other, but removes the outer row of pigment cells, leaving the retinophorae and their rods still surrounded by the inner row of retinulae. The whole group of cells has a conical shape, the rod forming the outermost and widest part (fig. 59). By further maceration, the inner row of pigment cells is isolated, and one may then distinguish, on each side of the flattened surface, from two to five refractive and colorless lines, which are seen to be distinct fibres, and not cell markings as might easily be supposed from the fact that, in almost every cell, some are either partly detached from, or project beyond, the inner end of the cells (fig. 60). With a good light, and a strong immersion lens, one can see exceedingly fine, cross fibrillae, which arise, at quite regular intervals, from the larger, longitudinal nerve fibres: where the latter project beyond the cell, the lateral fibrillae may still be seen, no longer as straight as before, but either so closely curled, or so strongly varicose, that one would hardly recognize them as fibrillae. In the usual macerated preparations, these pigment cells extend only about two thirds of the way from the basal membrane towards the outer surface, where they appear to cease abruptly. If, however, the cells be isolated in weak sulphuric acid, their outer thirds are retained as thin and transparent membranes, along which one may see several fine lines, undoubtedly the continuation of the nerve fibres, seen more distinctly on cells prepared in other ways. The inner ends of these pigment cells end in a rather blunt point, on which I have not been able to distinguish those root-like fibres, so common upon the inner ends of most epithelial cells. But this very circumstance makes it much easier to follow those nerve fibres, just described, through the basal membrane inwards, a considerable distance, until they are lost in the mass of scattered fibres which supply the eye.

It is difficult to obtain isolated retinophorae intact, and in a condition to show the nerve endings. It is necessary to seach until a good example is found. The best way is maceration in $1/20 - 1/30$ % chromic acid, for ten or twelve days. The rods are somewhat shrunken in the centre by this process, but are provided with a number of long fibres, whose free ends project some distance beyond the inner edges of the rods. These free ends are covered with a great number of fibrillae, which branch from the main fibre at right angles, and, projecting a short distance, end in a minute, refractive globule (fig. 48). The fibres may be followed along the outer surface of the rod, where they form a complete network of distinct, longitudinal fibres, and small, irregularly distributed, cross ones, or fibrillae. At the outer end of the rod, the longitudinal fibres become continuous with each other by means of connecting loops, as I have distinctly seen in several cases. The loops may be distinguished from the other cross fibres, by their greater size and distinctness (fig. 59). It is very difficult to find retinophorae, treated in this manner, which have the rod still attached, therefore it is not possible to follow the nerve fibres along the whole length of the cell, because they are so intimately united with the rods that, when the latter are detached, the nerve fibres are carried with them. Yet I have seen the retinophorae with the rod still attached, and have followed the nerve fibres almost down to the base of the cells.

In sections, one can, under favorable circumstances, see a special aggregation of nerve fibres, passing to each retinophora, and ascending along the outer surface, between it and the inner pigment cells, until, towards the outer ends of the latter, they disappear. It is therefore only on macerated specimens, that I have been able to follow the nerve fibres over the surface of the rods, where they terminate as already described.

The retinophorae are, moreover, supplied with a second form of nerve fibres, which I believe to be characteristic of these structures, and not to be found in the other elements of the retina, namely, a central nerve fibre, or bundle of nerve fibres, which extends, through the axis of the retinophora, into the rod. Now, if we suppose that each cell was supplied with a number of external nerve fibres, like those described for the pigmented ones, and that a special cluster of such fibres was formed between the juxtaposed walls of two retinophorae, it is evident that, with the fusion of the two cells, and the disappearance of the apposed walls, the bunch of nerve fibres will come to lie in the centre of the retinophorae; and since, according to our suppositions, the nerve fibres extend to the summit of the cell, — as we have always found to be the case, — they will therefore penetrate the centre of the rod. It is difficult to follow the nerves through the retinophorae, on account of the mass of refractive globules, but here, as in other similar cases, it is only necessary to find favorable examples, where one may distinguish a bundle of at least two or three nerve fibres extending upwards from the base of the cell, beyond the refractive granules; near the nuclei, they become varicose and irregularly distributed. I have not succeeded in tracing them directly into the rods, although I do not doubt that they terminate there. The inner ends of the retinophorae are always pointed, lacking the root-like fibres of the pigment cells; their transformation into the issuing nerve fibres is so gradual, that it is impossible to say where the one begins and the other ends. This nerve fibre, which is really a nerve bundle composed of several smaller fibres, is larger than those seen connected with the pigment cells. In some cases, the varicosities of the axial nerve, at a short distance from the cell, become so large as to form one or two vesicular swellings, which I thought might contain nuclei, but I have never been able to determine this point with certainty. The very small size of the rods has rendered the observation of the ultimate nerve endings there a matter of extraordinary difficulty. That the outer fibres send their ultimate fibrillae into the substance of the rod is shown by the persistency with which they invariably adhere to its surface, while, on the other hand, they are always torn away from the surface of the retinophorae. If we accept the supposition that the retinophora is formed by the fusion of two cells, — which, in fact, can hardly be called a supposition, since we have incontestible proof of it in the double nature of the rod, and the presence of two nuclei, — then the central bundle of nerve fibres belongs to the same category as the external ones, and we may presume that they, like the outer nerve fibres, also extend to the outer ends of the rods, that is, they form a system of axial nerve fibres in the centre of the rod, just as is the case in the rods of *Pecten*. Moreover, analogy with *Pecten* and *Haliotis* will allow us to suppose a similar system of horizontal fibrillae uniting the inner and outer system of nerve fibres.

Having obtained a more complete knowledge of those complex elements, or ommatidia, of which the most specialized eyes of *Arca* are formed, we are now in a better condition to understand the structure of the second form, and the origin of both types from the aggregation of elements found scattered in the pigmented portions of the mantle.

The Invaginate Eyes.

The general characters and distribution of the invaginate eyes have already been alluded to, and it now remains for us to give a more accurate description of them.

When seen from above, in living specimens, they appear as very dark brown or black spots. They may be sharply defined, oval, or round, or they may be surrounded by a circle of lighter pigment cells, which gradually pass into the surrounding, colorless epithelium. In the midst of each pigment spot, one always sees from three to six or more brilliantly refractive and colorless points, all the more striking from being situated in the midst of the dark pigment. The intense black color of the pigment is often reduced by the invagination of the eyes below the surface, the more or less transparent lips of the cup thus formed folding over, and partly hiding, the sunken eye. The deeper the cups, the greater is the tendency for their lips to approach each other, forming a long, slit-like opening (Pl. 30, fig. 47). Whether this iris-like fold is capable of regulating the amount of light by contraction or expansion, I am unable to say. I have not observed any movement, which would indicate such a function. WILL has described an iris-like, contractile opening in *Pectunculus*, which has faceted eyes similar to those of *Arca*, but no invaginate ones. It is possible that he had in mind the invaginate eyes of *Arca*, when describing those of *Pectunculus*. Sections of the invaginated eyes show that they are simple, thickened portions of the hypodermis, sunken below the surface, sometimes forming wide-mouthed and shallow depressions, or deep funnel-like pits; in the latter case, the axis of depression is not perpendicular to the surface, but at an angle of about $50°$ or $60°$ with it, the deepest part being directed toward the shell (fig. 42).

The retineum is composed of broad, square-ended cells filled with dark brown, or black pigment, and a smaller number of colorless ones. The latter contain a highly refractive, granular substance, and are usually conical, or wedge-shaped, the smaller end being directed outwards, while the widened base is turned in the opposite direction and contains a large nucleus. The latter is distinguished from the nuclei of the surrounding pigment cells, in the same way that those of the retinophorae in *Haliotis*, or in the faceted eyes of *Arca*, are distinguished from the nuclei of the retinulae, i. e. by the clearness with which they stain, and the presence of a nucleolus. The nuclei of the retinulae are filled with a quantity of chromatine, which, although staining deeply, produces a dull and heavy effect when contrasted with the brilliantly and sharply stained nuclei of the retinophorae. This difference alone would enable us to distinguish the two kinds of cells. I have sought for traces of a second nucleus in the retinophorae, but in vain: this is probably due to their small size, and the difficulty of macerating them properly. On account of the paucity of these cells, they may be easily overlooked, or confounded with colorless ones of the surrounding epithelium. These difficulties, coupled with the fact that under the most favorable circumstances the aborted nucleus is very hard to observe, render it more than probable that such a nucleus has been overlooked, rather than that it is not present at all. The number of these cells is comparatively small; I have never seen, in sections of one eye, more than three. Looking into the eye from above, on surface preparations, six or seven colorless cells are seen as bright, refractive spots, while it is probable that there are two or three more, that could not be seen, on the sides of the pit; therefore a typical invaginated eye would consist of from seven to ten ommatidia.

The remainder of the retinal layer is composed of large, cylindrical cells filled with dark brown, or in some cases nearly black pigment. Only their bases are colorless, so that one can see the lower portion of the deeply stained nuclei, the outer parts being closely enveloped in pigment (Pl. 30, fig. 49).

The nuclei of both pigmented and colorless cells are so deeply situated that they seem, in some cases, to rest upon the basal membrane, which is hardly more developed here than below the ordinary epithelium (fig. 42).

Below, and parallel to the basal membrane, is a number of connective tissue fibres, besides many large gland cells with refractive and granular contents, and excentrically placed nuclei.

The cuticula — bearing in mind that it is by no means certain that all the structures with this name are homologous, or chemically identical — is well developed over all the pigmented cells, while it becomes especially thickened over the sunken, retinal layer of the invaginated eyes. The thick cuticula over the pigmented areas is formed of two layers: a thin, external one, dense and refractive, and a thicker, less refractive, inner one, which has not so completely lost its vital properties. In, and below the latter layer is found the network of nerve fibrillae constituting the retia terminalia. It is this layer which is so greatly developed over the retinal cells of the invaginated eyes, while the outer and thinner one remains unchanged. Over the invaginated eyes. the retinal cuticula is composed almost entirely of innumerable and distinct nerve fibres, which may often be traced below the cuticula, between the retinal cells (Pl. 30, fig. 42). At the basal ends of the cells, there are often considerable spaces in which may be seen continuations of the same fibres, which pass through the basal membrane into the underlying tissues as isolated branches, not united to form a special optic nerve. When the nerve fibres have once passed beyond the basal membrane, it is difficult to distinguish them from those of the connective tissue.

These eyes are so difficult to macerate that I have not obtained many data in that way, but still enough to convince me that the same arrangement of nerves is found here, as in *Haliotis*, which will be described in greater detail further on. For example, when I was fortunate enough to isolate some of the retinal cells uninjured, almost without exception, two or three nerve fibres were seen attached to their sides, with the free ends projecting some distance beyond either end of the cells. This shows that, when the latter were in position, the nerves extended into the cuticular layer, which is merely an exaggerated form of the ordinary cuticula containing the nervous retia terminalia found everywhere above the pigmented hypodermis. The ordinary cuticula represents the sum of the products of the individual cells, and, in most cases, the outline of each cell is distinctly visible upon it. This goes so far that it is often possible to separate the cuticula into its component elements; but especially is this the case on the modified, retinal portion of the hypodermis, where the product of each cell has attained a high stage of individuality, giving rise to the rods.

The invaginated eyes, therefore, are composed of the same elements as the faceted, that is, a central colorless cell, probably containing an axial nerve fibre and two nuclei, together with a cuticular rod supporting a specialized part of the retia terminalia (a retinidium);

around each of these central cells, or retinophorae, is arranged a number of pigmented ones, — in this case more than a single circle, — which also support nerve-bearing, cuticular rods (Pl. 30, fig. 49).

Such circles of cells, or ommatidia, form groups varying greatly among themselves, either in the number of ommatidia, or in the precision with which they are separated from the surrounding epithelium. A very common form of invaginate eye is that in which from two to four or more closely placed ommatidia form a central, dark area, surrounded by a zone of lighter colored pigment cells, in which are several, irregularly scattered ommatidia, decreasing in number towards the periphery of the band. In surface preparations, one may easily recognize these scattered ommatidia by the color of the retinulae surrounding the retinophorae. Although these isolated ommatidia are usually seen in greater abundance about the invaginated eyes, they are often found quite independent of them scattered irregularly over the ophthalmic fold, and even in the other portions of the mantle. The cuticula over these isolated retinulae, does not seem to be especially thickened.

Pseudo-lenticulate Eyes.

I have found an interesting transitional form of eye, which belongs neither to the invaginated nor faceted type, and which, for lack of a better name, I shall call the pseudo-lenticulate eye. In sections, for instance, through that portion of the mantle where the invaginated eyes are most abundant, I have found quite sharply defined groups of non-invaginated ommatidia, provided with a prominent lenticular thickening of the cuticula, containing vertical fibres undoubtedly of the same nature, i. e. nerve fibres, as those found in the cuticular layer of the invaginated eyes (Pl. 30, fig. 54).

A retinal cuticula seems to be formed by the pigmented cover cells, as well as by the retinophorae, and hence, in this respect, these eyes resemble more closely the invaginated ones. On the other hand, these intermediate forms, which greatly resemble the ocelli of the Coelenterata, offer some similarity to the faceted eyes, in that they tend to form a protuberant, convex surface, instead of a concave, invaginated one.

Just as the invaginated eyes, composed of a varying number of ommatidia closely or loosely arranged in groups, show all grades of invagination, so may one find a parallel series of changes in the pseudo-lenticulate eyes, together with all grades of convexity. In the faceted eyes, the ommatidia, whether single or united in groups, show the same composition. It is rather remarkable that the ommatidia of each type of eye should retain so constantly their specific characters, even in cases where the two types which they produce are so little differentiated from each other. I believe that, in both cases, the ommatidia are different phases of the same structural elements, those of the faceted eyes being undoubtedly of a higher order than those of the invaginated ones, the latter being almost identical in structure with those isolated ommatidia, found irregularly distributed over the exposed portions of the mantle. The isolated, faceted ommatidia are only found — and then rarely — in the immediate vicinity of what appear to be degenerate evaginate eyes. It is more probable that the higher structure of the faceted ommatidia was attained, after they were united into distinct groups, than when in the isolated condition. If this is the case, we should expect to find in those imperfectly formed faceted eyes, the peripheral ommatidia in a less perfect stage of development, in proportion as they were more distant from the centre of the eye. But this is not the case, for I have often seen isolated ommatidia on the periphery, as highly developed as any ever found in the centre. For this reason, I consider such eyes as retrogressive, rather than progressive, and possibly analogous with those cases in *Pecten*, where fully formed eyes become functionless, by the complete pigmentation of the cornea.

It is probable that during the phylogenetic development of the visual organs of *Arca*, those portions of the mantle, most exposed to light, developed pigmented cells, among which were numerous colorless (gland?) cells. By the fusion of two such pigmentless cells, and the accumulation around them of a definite number of pigmented ones, the isolated ommatidia were formed; they in turn united into special groups, where the ommatidia became modified in certain directions according to the form and position of the organs they composed. The number of the isolated ommatidia must have been, at first, very great, but probably diminished, as they accumulated to form more complex organs of greater functional activity; after the formation of these groups, the development of the ommatidia continued, until an enormous number of visual organs was formed, in a high stage of perfection, and of a functional activity disproportionate with the requirements of the animal; a tendency for certain of the eyes to degenerate would therefore arise. Such is at present the condition in *Arca* and *Pecten*. It is probable that in both cases, peculiar, favorable conditions were present, which carried the development of these organs beyond the requirements of the animal. The development was so rapid, and the inertia — if we may use the expression — so great, that a state of inequilibrium was attained, now returning to a more stable condition by a reduction in the number of eyes. This furnishes us with a remarkable instance of reversed degeneration, in which the degradation begins, not with the loss of the most recently acquired characters, that is, the reduction of the ommatidia to a simpler condition — but by the isolation of the perfected ommatidia; therefore retracing that developmental step which was the first to give rise to the eyes.

The faceted eyes probably arise as modifications of the invaginated ones: during this process, the latter become shallower, and the nervous network reduced entirely to the rods of the retinophorae, while the retinulae, whose rods disappear, are used solely to protect the retinidia of the retinophorae from the lateral rays of light.

Pectunculus.

The thick mantle edge of *Pectunculus* contains an enormous number of gland cells, which secrete a quantity of thick slime, materially adding to the difficulty of studying the eyes of the living animal. Although the edge of the mantle is thus enlarged, the three folds, which are present here as in *Arca* and *Pecten*, are but slightly developed. The inner wall of the ophthalmic fold is much extended and constitutes the greater part of the pigmented portion of the mantle. It is studded with numerous oval, or round, madder brown, pigment spots, which, in many cases, are sharply defined areas of nearly black pigment that might easily be taken for eyes; in other instances, they are more irregular and lighter colored, without the sharp boundaries of the former. With the exception of these pigment spots, the hypodermis of the ophthalmic fold is nearly colorless, or of a faint, yellowish white tinge, intensified at the base of the velum to form a distinct band of brownish pigment, parallel with the edge of the mantle. The velum is reduced to a colorless, and inconspicuous ridge thrown into many irregular folds. At the base of the ridge, on the proximal side, is a distinct band of brown pigment, in the median portion of the mantle, broken up into wedge-shaped patches, each one consisting of radiating, pigmented lines. At the anterior end of the mantle, the pigment is darker and forms a continuous, but narrow band. The cuticula is slightly thickened over the pigmented spots, and, in some cases, has a faint wavy outline, each curve corresponding to the outer end of a pigmented cell. The spots are provided with colorless sense cells, for on surface views one sees numerous refractive and colorless points of varying size; the light, which is often silvery white, appears to be reflected from the refractive granules within the cells. The refractive points are only (?) to be seen in the colored areas, where, surrounded by and contrasted with the dark pigment cells, they are especially striking. Towards the anterior edge of the mantle, the spots become smaller and, assuming a lineal arrangement at the summit of the ophthalmic fold, by a series of easy gradations, pass into the faceted eyes, the only kind present in *Pectunculus*. Being confined at the summit of the ophthalmic fold to a space about 7 or 8 mm long, they are necessarily less numerous than those of *Arca*. As in the last named genus, the number is greater on the right, than on the left fold of the mantle. For instance, in twelve specimens, the eyes varied in number from 17—25 on the left valve, and from 20—30 on the right; the average being about 25 and 22 on the right and left mantle respectively. The largest eyes are not situated in the middle of the row, as one might suppose, but at that end farthest away from the hinge. The same tendency to form pairs is seen here as in *Arca*. Usually two large eyes are followed by two small ones, then two large ones with a small one between; those of equal size being closest together. I have observed cases, however, in which as many as six or seven fully formed eyes had united to form one large group, whose origin was indicated by the number of component parts, which had not entirely lost their individuality.

The eyes of *Pectunculus* are easily discernible since they are not surrounded by such quantities of pigment as in *Arca*. There are other, but slight differences, which distinguish them from the eyes of the last named genus; the lens-like rods are larger and more protuberant; the cover cells of the outer row are thinner and less deeply pigmented; and the eyes seem to have arrived at a more stable condition, for there is a diminution in the number as well as variety of intermediate forms: the few remaining eyes, having reached the height of their development and being sufficient for the requirement of the animal, have been retained, while the less useful, intermediate forms have disappeared.

The eyes may be easily overlooked when the animal is irritated, for the mantle is then contracted in such a manner, that the pigmented outer edge is folded in against the shell, and only the inner side of the thickened mantle, quite devoid of pigment, is seen. But when undisturbed, the shell is slightly open, and the mantle brought forward, exposing the eyes, as well as the pigmented portions, to the light.

WILL (5) was the first who (in 1844) claimed to have found eyes in this genus: his description, incomplete as it was, is still better than any which has been published since that time; being short, and the original difficult to find, I will quote it in full. »Der Raum des Mantels von *Pectunculus pilosus* hat zwei dicht an einander liegende Falten, welche, wie bei anderen Bivalven, in der Nähe des Schlosses in eine zusammenlaufen. Am Vorderrande ist diese eine dunkelbraun gesäumt, was größtentheils von den darauf befindlichen, sitzenden Augen herrührt. Dieselben stehen theils einzeln, theils in Gruppen vereinigt, auf dunkelbraunen, orangenartigen, wiewohl nur wenig hervorragenden Erhöhungen. In den Gruppen, welche beiläufig $1/4$—$1/6$''' im Durchmesser haben, liegen die Hornhäute so eng an einander, dass sie im Zusammenhange bleiben, wenn man sie von den unterliegenden Geweben losreißt. Die einzelnen Hornhäute sind jedoch rund. Man könnte diese Häufchen aggregirte Augen nennen, denn sie haben alle Merkmale derjenigen zusammengesetzten Augen, welche man mit diesem Namen bezeichnet. Die Anzahl der einzelnen Augen in einer solchen Gruppe beträgt 20 bis 30. Sie sind etwas kleiner als die einzeln stehenden, und die Durchmesser beider verhalten sich wie 5:7 oder wie 5:8. Die Pupille ist in allen Augen rund; die Chorioidea roth; Glaskörper und Linse sind selten deutlich zu sehen. Am unteren und hinteren Rande des Mantels scheinen die Gruppen häufiger, dagegen die einzelnen Augen seltener zu sein. Nicht zu verwechseln mit den augentragenden Erhabenheiten sind die zwischen ihnen liegenden Pigmentflecken. Abgesehen davon, dass letzteren die charakteristische Hornhaut fehlt, sind auch die in ihnen enthaltenen Pigmentzellen kaum die Hälfte so breit, als die Augen und laufen nach innen spitzig zu, so dass sie wie kleine Kegel aussehen, deren Basis und Spitze eine helle pigmentlose Stelle haben.«

It is not difficult to harmonize this description with what may be observed by an examination of the mantle edge of *Pectunculus pilosus*. The eyes, that he refers to as being found singly and united in groups, are in the latter case undoubtedly the faceted eyes, while in the former they are probably either minute pigment spots or isolated ommatidia. In all other respects, the description, as far as it goes, is clear and accurate and shows plainly that, even at that early date, the resemblance of these eyes to the compound ones of Arthropods was fully recognized. Just as was the case with *Arca*, no one deemed it worth while to give a more accurate description of them. SIEBOLD (7) simply reiterates the statements of WILL, as do also SCHMIDT (**17**) and GEGENBAUR (**14**). CARRIÈRE'S (**19**) recent description, accompanied by a drawing, is of little importance, since it contains nothing new but what is wrong, and nothing right that was not already known. The description given of the finer anatomy of the faceted eyes of *Arca* will, with the exception of the slight differences already mentioned, apply equally well to *Pectunculus*.

Pecten.

Historical.

It is not to be expected that the remarkable organs, which we shall here consider, so prominent and so brilliantly colored, could have long escaped the attention of the older Naturalists.

Nearly a century has elapsed since they were first described by POLI (**1**), in 1795, who noticed their arrangement in pairs (a fact overlooked by subsequent writers) and their position at the ends of short tentacles; he thus unwittingly introduced the theory that they were modified tentacles, an opinion held by some even to the present day. He could hardly have failed to recognize the resemblance of these organs to the human eye, as in fact he did, and applied corresponding names to what he considered to be corresponding parts. This had its effect upon succeeding writers, — to whom the terms homology and analogy were unknown, — who, upon the discovery of new parts, saw in them the structures known to occur in the human eye. To them there was but one visual organ, that of the Vertebrates, and, having once recognized in the eye of *Pecten* a superficial resemblance to that of the Vertebrates, they believed that there must be a corresponding agreement in all the remaining parts. This led to results which, as far as *Pecten* is concerned, are less striking, since there is indeed a remarkable agreement in more ways than one; but in less complicated visual organs, such as described by WILL for other Lamellibranchiata, where the so-called eyes in reality consist of hardly more than pigment spots, one is surprised to learn that in these simple organs they were able to recognize a lens, vitreous body, choroid, iris etc., all of which are terms borrowed from human anatomy.

Although it appears that the existence of these minute eyes was not forgotten, further mention of them was not made until 1837, when ROBERT GARNER (**2**) described the »Brilliant emerald-like ocelli, which from their structure, having each a minute nerve, a pupil, a pigmentum. a striated body, and a lens, and from their situation at the edge of the mantle, where alone such organs could be useful, and also placed as in Gasteropods with the tentacles, must be organs of vision«. To his concise description[1], where by the »pigmentum« is meant the red pigment layer. and by the »striated body«, the retina, not very much was added until HENSEN (12) published his paper of which we shall speak later.

KROHN (3) and GRUBE (4) published, almost simultaneously, an account of visual organs in the Lamellibranchiata, in which the optic nerve and argentea were described with tolerable accuracy. To the former is due the credit of having first seen the septum, a name which he himself introduced.

We are indebted to the vivid imagination of WILL for the greatest number of accurate observations, as well as for many mistakes, concerning the visual organs of Lamellibranchiata. In some cases, he has very accurately described the external characteristics of the eyes of *Arca*, *Pectunculus* and *Cardium*; in others, he has scattered, with lavish hand, high sounding names to organs, which, if they once existed, now seem to have disappeared. To him, however, is due the credit of having first accurately described the cellular structure of the lens of *Pecten*. The observations of WILL appear to have been accepted without comment by SIEBOLD, LEYDIG, BRONN, and even by still later writers.

KEFERSTEIN (11) recognized in the so-called viteous body, the fibrous structure of which had been known since GARNER, the real retina, the rods of which he believed to be turned inwards, as in Vertebrates.

The classical researches of HENSEN carried our knowledge, at one bound, to the position which it occupies to-day. He has described with the greatest detail the structure of the component parts of the eye, — especially the retina, where his acute vision enabled him to distinguish the central nerve fibre of the retinophorae, an observation which his successors were not always able to repeat. The general course of the other nerve fibres, especially those proceeding from the ganglionic branch, he was likewise able to follow with wonderful accuracy, when we consider his means and methods of study.

---

[1] The reference of GARNER to the eyes of *Ostrea*, in which we are led to assume that they are similar to the eyes of *Pecten* and *Spondylus*, is probably due to the fact that he had in mind another species of *Pecten*. POLI speaks of *Pecten* as *Ostrea*.

HICKSON (15 and 16) and CARRIÈRE (19) have only been able to add to the excellent work of HENSEN a few corrections of minor importance, concerning the structure of the lens, cornea etc.

SHARP (18), without making any contribution to our knowledge on the subject, has come to the conclusion that the external pigmented ring of the eye is really the sensitive part, while the eye itself, he considers to have another function than that of vision.

It is interesting to follow the fluctuations in Zoological opinion, caused by the accession of new knowledge concerning these organs. At first, the superficial resemblance between these structures and the human eye was so great that an equivalent functional power was likewise tacitly ascribed to them. With increased knowledge, the structural similarity was seen to disappear, and less importance was then attached to their functional powers, until, finally, the careful researches of HENSEN showed a remarkable discrepancy between their highly complicated structure, and their apparent lack of visual power. This difference is heightened by the great number of eyes present, which appear to far exceed the simple requirements of such an animal.

Thus many were led to believe that the organs in question were not eyes at all, but luminous organs, or they were placed in the category of structures, the functions of which were unknown.

General structure.

After comparing the complex organs just described with the simpler eyes of *Arca*, and the infinitely less complicated ones of *Avicula*, we are led to expect a corresponding difference in their functional powers. How far this expectation is realized will be seen from what follows.

If we study the structure of the eyes of *Pecten*, we shall find that the parts really have the function that their names and composition indicate.

We see a constant purpose in view; the concentration of the rays of light, and formation of inverted images of external objects upon a sensitive nervous layer, the arrangement of whose elements shows a definite relation to the direction of the rays of light.

First, let us consider the cornea and the colorless opening, or pupil, surrounded by the pigmented iris. The curvature of the former (which in *Pecten Jacobaeus* and *Pecten opercularis* projects but little above the level of the iris), and the size of the pupil, may be regulated, according to the conditions to be fulfilled, by means of contractile fibres. By the simultaneous contraction of the ciliaris (Pl. 29, figs. 18 and 19 *s. b.*) and the superficial circular and radiating fibres of the lens, the edges of the cornea and iris will be drawn inwards, and the convexity of the former and of the outer surface of the lens increased, while the opening of the pupil may be diminished to almost half its previous diameter. In the living condition, all stages of contraction may be observed. Strong irritants cause contraction, and an increased convexity of the cornea. If the mantle is treated with weak chromic acid, the muscles relax, the cornea becomes nearly flat, and the pupil widely extended. Contraction of the longitudinal muscles, extending along the inner wall of the iris and attached to the suspensory ligament (Pl. 29, fig. 19 *s. b.*), would cause a flattening of the outer surface of the lens, accompanied by a bodily movement of the latter toward the retina. We now see the object of the peculiar layer of vertical nerve fibres: for without this, any movement of the lens, attached to the septal membrane, would necessitate a disturbance of, or injury to the retinal cells. But with the present arrangement the lens, accompanied by the septal membrane, may be elevated or depressed, without contact with the retina, simply by the flexion of the nerves of the fibrous layer. The latter was considered by HENSEN to be artificially formed by shrinkage, and the consequent drawing out of the nerve fibres from the septal membrane. CARRIÈRE has described it as forming a layer of small columnar cells. That both of these statements are incorrect, and that the condition represented in figs. 10 and 19 is a natural one, may be seen by examining this layer, in the living condition, through the choroid fissure. It is very probable that the inward movement of the lens is accomplished by the contraction of the ciliaris and the muscles attached to the suspensory ligament. This movement is facilitated by the contraction of the circular fibres on the periphery of the septal membrane, so that the thick, structureless, central portion, upon which the lens rests, will fall by its own weight, or by the pressure of the lens. But how is the elevation of the latter accomplished? It might be done by the contraction of the relaxed, septal membrane; but that is only provided with circular fibres, which could not produce any such effect. Neither could the lens be raised by the contraction of any of its own muscles, or of any attached to it. It is produced by the tendency of the elastic septal membrane to return to its natural position, after the contraction of its peripheral, circular fibres has relaxed the tension upon the central portion. There is good evidence of the elasticity of this membrane, for in certain reagents, as chromic acid, the muscles being gradually deprived of their power, the tension of the septal membrane acting upon the lens presses it almost flat, and two great folds are produced in the periphery of the retina. But, by isolating the lens and subsequently hardening it in chromic acid, its original shape is perfectly preserved. Muscular contractions which, caused by the irritation of reagents, produce such a great difference in the shape of the lens, must be able, in the living condition, to produce the extremely slight changes necessary for focal adjustment! This process may be produced then in two ways: by an increased convexity, causing a shorter focal distance, and by the bodily movement of the lens itself. But it will be asked, is this body really a lens? Does it actually form an image, or concentrate the rays of light at a certain point, and does this point fall within the retinal layer which, morphologically, we must consider to be the essential and percipient one?

These questions are pertinent, and the answer to them will show whether the body in question is really entitled to be called a lens, and whether the function of these eyes of *Pecten* is as perfect as their complicated structure indicates.

The following experiments will prove that all the above questions may be answered in the affirmative. The body in question is a true, optic lens. it forms a perfect inverted image falling upon what must, morphologically, be considered as the percipient elements, namely, the rods with their contained retinidia. In order to see the images formed by the lens, and determine their position, one of the large eyes, containing little pigment, must be selected from the anterior or posterior edge of the mantle: one may then easily look into the interior of the eye, when it has been carefully removed from the shell. The eye must then be fixed with the optic axis nearly vertical, but with a slight inclination toward the window whence the light comes.

The images of white objects are most easily visible. I have, therefore, dipped a fine needle in white paint, leaving a small globule at the point. If the needle is now inserted between the eye and the objective, a perfect inverted image will be seen in the depths of the eye; the globule at the end of the needle serves to orient the image. That the image of a much larger and distant object will be formed with exactly the same precision may be proved by holding the fingers of the hand at the level of the ocular, when an upright image of the fingers, or a part of the hand, will be seen with perfect distinctness, below the inner surface of the lens. An upright image is seen in the latter case, because the inverted image, formed by the lens, is rectified by the microscope. In the former experiment, both the needle and its inverted image are reversed by the microscope, so that the relation between the two is retained. Any other object, when held in the right position, may be seen with equal distinctness. For instance, if one of the numerous tentacles, supplied with sense hair papillae, be placed over the pupil, its inverted image, with all the details of structure, will be seen below the surface. One may also paint several white lines on the base of the objective, the images of which will easily be seen in the eye. That these images are not formed by reflection from the cornea, or surfaces of the lens, is proved: first, by the fact that the images are inverted and are formed below the lens; and, secondly, by comparing them with the reflected images formed by the surface of the lens, or cornea. For instance, by focusing upon the latter, or inner surface of the lens, an inverted image of the moving tree tops in front of the window, or the base of the latter will be seen. When seen with the microscope, these images are inverted, and therefore are formed by the cornea and surface of the lens, as upright and reflected images. Only a part of the image, that formed in the centre of the eye, is perfect; the image of a large object, as the hand or fingers, about twelve inches from the eye, will be enlarged and curved at the periphery. Only the end of the horizontally held finger will be perfectly reproduced, while the basal part appears enlarged and bent; but a tentacle, just above and extending entirely across the pupil, will be quite perfectly reproduced as a concave image. In trying this simple experiment, the utmost care is necessary to have a perfectly fresh and uninjured eye, as the slightest pressure appears to be sufficient to prevent the formation of any but reflex images. But where is the image formed? This may be easily determined by following successively the layers of the eye as far as the tapetum. First, are seen the minute hexagonal ends of the corneal cells, then the radiating and circular fibres of the pseudo-cornea and outer surface of the lens, followed by the large, irregularly shaped cells of the latter; then the outer layer of ganglionic cells above the perfectly regular but faint outline of the rods (which may be recognized by their resemblance to the figures seen by viewing the prepared isolated retina from above or below), — and lastly, the tapetum itself, from which issues the red light from the pigment below. Just before reaching the tapetum, the image of any object in front of the pupil will be seen with the greatest distinctness, diminishing in definition according as the objective of the microscope is raised or lowered. But the rods also lie just above the tapetum, so that upon them the image must be formed. A remarkable phenomenon may be observed, by focusing between the argentea and the place where the image formed by the lens is seen with the greatest distinctness, for there one sees a double image, less distinct towards the argentea, but increasing in sharpness towards the focal point of the eye, where the two images ultimately fuse to form a single one. The only explanation I have to offer for the origin of this second image, is that it is a reflected one of the first, formed by the curved surface of the argentea. A plain mirror would never reflect an image formed by a lens, since the rays of light would be dispersed; neither would the image be reproduced by a concave mirror, unless the curvature was such that the divergent rays coming from the lens impinged upon the reflecting surface, at right angles to the tangent at that point. In that case each reflected ray would coincide with the incident one, and a reflected repetition of the lenticular image would be reproduced, both being formed at the same point. The exact relation between the focal distance of a lens like that of *Pecten*, and the radius of the concave mirror which would again unite the rays, has not been determined (Pl. 32. fig. 149).

Anatomy of the Eyes.

The mantle of *Pecten* would serve very well as a type, since it possesses all the structures found in any Lamellibranchiata, with the exception of the various forms of faceted eyes so characteristic of *Arca*. The shell fold is separated from the ophthalmic, by a very deep furrow, the bottom of which is occupied by a continuous, double ridge of thickened cells which secrete the cuticular covering of the shell. The outer of these ridges, both of which extend the whole length of the mantle, is large and heart-shaped, while the other is high and narrow (Pl. 28, *c. g.*).

The ophthalmic fold projects considerably above the edge of the mantle, and is deeply forked at its free end. From the inner wall of its base, arise the innumerable tentacles, and, at certain intervals, the stalked eyes, which it is our purpose to consider. The tentacles are usually situated between the eyes and the ophthalmic fold (Pl. 28, fig. 7), but occasionally the reverse may be the case.

The inner edge of the mantle is continued inwards to form the enormous velum, the free edge of which is beset with small tentacles: Pl. 28, fig. 2 represents a section through the mantle edge of a young *Pecten opercularis*. If one imagines all of these folds increased, and a greater development of the tentacles, a very good idea of the adult condition will be obtained. Only the ophthalmic fold is ciliated, the remaining portions are, however, studded with sense hair papillae.

The distribution of the eyes offers several interesting peculiarities that have not been sufficiently treated by previous writers. They are largest and most numerous at the anterior and posterior ends of the flat, left valve; at those points also, the pigment ring of the eye is lighter and less developed, while the eye stalks are short. The pigmented ring is larger and blacker, and the stalks longest, in the median part of the mantle, but, at the same time, the eyes are farther apart, and placed at pretty regular intervals. One of the most remarkable things, is their arrangement in pairs, something in the following manner: two large ones are followed by two smaller ones, all at regular intervals; then follow two large ones, farther apart, with a single one between, and so on: although the sequence may not always be the same, still the paired arrangement is never disguised. I thought, at first, to recognize a definite law in the succession of large and smaller ones, but was finally compelled to admit that the number of eyes not only varied considerably, but that the sequence of the groups was not at all constant. We will show, in speaking of the development, that, although the number and size of the eyes may differ in individuals of the same age, no formation of new eyes takes place, after the attainment of more than a couple of centimetres in size.

Another fact worthy of consideration is that, on the posterior edge of the mantle, and therefore near the rectal opening, there is a special group of six or seven large eyes closely placed, and all nearly equal in size to the largest eyes in the group near the mouth opening; some of the eyes in the latter group are distinguished by being much smaller than the others. Although it is difficult to define exactly the difference between the two groups, — since they often vary considerably, — still they may be always recognized by the characteristics given above.

The eyes of the right mantle are much smaller, and almost uniform in size; they are situated at the summit of long stalks arranged at nearly regular intervals.

In no species of *Pecten* is the difference between the curvature of the right and left valves so strongly marked, as in *Pecten Jacobaeus*, and in no species is to be found an equally strong, corresponding difference in the size and arrangement of the eyes. I have made a great many experiments with *Pecten Jacobaeus*, and have found that, when turned upon the flat side, after a few hours they invariably succeeded in turning over. Among the large number constantly kept in the Aquarium at Naples, I have never seen one resting on the flat valve. In other species of *Pecten*, where there is no difference in the curvature, still there is a tendency to rest upon the right valve; and then, also, one finds a corresponding difference in the development of the eyes, those on the right valve being, if not always smaller, at least less numerous. In *Arca barbata* as well as *Arca Noae*, an exactly similar condition is to be found.

In attempting to account for this difference between the two sides of the mantle, the first thought suggested is that the animal has become accustomed to lie upon one side, so that one part is more exposed to the light than the other; therefore the eyes would attain their greatest development at that point. It is true that, when such a difference was once started, the advantage given to one side of the mantle would lead to a still further differentiation of the two parts. But why is it that animals, which are capable of resting upon either one side or the other, and between which there is no apparent difference in size or curvature, have more and better developed eyes upon the left, than upon the right fold of the mantle? Why is it, for instance, that in *Arca Noae*, or *Arca barbata*, the left half of the mantle is more richly supplied with eyes, than the right, although the right, left, or ventral side may be turned downwards? In *Pecten opercularis*, *P. varius*, and others, there is a well marked difference between the mantle edges, but in a great many cases it is difficult to observe any diversity in the color and curvature of the two shell valves. It is probable that there is a tendency for these species to rest more upon one side than the other, but this cannot be so constantly the case as in *Pecten Jacobaeus*, otherwise, there would be a greater, and more constant difference between the valves of the shell. There are, therefore, two factors which must influence the development of the eyes at certain points: the first is an unknown one, by whose agency a greater development of the pigment and visual organs upon the left side is produced; it is also possible that the same factor might cause a tendency to rest upon the right side; the second moment, which could only come into play after the action of the first, is the advantage gained by having one side nearer the light, and more removed from the sediment of the bottom. The best example of this effect is seen in *Pecten Jacobaeus*, which always rests upon one side, and where a maximum difference between the curvature of the shell valves is accompanied by a maximum difference in the development of the visual organs of the two mantle folds. But I must confess that the apparently doubtful advantage, gained by the eyes of the upper valve, does not seem sufficient to account for the great ascendency they have gained over those of the other side; for, unless the upper mantle edge, or the stalks of the eye, are sufficiently developed to carry the latter beyond the edge of the shell, the lower mantle would receive the more direct rays of light from above. But the eyes of the lower mantle have as long, if not longer, stalks than the upper ones, and project as much beyond the edge of the shell; so we seem to be left just where we started from; that is, without a sufficient reason for the greater development of the eyes upon one side than upon the other.

One finds in those species in which the eyes are especially numerous, — *Pecten varius*, and *P. opercularis*, — a number of eyes, the pupils of which are entirely covered with pigment. I have taken especial pains to examine these organs, which could no longer function as eyes, and have found that the retina, with its rods and nerve fibres, is as perfectly developed, as in the most perfect eyes!

In *Pecten Jacobaeus*, the left side of each eye stalk in the right valve, as well as in the left, is the longer and therefore, when the animal is in its natural position, the pupil is directed upwards.

The stalk of the eye has been described as colorless (except by HENSEN, who says that the stalk, as well as the eye itself, is covered with a pigmented epithelium); but this is not so, for, on the upper side of the eyes on the left valve, is a longitudinal band of pigment exactly similar to the one over the corresponding side of the tentacles. In the lower mantle fold, the bands are, morphologically speaking, on the opposite side, or on that part away from the shell. In both cases, when the animal is in its natural position, the pigmented bands are on the upper side of the eye stalks, and therefore towards the light.

The pigmented ring, around the apex of the eye, offers certain peculiarities which have heretofore escaped notice, or perhaps were not thought worthy of consideration. For instance, in the eyes on the median part of the mantle, the cells on the upper side of the iris are completely filled with a nearly black pigment, most deeply colored at the inner ends of the cells (Pl. 29, fig. 19). When seen »in toto«, this portion forms a specially dark area, continuous with the pigmented band on the same side of the eye stalk. In these median portions of the mantle, the under side of the iris has little, or no pigment, and then the red tapetum may easily be seen through the transparent epidermis, giving to the eyes a characteristic red color. In all cases, the cells on that side of the iris toward the light are darker, and completely filled with pigment; on the opposite side, only the inner ends of the cells are colored.

In the young eyes of *Pecten Jacobaeus* and *P. opercularis*, the pigmented ring, or iris, is broader on the branchial, than on the shell side. In the development, the pigment first appears on the branchial side and grows around the eye. But it often happens that the closure of the ring is not completed even in the fully formed eyes. The incomplete closure gives rise to a narrow, colorless fissure, the choroid fissure, appearing like a triangular extension of the cornea toward the shell side of the iris. By selecting those eyes with a large choroid fissure, one may look through it into the eye, and study the shape of the lens and the general features of the retina.

Since the general structure of the eye has long been so well known, it will not be necessary to give an introductory description, before discussing, in detail, the structure of the various parts.

The beautiful silvery, emerald, violet and purple reflections, caused by the combined effect of the tapetum, argentea and lens, early excited the admiration of Zoologists, and, among all the remarkable objects which the prying eyes of the older, or more recent Naturalists have managed to discover, few are more beautiful, or worthy of admiration than these. When one looks into the pupil, at an angle of about 30° to the optic axis, the emerald and violet reflections are predominant; if, on the other hand, one looks at an angle of 90°, or directly into the eye, the former color disappears, and only the brilliant sparkle of the refractive lens, or the white light of the argentea, is seen.

The tapetum, as is well known, is somewhat concave, and furnishes a perfect mirror for incident rays. But if the microscope, with which one looks directly into the eye, is focused upon the argentea, the red light from the underlying tapetum may be distinctly seen, thus indicating that, although light may enter the eye from below, very little may pass the argentea from above. When the lens is removed, the silvery glance of the argentea is retained, but the violet and emerald colors have disappeared.

The whole external surface of the eye is covered with a continuous layer of columnar epithelium, lowest near the base of the stalk, whence it gradually increases in height as far as the iris, at whose edge it is suddenly reduced in thickness and, losing its pigment, becomes transformed into the transparent cornea, the central part of which is the thickest.

The corneal cells (Pl. 29, fig. 31) are columnar, constricted in the middle, and slightly expanded at either end; the outer one is capped with a layer of cuticula, while the wall of the inner is thrown into a number of narrow folds, which fit into corresponding indentations of the neighboring cells. These folds extend nearly to the middle of the cell, and end about opposite the oval nucleus. An excellent method of studying these structures is either to remove the cornea as a whole by hardening and subsequent maceration, or to isolate the individual cells. In the former case (Pl. 29, fig. 37), when viewed from the inner side, the round serrated ends of the cells may be easily seen, while, by focusing more deeply, the nuclei, and finally the hexagonal or pentagonal outer ends of the cells, appear. In the latter case (by maceration), besides the inner folds of the cells, there will be seen, in the median constricted part, a number of irregular, horizontal teeth (Pl. 29, figs. 31 and 19). They are probably modified, longitudinal folds, which, at this point, are broken up into irregular, spine-like projections, interlocking with those of the adjacent cells. The inner ends of the longitudinal folds are continued inwards as fine fibres, crossing the pseudo-cornea, and uniting with the outer surface of the lens (Pl. 29, fig. 19). This interlocking of the corneal cells, which is also found — but in a less perfected form — in the hypodermis of the eye stalk, gives greater firmness and flexibility to the cornea, a condition necessary for the peculiar movements produced by the ciliary, and other contractile fibres, which we will describe more fully hereafter.

The cells of the iris only differ from those of the cornea, in their greater size, and in being completely filled with pigment. When isolated, they seem to possess the same plicated inner ends, as those of the cornea, except that the folds assume more the character of fibres continued into the subjacent connective tissue. The outer ends are capped with a rather thick cuticula. HENSEN (12) seemed inclined to regard them as sense-cells, which had something to do with the optic function of the eye. SHARP (18) held a similar opinion, ascribing to them the power of distinguishing light from darkness, just as do the cells in the pigmented spots and grooves in the mantle and sipho of *Venus*, *Mactra* and *Solen*, while, to the complicated organ within, — the eye, — he would attribute another function than that of vision. SHARP's supposition arises from a mistaken notion of what the visual elements, in the pigmented areas he has described, really are. It has not, in any case, been proved, that simple, pigmented cells are sufficiently sensitive to changes in the amount of light to cause muscular contractions (the only evidence that we at present possess to show that such a function is present); on the other hand, it is extremely probable, from my observations, that the irritability to light is only found, to a perceptible degree, in what I have called the isolated ommatidia.

The much deeper pigment of the iris on the side toward the light, and the absence of nerve fibres, or isolated ommatidia, indicate that the iris is merely a structure for the exclusion of lateral rays of light from the retina.

The cilia, which HENSEN believed to have seen on the outer ends of these cells, were probably ragged ends, caused by maceration or tearing away of the cuticula, or they belonged to ciliated cells from some other part of the mantle. since no cilia, or sense hairs are to be found on any part of the epithelium of the eye.

The stalk itself consists of loose, connective tissue, often containing enormous blood spaces. Besides the connective tissue forming the wall of the lacunae, there is an upper and lower group of long, striated, muscular cells, serving as erectors and depressors of the eye. They are continued from the stalk toward the anterior pole of the eye, into the connective tissue layer (Pl. 29, fig. 19 *c. t. c.*), where, the cross striae disappearing, they are replaced by numerous, fine, smooth fibres, interspersed with nuclei. The fibres decrease in size and distinctness, until, just beneath the cornea, they form an almost structureless and hyaline layer — the pseudo-cornea, — in which nuclei are seldom found. Beneath the iris, some of the fibres are seen to originate from the ends of pigment cells, while, at the edge, many fibres which, up to that point were distinctly visible, appear to terminate with an outward curve, as though attached to the epithelium at that point, forming what we shall call the ciliaris (Pl. 29, fig. 19 *c. l.*).

The lens which, as the development shows, consists of a modified group of mesodermic cells, continuous with those of the pseudo-cornea and connective tissue capsule, is round and biconvex, with the inner surface much more curved than the outer. It consists of large, irregular, granular cells with very distinct walls and excentric nuclei. The elongated cells in the middle of the lens are the largest, the long diameter being parallel with the optic axis. Toward the inner surface, they become flattened and strap-shaped to form cells, the nuclei of which seem, in many cases, to have entirely disappeared. On the anterior side, the cells are smaller, but not flattened, while, where the two surfaces of the lens meet, they are so minute as to be distinguished only with great difficulty. By isolating the lens, this part is seen to project as a ragged membrane, composed of fibres continuous with those of the connective tissue capsule (Pl. 29, fig. 23 *c. l.*). This membrane will be called the s u s p e n s o r y l i g a m e n t. The outer surface of the lens is covered with two sets of fibres, most conveniently observed in the isolated cornea, or on the surface of the lens, to either of which they may remain attached Pl. 29, fig. 37). They form a layer of strong, circular fibres, concentrically arranged, and superimposed by a smaller number of radiating ones extending from the periphery of the lens to the centre, toward which they gradually diminish in size. In cross sections, the circular fibres of the lens appear as a row of dots, forming a sharp demarkation of the outer surface of the lens (Pl. 29, fig. 19 *c. f. l.*).

The inner surface of the lens is sparingly supplied with branching fibres, which in *Pecten opercularis* accumulate near the centre to form a fibrous mass containing an occasional nucleus, and connecting the lens with the septal membrane (Pl. 29, Fig. 23 *l. l.*). This internal ligament I have been unable to find in *Pecten Jacobaeus*, where, if present at all, it is much less developed: one may, however, observe on the surface, the branching fibres which, becoming more abundant towards the exterior, finally unite with the radiating, or circular, ones to form the s u s p e n s o r y - l i g a m e n t.

The lens of *Pecten opercularis*, being smaller than that of *Pecten Jacobaeus*, is more favorable for observation, and here one may see, what probably exists in the latter genus likewise, a special accumulation of circular fibres to form two contractile rings, close together on the inner and outer surface of the lens (Pl. 29, fig. 23 a^1 and a^2). In *Pecten pusio*[1], the lens is relatively small, and the inner surface less convex on account of the enormous development of the cornea (Pl. 29, fig. 10). In *Pecten varius* the high, conical lens is firmly attached by a connective tissue ligament to the septum, and the pupil is proportionately small.

Recent authors have hardly been more successful than the earlier ones, in determining the true shape of the lens. KEFERSTEIN (11) believed it to be spherical, while HENSEN (12), who in this respect is less accurate than usual, represents it as filling the entire space in front of the retina, and, although his own observations agree with those

---

[1] Fig. 23 represents more correctly the shape of the lens than fig. 19, where it is not quite deep enough.

of KROHN (3), who considered it biconvex, he cannot see sufficient reason to combat the definite description and drawings of KEFERSTEIN. The flattened appearance of the lens, drawn by HENSEN, is caused, as he rightly supposed, by the chromic acid, since I have myself observed that an exactly similar shape is produced by treatment with this reagent. A similar result also appears to have misled CARRIÈRE (19), whose drawing represents exactly the effect certain reagents produce upon the shape of the lens. HICKSON (15), who was surprised at the failure of his predecessors to determine such a simple point, has himself been equally unfortunate, for he considers the lens to be elliptical, a cross section being circular, or equally biconvex, according as it passes through the major, or minor axis. SHARP was led to believe, from the researches of HENSEN and his own observations, that the lens filled the entire space between the retina and cornea.

The soft nature of the lens renders it almost impossible to isolate uninjured, before it is hardened; the majority of reagents destroy its original shape, by causing violent contractions of the muscular walls of the eye. Treatment in weak sulphuric acid for twenty-four hours will enable one to isolate the lens in its perfect and normal condition. By examining many specimens, some eyes will be found with large, choroid fissures, through which the real shape of the lens may be studied and compared with those treated in sulphuric acid.

Neither HENSEN nor HICKSON could find any membrane covering the lens, or any fibres connected with it, although the latter described a ligamentary support for it, ignorant of its having been already more correctly described by KROHN, as the septum, or septal membrane.

The lens is suspended in a large, blood sinus, which has been regarded as a »vitreous humor.« CARRIÈRE first saw the isolated cells in this space, and correctly interpreted them as blood corpuscles. I am at a loss to account for their presence there, since the retina seems to shut out all communication with the blood cavities of the eye stalk. They probably enter through the narrow spaces between the lateral branch of the optic nerve and the surrounding connective tissue. At times, a great many blood corpuscles are found in these spaces, while, again, they may be entirely absent. It is possible that they are forced into the cavity artificially by the violent and unnatural contractions of the connective tissue, caused by reagents.

The lens and the two corneas form the anterior, dioptric part of the eye. The posterior portion consists of a thick, concave disc, completely enclosed within a membranous sac, which we shall call the ommateal sac. The thick, anterior, concave wall, or septal membrane (Pl. 29, fig. 19 *s.*), serves at once to protect the ends of the retinal cells, and as an elastic cushion, upon which the lens rests. The inner wall is still thicker, and constitutes the tough, double-layered sclerotica (fig. 19 *sc.*). At the confluence of these two membranes, the wall of the sac is much thinner, and perforated by innumerable passages for the entrance of nerve fibres from the axial branch of the optic nerve. Within the ommateal sac, the cells constitute a closed vesicle, whose anterior and posterior walls are so closely approximated as to touch each other, thus obliterating the central cavity. The wall of the vesicle, for theoretical reasons to be hereafter enumerated, we shall consider as composed of a single layer of cells, although this simple arrangement is obscured by many changes, resulting in the division of both anterior and posterior walls into several secondary layers. The posterior wall of the ommateal vesicle, then, consists of four layers: an outer vitreous network; a double layered argentea, and the red tapetum. The anterior wall is likewise composed of four layers: an outer ganglionic layer; an inner ganglionic layer; the retinophorae, and the rods containing the retinidia.

We shall first consider the retinophorae, which constitute the largest and most important part of the retina. Their attenuated outer ends, which become insensibly transformed into single nerve fibres, are attached to the periphery of the retina, whence they are directed inwards towards the optic axis (fig. 19 *n. rf.*). The most superficial of these cells, after describing a long curve, bend suddenly at their expanded inner ends almost at right angles, and terminate in the centre of the retina. As the remaining cells end nearer the periphery, their expanded inner extremities become relatively larger, longer, and less sharply bent, until, finally, the shortest and peripheral cells describe a nearly perfect semicircle (Pl. 29, fig. 19). A saucer-shaped layer of cells is thus produced, whose edges are formed by the curved, fibrous ends of the retinophorae, the large, oval nuclei of which (containing a nucleolus) are crowded together at the periphery of the retina. Beyond the nuclei, the cells are continued as slender stalks which, before reaching the ommateal sac, through which they pass as a single nerve fibre, become expanded into a delicate, oblong vesicle, containing a second, faintly stained, and often invisible nucleus (Pl. 29, figs. 34. 35 and 36 *b.*). The expanded, inner extremities of the cells, filled with fine, granular protoplasm, and containing a very faint and minute vacuole, only conspicuous by the constancy of its presence and position, terminate at the same level, and form a gently undulating line of division (the pseudo-membrane, or sieve-membrane of CARRIÈRE) between the cellular layer of the retina, and the underlying rods. The sharpness of this line is enhanced by the fact that the flanged walls of the inner ends of the cells unite with those of the neighboring ones. An exceedingly small space, or canal, surrounding the inner ends of the cells, is thus formed.

A delicate, structureless wall separates the retinophorae from their rods, thus tending still more to produce the impression that a membrane is present. HENSEN and CARRIÈRE called attention to this effect, in order to warn against it. HENSEN attributed it to the fusion of the walls of the neighboring cells, but failed, as did also CARRIÈRE, to see the dividing wall. By studying a series of cross sections at the niveau of the pseudo-membrane, some cells will be seen containing, instead of the granular protoplasm, a thin, homogeneous partition, — the terminal membrane, — the centre of which is perforated by the axial, nerve fibre (Pl. 29, fig. 26 *x*).

The large, abnormal folds figured by HENSEN, HICKSON and CARRIÈRE, especially the two former, are produced by the contraction of the elastic septum, which, in the living condition, is always in a state of tension.

Most of the retinophorae have the peculiar shape indicated in the figures, but a comparatively small number of modified forms, which have escaped previous observers, are mingled with them. They are retinophorae containing the axial nerve fibres and the two nuclei, but differing from the others in being reduced almost to a fibre (Pl. 29, fig. 36). They are not easily seen in sections, but may be found quite frequently among the macerated and detached cells of the retina.

Although I have found some very long ones, which must have terminated near the centre of the retina, they are most abundant near the periphery, where they become gradually transformed into the short, fibrous cells, without rods, which, for lack of a better name, I shall call the pseudo-retinophorae (Pl. 29, fig. 38 *ps. rf.*).

The rods of the retinophorae, which are at once the most interesting part of the eye, and that most difficult to understand, have long resisted all attempts to harden them in anything like a perfect condition. The only method which gives satisfactory results is treatment in hot chromic acid as described at the end of this paper.

My first studies upon the rods of Mollusca were made upon those of *Pecten* prepared in this manner, and the facts thus obtained formed the basis of further observations in other genera of Mollusca, as well as Arthropods.

Although the rods of *Pecten* have been described by HENSEN, CARRIÈRE and HICKSON, they had a very inadequate notion of their structure, or even shape, owing to the lack of proper means of preparation. They are columnar-shaped bodies of a faint, yellowish-red color, largest near the optic axis and gradually diminishing in size toward the periphery of the retina. They consist of a hyaline, refractive cap, or sheath, surrounding a pyramidal, axial core filled with a watery, non-refractive fluid, and, a short distance from the inner ends of the rods, terminating in a rounded apex (Pl. 29, fig. 20).

Each retinophora contains an axial nerve fibre ($ax. f.$), which, entering the attenuated end of the cell, is continued through the first vesicle-like swelling (to whose wall it seems to cling), past the second nucleus, and on, through the centre of the cell, to the inner end of the rod, whence it issues, and, dividing into two main branches, becomes united by connecting loops with the axial fibres of neighboring cells (fig. 20 $l. ax. f^2$.). In order to study these highly interesting conditions, it is necessary to remove the rods »en masse«, and then study their inner ends. From the dark, oval area, representing the apex of the axial cone (Pl. 29, fig. 22) seen in optical section, arises a large nerve fibre, which issues from one side of the rounded inner ends of the rods, and divides into two principal branches, one of which unites with a branch from a neighboring rod to form a »nerve loop«, while the other, bending nearly double, passes between the rods, there giving rise to innumerable fibrillae which surround their outer walls. The ends of the rods are also supplied with minute nerve fibrillae arising from the loops, as well as from the other branches (Pl. 29, fig. 22).

Toward the inner ends of the retinophorae, the axial nerve fibre begins to give off radiating fibrillae, which, in the rods, are so numerous as to constitute the greater part of their substance. When perfectly preserved, which is seldom the case, they form an almost solid core of straight, radiating fibres, some of which, at the inner wall of the sheath, become continuous with circular fibres, while others are continued on, through the sheath, to the surface of the rod, there uniting with branches from the external nerves arising from the ganglionic layer or from the ganglionic branch of the optic nerve (Pl. 29, figs. 20 and 24). In some preparations, the core seems to be filled with fine granules, produced by the coagulation of the fibrillae. In others, the fibrillae are seen to be strongly varicose, so that, with a lower magnifying power, the same granular effect is produced, while, with the strongest immersion lens, $1/20$ LEITZ, the connection between the varicosities may be distinguished. In the most perfect examples, the fibrillae are in the majority of cases smooth. Another and better proof that the structures in question are real fibrillae, proceeding from the axial nerve, may be obtained in the following manner. By treatment, for 18 hours, in chromic acid, $1/4$ or $1/5 \%$, a peculiar effect is produced, for, upon sections of such material, or by teasing in dilute chromic acid, it will appear as though the rods were destroyed, or at least so badly distorted and broken, as to lose all trace of their former shape. The fact is, however, that the rods have burst, the inner ends broken off, and the contents been forced out, or left hanging in various positions. The ragged sheaths of the rods are usually left attached to the ends of the retinophorae. It is the nervous cores of the rods which interest us most, and many of them may be found as oval, or egg-shaped masses, with one end drawn out into a coarse fibre, either perfectly free, or showing all stages of detachment from the rods; there can be, therefore, no doubt of their origin. On closer inspection, it will be seen that the fibrous prolongation, which is the detached, axial nerve. is continued into the centre of the mass, and there gives rise to lateral branches, which on the periphery become continuous with irregular, circular ones. The relation, which these three series of fibres bear to those of the axial core, is so evident as to be beyond question and furnishes a proof that the nervous structure, attributed to the rods, really exists and is not produced by the coagulation of the rod substance. In osmic acid, the rods are stained a deep blue, or black, not due to any fatty substance contained in them, as is shown by their determined resistance to all fat solvents, but to the innumerable nerve fibrillae, with which the entire rod is permeated. HENSEN first saw the axial nerve fibre in the retinophorae, and was able to follow it a short distance into the cell. His remarks lead one to believe that it was a disagreeable duty to record his observations, on account of the difficulty of bringing them into agreement with his remarkable theory upon the connection between sense cells and nerve fibres! CARRIÈRE (19), also, saw what was probably the axial nerve, but did not consider it as such because, in focusing, it moved back and forth (p. 106)!

Finally, a word in regard to the nuclei of the retinophorae. No one was able to determine, among the confusion of nuclei, which of them belonged to the retinophorae. HENSEN does not mention the subject in the text, but, from his figure 95, Pl. XXI, one sees that he regarded the inner ganglionic cells as nuclei. CARRIÈRE, also mistook them for the nuclei of the retinophorae while, the real nuclei, he regarded as those of a circular ganglion, to which he attached considerable importance. The observations of HICKSON are so poor, that it is impossible to determine exactly what he did think.

Besides the retinophorae, two other groups of cells, the inner, and outer, ganglionic layers, are found, adding to the complication of this minute organ. The outer layer, which in its median, thickest part is two, three, or even four cells deep, and toward the periphery, gradually diminishes in thickness to a single cell layer, entirely fills the saucer-shaped cavity formed by the retinophorae.

Although the cells show all variations in size and shape, three types may be distinguished.

(1) The larger, outer ones, whose broad ends terminate in many fibres which penetrate the septal membrane and unite with the superior branch of the optic nerve. Their blunt inner ends, containing large, oval nuclei, are drawn out into several fibres, which, with many others from the deeper cells, extend, radiatingly, towards the inner ends of the retinophorae, after crossing which, at right angles, they are continued along the walls of the cells, to the rods (Pl. 32, fig. 140 gc^1.).

(2) The second kind are large, irregularly shaped cells, drawn out into several fibres, a single one, directed toward the lens, being the largest, and dividing, just before entering the fibrous layer, into several small branches, which are continued onwards to the ganglionic branch of the optic nerve. The outer arms of these cells may be as fine as any nerve fibre, or much thicker, resembling an elongated cell; in this case, it terminates abruptly at the beginning of the fibrous layer, where it breaks up into a number of fine fibres. The inner ends of the cells, which contain large and nearly round nuclei, are drawn out into several fibres, like those of the first type, extending towards the inner side of the retina (Pl. 29, fig. 33 b, and Pl. 32, fig. 140 gc^1.).

(3) The cells of the third form are small and provided with numerous nervous prolongations, one of which passes through the fibrous layer into the outer branch of the optic nerve, while others extend inwards towards the rods (Pl. 32, fig. 140 gc^1.). All these kinds of cells, which show no very definite arrangement except that the first generally constitute the outer row, are evidently modified forms of the same elements.

At the periphery of the retina, the outer ganglionic cells are reduced to a single layer, extending as far as the thin wall of the ommateal sac, where the fibres from the axial branch of the optic nerve enter the retina. These cells are drawn out into two long fibres, which, instead of penetrating the deeper parts of the retina, form an irregular layer of superficial, circular fibres. By isolating the entire retina and examining it from above, the large, oval nuclei will be seen and the prolongation of the spindle-shaped cells may be followed a short distance (Pl. 29, fig. 32 d). Toward the centre of the retina, the cells grow large and round, until transformed into those of the outer, ganglionic layer.

The inner ganglionic layer is composed of a single row of very small, flattened cells, which, when seen at all, were mistaken by previous writers for the nuclei of the retinophorae. This mistake is readily made, since the small cells, almost completely filled with a flattened and deeply stained nucleus, are squeezed flat between the walls of the retinophorae. The best method of studying them is by teasing macerated eyes; the minute cells in question will then be seen closely attached to the side of the retinophorae, — near the angle formed by their bent, inner ends, — by means of several (6 or 7) radiating arms, which, adhering closely to the wall of the cell, extend nearly parallel to each other, towards the rods (Pl. 29, fig. 38). On the outer side, one or two large fibres extend towards the lens and become continued into the ganglionic branch of the optic nerve (Pl. 32, fig. 140 gc^5). Thus the enlarged, inner ends of the retinophorae are surrounded by innumerable, longitudinal fibres, which extend beyond the cells to the inner ends of the rods, over the surface of which they form a network of fibres. One will often be struck with the difficulty of separating these ganglionic cells from the retinophorae, the reason being that the outgrowths of the cells are provided with innumerable, lateral branches completely surrounding the retinophorae with a network of closely united fibrillae, which probably penetrate the cell wall. When one has finally succeeded in isolating them, either by prolonged maceration, or by persistent tapping upon the cover glass, many of the fibrillae will be seen still attached to the fibrous prolongations of the cells (Pl. 29, fig. 36 y). There are, moreover, many nerves arising from the outer layer of ganglionic cells and continued directly onwards to the rods, while others, breaking up into numerous smaller fibres, terminate in the walls of the retinophorae. The nerves terminate in two ways. In the first method, which rarely occurs, a single fibre impinges directly upon the cell wall and there divides into several short fibrillae, connected at their distal extremities with a circular fibril enclosing the whole (Pl. 29, fig. 36 x). In the second method, a nerve fibre, after following the cell wall for some distance, giving off at irregular intervals smaller, lateral branches, finally becomes so minute as to disappear. Many small nerve branches, instead of penetrating the pseudo-membrane, unite with each other to form a network of fibrillae, lodged in the circular spaces formed by the flanged walls of the retinophorae.

There are still other nerve fibres, surrounding the attenuated outer ends of the retinophorae, which could not have originated from either of these ganglionic layers. They probably arise from the angle of the ganglionic nerve (Pl. 29, fig. 19), and, entering the periphery of the retina, follow the general direction of the axial nerves to the inner ends of the retinophorae, where they are lost among the other nerve fibres from the ganglionic layers. It is well nigh impossible to follow a single fibre any distance from its source of origin, but we can say with certainty that most, if not all, of the large fibres from the inner ganglionic cells extend directly inward, over the surface of the rods, while others, from the same cells, extend in the opposite direction to the ganglionic nerve. The inwardly directed fibres may terminate on the wall of the retinophorae, or be continued beyond the pseudo-membrane to the surface of the rods. Their outwardly directed ends may vary from thick, cell prolongations, terminating in many fine fibres, to attenuated processes, themselves no larger than fibres, and which are then continued outward, without branching, to the ganglionic nerve.

There are still other kinds of nerves found in the retina, which, instead of originating from one of the layers of ganglionic cells, may arise from the ganglionic branch of the optic nerve, and proceed directly to the retinal layer, without the intervention of a ganglionic cell (Pl. 32, fig. 140).

The fibrous layer has been described by CARRIÈRE, as a thin layer of nucleated, columnar cells; HENSEN believed it was produced by shrinkage and a consequent drawing out of the nerve fibres from the septum.

Many of the inner cells of the outer, ganglionic layer present a most interesting and instructive sequence of forms. Their inner ends are drawn out into several fibres, while the outer end shows all stages in the transformation of a thick cell body into one or two nerve fibres. One often finds parts of cells, not quite reduced to a nerve fibre, but giving off lateral branches, which unite with the neighboring cells (Pl. 29, fig. 33, Pl. 32, fig. 140 $gc.^4$). I have also found minute, inner, ganglionic cells, to whose surface was attached a nerve fibre ending in a manner exactly similar to those upon the surface of the retinophorae (fig. 140 x). The ganglionic layers, therefore, contain cells in all stages of metamorphosis, from ordinary cells, to the most highly modified ganglionic ones. Those nerve fibres, which arise directly from the ganglionic branch, may be considered as the inner ends of ganglionic cells, the nucleated bodies of which in the earlier stages have become entirely separated from the retina. The ganglionic layer then contains cells in all stages of ganglionic perfection, and showing all grades of union with themselves and with the real sense organs, — the retinophorae and their rods.

Having traced all these fibres to the rods, it remains to see how they terminate there. In cross or longitudinal sections, they are extraordinarily difficult to see, but, by isolating the rods hardened in hot chromic acid, the difficulties will be materially diminished. By the latter method then, one may see the surface of the rods covered with longitudinal fibres, from which arise innumerable, smaller branches encircling the rods with a meshwork of fibrillae (Pl. 29, fig. 20). The larger, longitudinal fibres, instead of growing gradually smaller toward the inner extremity of the rod, retain their original size, and, dividing into one or two branches, unite with each other by arched loops (Pl. 29, fig. 22). From these external loops may arise a few minute fibrillae, which extend over the inner end of the rod. All these fibres adhere so firmly to the surface, that it is extremely probable the ultimate fibres penetrate the rod and become continuous with the cross fibrillae of the axial nerve. The latter, as we have already said, after issuing from one side of the extremity of the rod, divides into two branches; one of which unites with the axial nerve of the neighboring cell, or, in some cases, passes over the end of one rod to unite with the nerve of the next; the other, bending completely double, passes between two adjacent rods, over the surface of which its branches are distributed.

A remarkable peculiarity will be observed by examining the inner surface of a group of detached rods; it will there be seen that the loops of the axial nerves are all turned in the same direction. It is not improbable that some relation exists between this fact, and the original arrangement of the two cells, by the fusion of which the retinophorae were formed. In the very best preparations, the most careful examination failed to discover any trace of a division in the rods, similar to that found in those of *Area*.

On the periphery of the retina, the rods are absent, and the retinophorae reduced to slender fibres, the nuclei of which are difficult to distinguish from those of the inner, ganglionic layer. In fact, at this point, the retinophorae, and the inner ganglionic cells, together with many nerve fibres from the outer ganglionic layer, form an inextricable mass of interlacing fibres, which are less intricate near the inner surface of the retina, where the prolongations of the first two sets of cells form a layer of parallel fibres, directed toward the inner surface of the eye.

At the periphery of the circular, rod-bearing area, the nuclei of the short retinophorae are situated near the pseudo-membrane in large vesicle-like swellings of the cell, whose narrow and rodless inner ends are surrounded by several large fibres from the inner, ganglionic cells (Pl. 29, fig. 38 *n. rf.*²). The latter, which elsewhere formed a single row above the rods, on the periphery of the retina become more numerous, and form, near the inner surface, several rows difficult to distinguish from the nuclei of the pseudo-retinophorae. It is worthy of notice that, on the periphery of the retina, there is much less specialization of the cells, the retinophorae being smaller, and the inner ganglionic cells larger, than in the middle of the eye.

There are certain points in the anatomy of the retina that may be studied to great advantage, by isolating it entire, and, after staining in picro-carmine, examining either from above or below (Pl. 29, fig. 32). In the former instance, one sees at the edge, first, the superficial, single layer of outer ganglionic cells (*d*); below them are the slender ends of the retinophorae, with the inner ring of their large, deeply stained nuclei, and the outer ring of vesicles containing the faintly stained ones (*c*): the nerve fibres continuous with the peripheral ends of the retinophorae are seen projecting in groups beyond the edge of the retina.

Beneath the retinophorae, is a small number of scattered nuclei contained in large spindle-shaped vesicles, filled with a mass of granular protoplasm in the centre of which is a clear space, containing an oval, sharply stained nucleus (*b*). These nuclei belong to those cells which form the transitional stages between the retinophorae and the pseudo-retinophorae. Whether the clear space surrounding the nucleus is produced by artificial shrinkage, I cannot say; it is, however, certain that the space is invariably present, and furnishes a means by which these cells may be easily recognized. Beneath the last layer, is a fourth, formed by numerous, small, sharply stained nuclei belonging to the inner ganglionic cells, and the pseudo-retinophorae. Toward the inner surface, to examine which it is better to turn the retina on the other side, these smaller nuclei begin to assume a circular arrangement, being placed with their flattened sides toward the centre of the retina (*a*). At the surface, the nuclei have disappeared, and we have, instead, a delicate membrane reaching from the edge of the retina to the beginning of the rods, and extending completely round the retina (Pl. 29, figs. 32 and

38 c.m.). In this manner a circular membrane — membrana circularis — is formed, composed of nearly concentric, circular fibres, often expanded into little knob-like swellings, which stain in haematoxylin, and have the appearance of nuclei. It is possible that they may be the aborted nuclei of those cells, by the fibrous transformation of which the circular membrane was formed; but the structures in question were so minute that it was impossible to arrive at any definite conclusion. The circular membrane seems to be divided into two, nearly equal zones, of which the inner is thicker and better defined, and terminates sharply at the edge of the disc-shaped layer of rods; the outer zone diminishes in completeness towards the periphery, where it gradually disappears.

The four layers just described, the outer and inner ganglionic layers, the retinophorae, and the rods, are all modifications of a single layer of cells forming the outer wall of the optic vesicle. Its inner wall is likewise composed of four layers; the vitreous network, the inner and outer argentea, and the tapetum. In each wall of the optic vesicle, three of the four layers are cellular, while one, formed by the rods in one instance and the vitreous network in the other, is non-cellular.

The vitreous network is extraordinarily difficult to preserve in its natural shape, and has, for that reason, been overlooked by previous authors. CARRIÈRE (p. 104) speaks of the rods as being immersed in a fatty substance (staining deeply in osmic acid), which extends between the rods as far as the sieve-membrane on the one side, and is limited by the tapetum (argentea) on the other. This fatty mass is formed by the fusion of the sheaths of the poorly preserved rods, while what he considered as the rods are simply the axial cores. The fatty mass of CARRIÈRE must not, therefore, be confounded with the vitreous network, which may be regarded as a very thin layer of hyaline substance, perforated by large holes into which the inner ends of the rods fit (Pl. 29, fig. 21). The holes, then, are as large, and have the same hexagonal or pentagonal shape, as the inner ends of the rods; they are separated from each other by narrow bars, provided at their points of union with short, vertical projections, which ascend a short distance between the inner ends of the rods. — The vitreous substance, therefore, forms a complete network, the meshes of which constitute a crown for the inner end of each rod, completely filling the narrow space left between their rounded edges and the argentea. On the periphery of the retina, where the rods are absent, the vitreous network is transformed into a thin plate filled with numerous and irregular holes (Pl. 29, fig. 21 a). The vitreous network, as is indicated by its development, is a cuticular secretion of the outer layer of the argentea, and is homologous with the cuticular rods secreted by the retinophorae.

The argentea is formed by the modification of two cell layers into refractive, laminated membranes. the outer being the most highly differentiated. Each membrane is composed of minute, square plates, whose edges are bevelled in such a manner that the outer faces are smaller than the inner, which rest upon the undifferentiated, under surface of the membrane by which all the plates are held together. In passing inwards, the membranes become thinner, less distinct and refractive, while the lamellated structure entirely disappears.

In sections, the retina is usually separated by a considerable space from the two, folded layers of the argentea, which, in the living condition, is perfectly smooth and concave; its thicker outer layer, in the adult condition, never contains nuclei, although one or two may occasionally be found in the inner, less refractive and less differentiated one. The argentea is thicker in the centre of the eye, whence it gradually diminishes to a thin layer, extending to the periphery of the retina, and terminating at the place where the fibres from the axial branch of the optic nerve enter the ommateal sac. In the outer membranes of the argentea, the spaces separating the squares from each other are not superimposed, but arranged so as to fall above the middle of the underlying squares (Pl. 29, fig. 29). In the inner membrane, where the square plates are either extremely thin, or entirely absent, it is impossible to recognize this arrangement. When the argentea is »in situ«, it reflects a soft, silvery light, like that from a highly polished mirror; the refraction of this light by the crystal-like lens gives rise to the well known, emerald and violet colors first seen and described by POLI. By removal of the lens, these colors disappear and we have instead the silvery light of the argentea and the colorless light from the lens. The iridescence produced by the lens, or argentea, depends greatly upon the condition of the animal, and the position of the eye as regards the light. The emerald and violet reflections are often entirely absent. The isolated argentea appears, by reflected light, like plates of polished silver. The transmitted light is differently refracted in various parts, producing red, orange, yellow, blue and purple lights. The optical properties of the argentea are not easily understood, but it appears that in general, while acting as a perfect reflector for incident rays passing through the lens, it offers no great impediment to the entrance of light into the retina, after passing through the colorless eye-stalk and red tapetum.

Although the septum, sclerotica and tapetum stain deeply in haematoxylin, the argentea never, to my knowledge, absorbs coloring matter. KROHN first described the argentea of *Pecten*, and ascribed to it the luminous appearance of these eyes. WILL appeared to confound it with the tapetum. HENSEN seems to have seen the minute, square plates of the membranes, for he mentions the »Stäbchenförmige Moleculc«, which he is inclined to regard as cells. HICKSON saw the play of color produced by the argentea, which he considered gave the eyes their »beautiful metallic lustre«. The argentea is formed according to him »of a great number of fine fibrils crossing at right angles«. CARRIÈRE states that. »Das Tapetum lucidum besteht aus feinen Fasern, welche alle in derselben Richtung verlaufen, und zwar, gleich den Seitennerven innerhalb des Auges, quer (senkrecht) zu der Oberfläche des Mantels«.

The tapetum, the red pigment layer of previous writers, usually consists of a single layer of cells, decreasing in thickness from the axial part of the eye toward the periphery, and terminating, with the argentea, at the entrance of the fibres from the axial branch of the optic nerve into the retina. The cells are large, many-sided bodies filled with coarse, red pigment granules, in the midst of which is a round, or oval, vesicle-like nucleus containing, in a clear fluid, two or three deeply stained and irregularly shaped granules, or nucleoli. The red color is preserved excellently well in hot sublimate, while it is dissolved or destroyed in alcohol, or in combinations of picric or chromic acid.

The tapetum forms one of the most conspicuous objects in the eye, and, for that reason, has long been known. It was first described by KROHN, but HENSEN was the first to discover its cellular nature. HICKSON was subsequently unable to confirm HENSEN's observations, and came to the conclusion that »the pigment contains no cellular elements at all«! CARRIÈRE has correctly described and figured the tapetum, which he erroneously considers to be a continuation of the nucleated septum. It must be considered, however, as continuous with the retina, and homologous with the outer ganglionic cells, as we shall explain more fully in treating the development of the eye; (see diagram. Pl. 32, figs. 151—152). A circumstance, which I cannot regard as accidental, is that, in the eyes of all the species of *Pecten* examined, the tapetum is not surrounded by pigment, but is exposed to the light from below. The iris always extends as far inwards as the outer edge of the tapetum, and there abruptly terminates. On the shell side, the iris, as has already been described, extends much further towards the mantle, and forms a narrow, pigmented band on that side of the stalk. We have failed to form any conclusion, as to what this apparently intentional exposure of the red pigment to the light, signifies.

The optic vesicle, with its eight layers, is contained in the ommateal sac. The anterior wall, the septum of Krohn, forms a stout and elastic cushion or spring, upon which the lens rests. The septum is formed of a double membrane; the thickened and structureless central part of the outer layer, a little to one side of the optic axis, is perforated by the ganglionic nerve branch (fig. 19); the peripheral part of the septum, gradually diminishing in thickness toward the edge of the ommateal sac, consists of numerous connective tissue cells modified into circular fibres. The nuclei of the cells are extremely difficult to find in the adult condition, on account of their minute size, and flattened shape. They are most easily seen in surface preparations of the membrane, which may be isolated without special difficulty. In young eyes, the nuclei of the septal membrane may be easily seen (fig. 10). The sheath of the ganglionic branch — according to Hensen — fuses with the septal membrane; but my own observations indicate that it terminates when the nerve leaves the connective tissue and enters the blood spaces surrounding the lens. The inner membrane of the septum is uniformly thin and structureless. The ganglionic branch forms a disc-like expansion upon its outer surface, over which the nerve fibres radiate in all directions. Toward the periphery, the nerve disc is so thin that the two membranes become closely united, and finally fuse with each other.

One may easily isolate this inner membrane, together with the disc-like end of the ganglionic nerve. It may then be seen that the outer surface of the membrane is smooth, but that the inner one is covered with the ends of the nerves which have penetrated the membrane. Carrière has attempted to show that the tapetum is continuous with the septum, to which he ascribes a cellular nature. The real nuclei of the septum, he did not see, for it is evident, from his figure 80, that what he considers to be the septum is composed of the septal membrane together with the single layer of cells formed by the continuation toward the periphery of the outer ganglionic layer!

The sclerotica, or inner wall of the ommateal sac, consists of a tough, hyaline, connective tissue membrane, thickest in the median parts opposite the pupil, whence it is continued, gradually decreasing in thickness, to the periphery of the retina, there becoming continuous with the septal membrane. The sclerotica has always been described as a single layer. According to my own observations it is formed of two layers, the inner of which is marked with short parallel cross lines; the thick, outer one consists of faint longitudinal fibres, the superficial ones of which may contain a few nuclei (Pl. 30, fig. 39). It has only been in three or four instances that the cross markings have been observed, but they were then seen so distinctly that there can be no doubt that such a structure was present. These lines produce the effect of plates of alternating density, rather than of fibres. This structure of the sclerotica seems to be best preserved by treatment with chromic acid, $1,5 \%$ for 24 hours. The sections must be examined in water, or some other medium with a low refractive index. The sclerotica has been considered to be continuous with the pseudo-cornea, by means of the connective tissue layer beneath the iris. The two latter structures are, however, merely continuations of the contractile tissue of the stalk into the anterior pole of the eye, while the sclerotica is directly continued into the **septal membrane**.

The **optic nerve** arises from the circumpallial nerve, and, after extending through the centre of the stalk, divides into two, nearly equal branches, of which the basal one abuts against the sclerotica, a short distance on the shell side of the optic axis, and then, losing its sheath, divides into many bundles of free nerve fibres, which, clinging closely to the sclerotica, ascend radiatingly towards the periphery of the retina, where they penetrate, in quite distinct groups, the ommateal membrane, and become continuous with the attenuated ends of the retinophorae, through the centre of which they are extended as axial nerve fibres. The **basal, or axial** branch of the optic nerve, therefore, consists entirely of the axial nerve fibres of the retinophorae. The division of the optic nerve takes place in a plane at right angles to that of the mantle. The lateral, or ganglionic branch, produced by this division, ascends toward the shell side of the retina, over which it is bent at nearly right angles, and is continued over the surface of the septum, the thick outer layer of which it penetrates just below the inner surface of the lens. After passing both layers of the septum, in the manner already described, its fibres either unite with the ganglionic layers, or pass between their cells to the surface of the rods. In the fibrous layer, two kinds of fibres may be distinguished, the most numerous are extremely fine, and arise from the outer ends of the oblong ganglionic cells; the larger and less numerous ones are the single prolongations of the more deeply situated ganglionic cells of the outer layer. Even in the disc-like expansion of the ganglionic nerve branch, one may see both kinds of fibres, and follow them a short distance into the more compact part of the nerve. That the sheath of the ganglionic branch is lost, before entering the blood spaces surrounding the lens, is shown by the fact that, as it bends inwards, it gives off numerous radiating fibres from its outer surface, which enter the periphery of the retina, without passing through the thickened central part of the septum. They are the fibres which surround the narrow outer ends of the retinophorae, and of which we have already spoken.

The optic nerve and the proximal parts of its two branches are surrounded by a delicate sheath, beneath which is a cortical, nucleated layer surrounding the central fibrous axis. The connective tissue of the stalk contains several large blood sinuses. The numerous radiating arms of the connective tissue cells, at the periphery of the stalk, become more regularly arranged, and constitute a system of circular and longitudinal muscular fibres. The latter, on the branchial and shell side of the stalk, form two, quite well defined groups of large, striated muscular fibres. Toward the base of the eye, are large, scattered, ganglionic cells, drawn out into several fibres, and filled with granular protoplasm Pl. 29, fig. 19).

Besides the tissues already mentioned, there are numerous long and refractive fibres, which arise from the mass of fibres at the periphery of the stalk, and, converging toward the base of the eye, penetrate the sclerotica and the superimposed layers, as far as the inner ends of the rods. In the stalk they are easily seen as single, seldom branched, wavy fibres, which, in the sclerotica, expand into refractive, spindle-shaped bodies, — often of a very faint pink color, — and are then continued still further inward, either as single fibres, or divided into several branches. These remarkable fibres, concerning whose origin and formation no very satisfactory explanation can be given, — see Pl. 32, figs. 151 and 152 — are as difficult to preserve, especially the ends with the spindle-shaped swellings, as the two layers of the sclerotica, and, like them, their preservation depends upon conditions, which I was neither able to understand nor control. In successful preparations, the number of the spindles seems to vary considerably: in one instance, in which they were preserved with remarkable clearness, I could only count three or four in each section: in other cases, as many as fifty or sixty could be seen.

Development of the Eyes of Pecten.

The following observations concerning the development of the eyes of *Pecten* were made upon young specimens, from 1–3 mm. long, of

Pecten opercularis. Other species, as *P. pusio*, *P. varius*, *P. flexuosus*, *P. inflexus* and *P. testae*, were also studied, but, in all except *P. pusio*, the differences were unappreciable.

The following description, with the exception of one or two remarks concerning *P. pusio*, refers entirely to *P. opercularis*.

The mantle edge of young Pectens has the three characteristic folds well developed. In the adult, these folds are enlarged and complicated by the presence of secondary ones, and several rows of tentacles. The walls of both the ophthalmic and shell folds are specially thickened, and ciliated on the shell side. The former, in *P. opercularis*, is short and thick, its free extremity being divided into two thick-walled and ciliated lobes: in *P. pusio* it is unequally forked, the outer division being much longer and thicker than the inner.

The pigment in the youngest specimens, 1 mm long, is entirely confined to the eye spots. In larger ones of 2 mm, the velum is covered with light yellow or red blotches, in which are many large, scattered ommatidia, usually single, but often united into pairs. They form irregular black spots, consisting of several darkly pigmented cells surrounding a central colorless one. These isolated ommatidia are larger and more conspicuous than any I have ever seen. In the adult, they are less prominent and may disappear entirely. Between the base of the ophthalmic fold and the velum is a narrow pigmented band, extending the whole length of the mantle, and, at places, deepened into longitudinal grooves, from the bottom of which are often developed the hypodermic thickenings, which constitute the rudiments of the eye. The thin branchial wall of the ophthalmic fold, usually colorless, with here and there a minute, yet black pigmented pit (fig. 2 *y*), is seldom provided with cilia, which are principally confined to the two thickened, terminal lobes and the opposite face of the fold. The pigmented pits consist of minute, deeply pigmented cups, sharply circumscribed, and not to be confounded with simple, irregularly shaped pigment spots upon the level surface of the ophthalmic fold. Not more than three or four cells, completely filled with black pigment, take part in the formation of these pits, which, in their position and general appearance, recall the invaginated eyes of *Arca*. The colorless cells, so universally present in the latter, could not be detected; but in spite of their absence (probably due to having escaped notice on account of their minute size and the difficulties of observation), I consider that these transitory pigmented cups are homologous with the invaginated eyes of *Arca*.

In cross sections of the very youngest specimens (1 mm long), may be seen, at the base of the ophthalmic fold, between it and the velum, a few large cells constituting small oval thickenings, the rudiments of a future eye (fig. 18)[1].

The cells of the thickening are large and columnar, striated at the outer extremities, while at the inner end they are clearer and bounded by faint lines. Instead of terminating in a sharply defined boundary, the protoplasm is often drawn out into many amoeboid-like arms, in the larger of which are nuclei. The boundaries between the cells are very faint and often invisible. The cilia, which are usually confined to the apical lobes (fig. 2), in this case extend over the optic thickening (fig. 18). On the outer edge of the rudimentary eye (that is away from the hinge), the nuclei are smaller and show a tendency to form a double row. In the next stage (fig. 14), an increased development is indicated by the greater number of nuclei on the outer side of the thickening, and their tendency to form several rows. They are likewise smaller than those forming a single layer on the opposite side. In this example also, the cilia have extended over the optic thickening, but they are fewer and smaller and appear to be degenerating. Both figs. 14 and 18 are sections of larvae, 1 mm long, in which no pigment was developed. In these young specimens, the absence of anything like a basal membrane, and the manner in which the inner ends of the cells are drawn out into naked, protoplasmic, amoeboid arms, some of which contain nuclei, is worthy of notice.

By continued proliferation of the cells on the outer side of the optic thickening, an oval, knob-like papilla is formed, the long diameter of which is parallel with the optic tract (fig. 11).

The optic tract is now pigmented, as well as the base of the papillae at whose summit (fig. 11) the pigment is absent. The wall of the thickening becomes better defined and consists of a single row of regularly arranged nuclei, except on the outer side where the proliferation to form the hypodermic core continues, thus, at that point, preventing the formation of any sharp line of demarkation between the superficial hypodermis and the underlying cells. The difference in the manner of division between the cells of the upper and lower side of the optic papilla gives rise to a change in form and direction of growth. At the point *h.y.* fig. 11, the plane of division is parallel to a tangent at the surface, and therefore the cells grow inwards to form the core.

---

[1] For the sake of convenience in the following description, we shall speak of the pigmented band, from which all the eyes originate, as the »optic tract«.

On the inner side, the plane of division is at right angles to the tangent, and consequently the hypodermis at that point increases in extent, but remains single layered. This causes an elongation, and flattening of the papilla, the proliferating point, *hy.* assuming a position more and more on the outer side. At first the hypodermic core is not at all sharply defined; several of the more deeply situated cells (figs. 11, 12 and 16) separate from the rest and mingle with the numerous connective tissue cells, from which they finally become indistinguishable. They are the ganglionic cells, which later provide the eye with nerve fibres. The division of the cells, on the outer side of the papilla, soon ceases, and the solid core of deeply stained nuclei becomes surrounded by a well defined, single layer of hypodermis, containing dark, homogeneously stained nuclei (figs. 12 and 16). Several connective tissue cells have grown, by rapid divison, between the hypodermis and the core, around which they form a single layered capsule of cells loosely connected by means of protoplasmic outgrowths. The nuclei are distinguished from those of the hypodermis by containing a clear, faintly stainable fluid, in which are several minute and intensely stained bodies, often collected into a flattened plate in the centre of the nucleus. Up to a late period in the development, these characteristics serve to distinguish the connective tissue cells from those of the hypodermis. At the base of the core are several large ganglionic cells, one of which is represented in fig. 12. After the core has been entirely separated from the hypodermis and enclosed within the connective tissue capsule, the whole papilla becomes elongated and somewhat flattened, while a disc-shaped cavity appears in the centre of the core, transforming it into the optic vesicle, the equally thick anterior and posterior walls of which, at first, consist of a single layer of cells. An inequality in the two walls soon appears, in that the nuclei of the outer, retain their radial arrangement, while those of the inner become tangentially disposed, at the same time forming a double layer of lighter colored nuclei (fig. 4). The outer layer of the optic vesicle develops into the retina, while the two inner ones give rise to the argentea, *ag,* and tapetum, *ta.*

The cavity of the vesicle, which becomes more and more flattened, in the earlier stages appears to be filled with a clear fluid, through which delicate, protoplasmic filaments pass from the inner to the outer wall.

In the following stages, the posterior wall becomes more sharply defined, and here, for the first time, the cells of the optic vesicle are provided with distinct cell walls (fig. 5). The outer row of cells, ag^1 and ag^2, becomes filled with refractive, yellowish green granules, some of which soon lose their color, and, at the outer surface of the cells, assume a regular arrangement in layers. With their loss of color and further development, the granules become more refractive and flattened, until they finally unite to form the membranes of square plates, so characteristic of the argentea in the adult. By the overlapping of the cells (fig. 5), the argentea is soon converted into a distinct double layer, of which the outer cells become most quickly transformed into the reflecting membrane, while the inner retain for a long time their nucleated, protoplasmic structure.

The retinal layer (fig. 5, r) increases in thickness, and its large, deeply stained, oval nuclei, containing numerous dark granules, become two or three layers deep: at the same time a slight indentation on the outer surface indicates the beginning of the saucer-shaped depression of the retina which, in the adult, is lined with the outer ganglionic cells. An extremely delicate structureless membrane forms the boundary of this depression and furnishes the first trace of the septum (fig. 5, s'). Just above the latter, the nuclei of four connective tissue cells are collected, being the first step toward the formation of the lens. The further development of the retina is accomplished by an increase in the depth of the central depression, below which the outer ganglionic layer becomes established by the arrangement of the nuclei in a single layer, and the appearance of the cell walls. The nuclei, on the thickened periphery of the retinal layer, are still characterised by being more deeply stained, and arranged three or four deep. As these changes become more and more marked, the retina divides into three zones, consisting of the fibrous (fig. 17 y'), the ganglionic (r), and the retinophoric layer ($n.rf.$). The fibrous layer is first seen beneath the septum, as a clear area, which gradually increases in width, until it has reached the condition represented in fig. 17. The ganglionic cells, which in the earlier stages we have seen separated from the hypodermic core, can no longer be distinguished; but, from the tissue of the ophthalmic fold arise numerous, varicose, nerve fibres which, reaching the eye, penetrate the wall of the optic vesicle, where they divide into numerous branches. These nerve fibres are the remnants of the outer ends of ganglionic cells, which — after the withdrawal of their nuclei and cell bodies from the eye into the underlying tissue — still remain united with the retina by a long nerve fibre, the end of which indicates, approximately, the original position of the ganglionic cells (figs. 4 and 5 $n.f.$). With the development of the retina these fibres increase in number and assume a more parallel arrangement. Whereas at first the fibres seemed to terminate indefinitely in the retinal layer, they now appear to end abruptly in the drawn-out ends of the ganglionic cells. Besides the nerves, the fibrous layer also contains numerous, minute and deeply stained particles, which, in the later stages, disappear entirely (fig. 17 *n. f.*). The middle, or ganglionic layer is formed of a single row of large, round nuclei, whose cells are filled with coarse, granular protoplasm. The periphery of the retina is filled with several rows of nuclei, imbedded in a clear protoplasm, a part of which gradually grows toward the centre of the eye, and forms a clear, narrow band beneath the ganglionic layer (fig. 17).

The lens has increased somewhat in size (compare figs. 5 and 17) and begins to show traces of its future shape; at its periphery, it still passes insensibly into the thin layer of connective tissue cells, surrounding the optic vesicle.

The epithelium of the eye consists of a thin layer of cells, the nuclei of which are widely separated. The greenish yellow pigment granules, which at first were only present around the base of the eye, have encroached upon the anterior pole, around which they form a deeply pigmented and nearly complete ring, the **iris**. The anterior pole remains colorless and forms the **cornea**. The iris is best developed upon the branchial side of the eye; on the opposite side only traces of pigment are to be found.

The **tapetum** forms a single layer, filled with **red pigment, before** the pigment of the iris has appeared. The cells **first become filled with coarse, colorless and refractive granules**, which soon acquire the characteristic red color of the tapetum.

The nuclei of the **retinophorae**, which at first form a thickened ring around the retina, gradually grow inwards towards the centre of the eye. It is not till quite late in the development, after the appearance of the **rods**, that the cell walls, containing the nuclei, become visible.

To determine the exact manner in which the **rods** develope, is an extremely difficult problem. Although my sections of that stage were most numerous and perfect, I was unable to come to any satisfactory conclusion as regards their origin. The clear space, represented in fig. 17, *y*, increased in thickness up to a certain point and then the faint outlines of the rods, together with the **pseudo-membrane**, suddenly appeared, only a little less distinctly than those of fig. 10. The only difference, between the rods when first seen and those of the adult, was in the large size of the **axial core** of the former, and the extremely thin shell, or sheath, scarcely visible except at the tips of the rods.

As soon as the latter could be clearly distinguished, they were seen to contain an axial nerve fibre.

The changes, by which an eye as complete as that represented in fig. 17 is transformed into the adult condition, are of no great morphological value, and are easily comprehensible without the use of figures. The lens increases in size, while between it and the cornea, the pseudocornea is formed by an ingrowth of connective tissue. The increasing convexity of the lens causes a space to be formed between it and the retina. The nucleated septal membrane is produced by the flattening and elongation of the connective tissue cells beneath the lens. The fibrous layer becomes more sharply defined, while the small deeply stained bodies (fig. 17 *y*) disappear.

The ganglionic cells increase in number, fig. 10, and form a double layer, from the periphery of which several small cells subsequently become separated and attach themselves to the ingrowing retinophorae (fig. 10, *d. c. c.*'. In this manner, the two layers of ganglionic cells become definitely established.

The argentea undergoes no great change after the condition represented in fig. 17. The nuclei simply decrease in size until they finally disappear, with the exception of those of the inner layer where, in the adult condition, one or two aborted nuclei may rarely be observed.

With the appearance of the rods, a fourth layer, the vitreous network, is produced, either by a secretion, or transformation of the outer argentea. The vitreous network, in contrast with its subsequent condition, forms a thick homogeneous and structureless layer (fig. 10, *i*). The innumerable, isolated fibres, which even in the earlier stages innervated the eye (fig. 4 and 5), subsequently unite to form a single, loose bundle of nerve fibres, the primitive optic nerve, which later divides into the more sharply circumscribed, axial branches of the definite optic nerve. All the nerve fibres supplying the optic vesicle are not collected to form the optic nerve, for many (fig. 10, *x*), terminating in the base of the vesicle, retain their primitive arrangement and appear to penetrate the sclerotica, tapetum and argentea, as far as the rods. Most of these fibres, in the opposite direction, are turned toward the shell side of the stalk, where they become loosely united with each other and connected with the ganglionic swelling of the circumpallial nerve from which the optic nerve originates (fig. 10, *cp. n.*). Even in the fully grown animals, these nerves, already described, may be seen as rather large, refractive, wavy fibres, which appear to have lost (?) their nervous function.

The circumpallial nerve contains as many ganglionic swellings as there are optic nerves. In many, if not all, of these ganglia, there is a peculiar infolding dividing them into halves (fig. 10, *cp. n.*).

The free edge of the ophthalmic fold contains at regular intervals, large ova-like cells, which may be seen in preparations of the whole mantle edge, as well as in section (figs. 2 and 7). I am unable to offer any suggestion as to their signification.

In the neighborhood of the hinge, the branchial wall of the mantle of younger specimens is thrown into a variety of thick ciliated folds, the nuclei of which are, in most cases, several rows deep (figs. 1 and 9). The outer of these folds is occasionally thinner and more protuberant than the others. It is likewise characterized by its innumerable cilia, so closely packed and equal in length that they appear more like a striated protoplasmic layer, than cilia; they also form little tufts or groups over each flattened cell (fig. 1). In some cases, one of the folds becomes especially enlarged at its extremity, the walls thickening to form a kidney-shaped body with a great many small, deeply stained nuclei (fig. 15). The surface is covered with a cuticula provided with minute papillae, from each one of which originates an enormously long cilium continued through the cuticula into the clear cortical layer (fig. 15, *a.y*). Toward the hinge, the ophthalmic fold may undergo a similar change, in that both its walls become greatly thickened and filled with several rows of small nuclei (fig. 13); in this instance, however, the cilia are absent. The tentacles are usually developed between the eye and the velum, but towards the later stages, it often happens that they may originate at the base of the ophthalmic fold, between it and the eye (fig. 7).

While in Trieste, I partially prepared a paper upon the sense hair papillae of Mollusca, the publication of which was delayed with the hope of finishing certain observations, not as complete as I desired. While studying the development of the eyes of *Pecten*, my attention was attracted by certain facts, concerning the origin of the tentacular nerves and the sense papillae, which promised to throw light upon the origin of the optic nerves. It was also necessary, for other reasons, that a comparison should be made between the development of the eyes, and that of the tentacles, in order to determine the relation between the two structures, and to see whether, as has been suggested, the eyes are modified tentacles or not.

The following remarks, concerning the origin of the sense papillae, do not properly belong here, and therefore only enough will be said to serve for comparison between the development of these fibres and those of the eye. A more detailed account of the sense hair papillae and their origin will be reserved for a future paper.

The sense hair papillae may originate at any place along the outer surface of the velum, or along the optic tract. They appear, at first, as thickenings of the hypodermis — similar to those of the eyes — which soon become conical, with a tuft of stiff sense hairs at the apex (fig. 6). The inward proliferation of the cells, at that point, gives rise to an ectodermic core, which becomes transformed into a longitudinal nerve with which every tentacle is provided. As the papillae increase in length, tufts of sense hairs are formed on the sides, each connected with one or two ganglionic cells (fig. 6). In those papillae, on the surface of the velum (fig. 8), which do not develop into tentacles, no nerve is formed; but two or three cells are separated from the summit of the papilla, and wander into the underlying tissue, there forming ganglionic cells, the nerve-like ends of which may terminate in a small number of sense hairs: or, if the cells are more highly specialized, the sense hairs may be absent, and the terminal fibres divided into numerous fibrillae, which supply the adjacent cells.

Many of the papillae are deeply pigmented; others on the contrary may be entirely colorless.

Ostrea.

I have not been able to find, in this genus, the eyes referred to by WILL and others, and, since more recent authors have been equally unsuccessful, we must, I think, believe that he was either mistaken, or examined some other species.

Besides the pigment scattered irregularly over the surface, I have observed, beneath the epidermis, a great many pigment balls (from .01 to .005 mm in diameter) smaller than, but similar to, those of *Cardium*. The tentacles are nearly pigmentless and ciliated. The hypodermis at the extremities, is thickened and supports a number of sense hairs; this is also the case with *Mactra*. In the pigmented areas, the same colorless cells, as in *Arca*, are seen surrounded by pigmented ones, and undoubtedly represent scattered ommatidia.

I can confirm the statement of SHARP, that *Ostrea* is sensitive to changes in the intensity of light. He has sectioned the pigmented areas and finds two kinds of cells, pigmented and colorless ones, which he compares to those found by FRAISSE in *Patella*, and believes, with him, that the latter secrete the cuticula, while the former are those sensitive to light.

Mactra.

The extremity of the sipho of *Mactra stultorum* is provided with a number of oval pigmented areas, varying in color from madder brown to dark purple, or even jet black; some, usually the darkest ones, are placed at the base of the tentacle, others, similar in shape, but lighter colored, are to be found on the free edge of the sipho. In the latter case, the pigment cells are arranged in small groups, in the centre of which is a clear, refractive spot. At the base of the tentacles, the cells are too deeply colored to admit of such a clear view. In the latter instance, it appears as though the pigment was deposited beneath the surface, but, unfortunately, the superficial examination that I gave them will not allow me to make any positive statement: I, however, believe that the clusters of pigmented cells, in the centre of which were the clear refractive points, are the same structures we have seen in *Arca*, that is ommatidia, composed of pigmented cover cells surrounding a central colorless one.

In *Mactra helvetica*, the pigmented areas are less numerous but apparently more highly specialized.

SHARP has examined *Mactra solidissima* and found the same sensitiveness to light and shadow, as in other genera with which he has experimented. I have tested *Mactra stultorum* and *Mactra helvetica*, in the same manner, and found that they also have this sensitiveness to a marked degree. His statement that the pigment cells tend to form shallow grooves at the base of the tentacles, I am neither able to confirm nor refute, having never studied them by means of sections, as he has done.

Pinna.

The bodies on the mantle of *Pinna*, first described by WILL as eyes, have in more recent times been supposed to possess some other function than that of vision. That they have the general shape and appearance described by WILL, can easily be seen on superficial examination. The slit-like fold, which he considers to form a kind of iris, is caused by muscular contraction of the mantle, and may, or may not be present. CARRIÈRE, after an examination by means of sections, concludes that the organs in question are not eyes, but peculiar glands.

Toward the expiration of the time at my disposal for the preparation of this paper, I was enabled to examine hastily some macerated preparations, and found the eyes (?) composed of an immense number of conical cells, expanded at the outer extremity and drawn out to a point at the inner; they were filled with a mass of refractive, closely packed, globules, — which, indeed, gave them the appearance of gland cells, — and were surrounded by narrow, ciliated cells, occasionally faintly colored at their expanded outer ends. Upon the external surface, the large cells were often provided with several, longitudinal fibres, which appeared like the nerve fibres seen in the retinophorae of *Arca*, but I could not decide whether they really were so or not. These organs present several peculiarities which render a more accurate study of them highly desirable. Their position on the edge of the mantle, and their hemispherical shape, show, at first sight, considerable resemblance to the faceted eyes of *Arca*, to whose retinophorae and cover cells, the large colorless cells, drawn out to a point at their inner ends and surrounded by smaller ciliated ones, might be compared. The absence of pigment does not offer any serious difficulty, and, if it could be shown that the innervation and composition of the large cells was the same as in the retinophorae of the faceted eye of *Arca*, we should be obliged to consider these problematical organs of *Pinna* as eyes, rather than glands. It seems, however, that in the absence of such observations, the question must for the present be left open. That *Pinna* has some organs of vision, is shown by the same simple experiments as have been tried upon other Mollusca; but whether the seat of this sensitiveness to light lies in the so-called eyes of WILL, or in the masses of dark pigment so abundant upon the edge of the mantle, is of course difficult to decide.

Avicula.

Avicula was examined very hastily, just before sending the proof sheets to the printer. It is extraordinarily sensitive to changes in the amount of light, the least shadow causing it to close the shell quickly, and with such force as to indicate that even this slight change acts as a considerable irritant. The simple, diffuse ommatidia, the only visual organs present, are sensitive to the difference in light produced by holding such a small object as a pencil between them and the window. Even a shadow, so faint as to be imperceptible to the experimentor, caused the immediate contraction of the mantle. The experiment is so simple, and the result so evident, that there is no possibility of a mistake in observation. This special case was of unusual interest to me, for here the simplest kind of eye known is accompanied by a sensitiveness to light and shade, not exceeded even in *Arca*, so lavishly supplied with much more perfect visual organs. We are here led to suspect the presence of some other factor which must, when known, account for the apparent agreement in functional powers between two organs so widely different in structure. Let us suppose a number of animals with equally perfect eyes, having the same structural perfection and functional powers, then, every thing else being equal, the same irritant would produce the same effect upon them all. But let us suppose that, after generations of existence under varying circumstances, the eyes remained stationary; then it would be found that the same cause would no longer produce the same effect. We may suppose that the results would be varied by the following factors.

1. By an inherited association of a sudden change in the amount of light with some danger, to escape which the animal must close its shell. Such an instinct would easily be acquired by Molluscs preyed upon by other animals, as e. g. Paguridae that are very expert in extracting animals from the shell by means of their peculiar shaped claws. Danger, in the shape of an approaching crab, would, like all other coming events, cast its shadow before, and the watchful Mollusc, that was fortunate enough to close its shell in time, would have the chance of transmitting to its descendants a tendency to be extremely sensitive to any slight change in the amount of light.

2. The results will be alike in both the following cases; (a) if there has been no such association between a difference in light and some impending danger; or (b) if by frequent repetition, the animal has become accustomed to the changes in the amount of light. In either case an ordinary shadow would not cause muscular contractions.

3. It is supposable that the same image will produce the same effect in two equivalent visual organs, but the effect may be transmitted to a nerve centre with different degrees of intensity, so that entirely different perceptions will be the result.

These suppositions, which have been merely outlined, so run into each other that they allow the interpolation of subdivisions, and a much more extended treatment; this will, however, suffice for my purpose, for it enables me to arrive at an important conclusion of practical value: if, for certain reasons, the same combination of light vibrations, acting upon the same visual elements, produces different perceptions, or different intensity of reflex actions, then it becomes actually impossible to determine the relative functional powers of two eyes, by the difference in effect produced by the same image, or by the same combination of light vibrations; and, conversely, neither can one determine what effect will be produced by the perception, through equivalent eyes, of the same image. There are plenty of cases to illustrate both sides of this proposition; therefore when a person attempts to judge of the perfection of an eye by experiments alone, his deductions are liable to be wrong, or at least to contain an abundance of uncertain elements.

The necessity of keeping these facts in mind is only too evident in the present instance. By experiment alone, we would be led to suppose that *Avicula* had eyes at least as complicated as those of *Arca*; but we are surprised to find that there are only a few scattered ommatidia, which would entirely escape the notice of one who had not seen them better developed elsewhere. But if we are led into such false conceptions by experimenting upon organs, which, the first glance tells us, are widely different in structure, how can we determine, by experiment alone, the relative perfection of organs which are nearly alike in histological structure?

Cardium.

The rather massive sipho of *C. edule* is beset with a double row of tentacles, which, in the expanded condition, form a radiating fringe around each of the siphonal openings. On the anterior and posterior side, the fringe attains its greatest development, while, between the anal and oral openings, it is reduced to a few, small, scattering tentacles; those on the anterior side of the oral opening are the largest of all, and one of these, from which the remaining ones differ but slightly, we shall select for description. It is extended directly away from the oral opening, with the exception of the expanded tip which is bent nearly at right angles towards the sipho (Pl. 31, fig. 113). On the side away from the latter, is a semi-circular band of brown pigment cells; the remainder of the tentacular hypodermis is colorless.

On *C. edule* I have counted fifty-one eye-bearing tentacles, — so large that one could distinguish the pigmented band with a hand lens, — about the oral or anterior opening, and sixty-two, around the anal one. At the tips of the tentacle, on the lips of the cup-like hollow, are tufts of stiff, sense hairs. Cilia, as far as I could see, were not otherwise present on the tentacles.

In the connective tissue of the sipho, beneath the hypodermis, are many irregular aggregations of large, round cells filled with dark brown pigment.

The remaining portion of the mantle is pigmentless, with the exception of a narrow band on the shell side of the mantle.

Most of the tentacles are single, but I have observed several cases in which the apex was forked, each end bearing an eye. The hypodermis is thrown into many irregular, circular folds; there are also two remarkable, longitudinal ones, extending the whole length of the tentacle, one on each side (Pl. 31, fig. 113 *x*). At the end of the tentacles, beneath the band of pigment, is an organ containing all the elements characteristic of an eye. It consists of a roughly spherical mass of large cells, — with sharply defined cell walls and nuclei, — when living, containing a faint red coloring matter. The periphery of the cells is filled with fine granular protoplasm, which gives them the peculiar appearance represented in the drawing (fig. 112). When fresh, they are transparent and refractive, so that one may see through them the silvery light reflected from the argentea. The former, in combination with the red light from the large cells, causes a brilliant iridescent play of colors similar to that produced by the red pigment and argentea of *Pecten*. The extremely simple retina, — which is oblong in shape, the short diameter being at right angles to the pigmented covering —, consists of five or six rows of cells, the ends of which are directed inwards, and rest upon the mass of connective tissue fibres which serve at once as a capsule and tapetum. The opposite extremities, near which are situated the large, oval and sharply stained nuclei, appear to terminate in single nerve fibres, which pass out of the capsule, on the side opposite the pigmented band, and, bending at right angles, extend along the axis of the tentacle as isolated fibres. At the angle of each of these cells, nearly opposite the large nuclei, is a small and poorly defined cell containing a minute, but deeply stained nucleus. It seemed, at times, as if I could distinguish an extremely delicate membrane between the retina and the red cells, but I cannot say with certainty whether it was really there or not.

The argentea (Pl. 31, fig. 112 *ag.*) is similar to that of *Pecten*, and consists of connective tissue cells, the bodies of which are flattened into membranes, composed of minute refractive squares much smaller than those of *Pecten*. In sections, it appears to consist of fibres with minute, refractive varicosities, and might easily be mistaken for a layer of nerve fibres. The best method to observe this »Plättchen« structure of the tapetum is by pressing the ends of the tentacles almost flat under a cover glass; one then sees beneath the hypodermis a layer of what appears to be fine refractive granules, the true form of which can only be distinguished with the highest powers. The cells of the tapetum are not so completely metamorphosed as to lose their nuclei; as is the case in the adult *Pecten*, the nuclei are quite numerous, and may readily be detected as minute, compressed bodies, conspicuous by the intensity with which they are stained in haematoxylin. The argentea envelops the whole eye, but is thickest on the sides next the pigment and toward the base of the tentacle; on the remaining two sides, it is reduced to a thin, hyaline membrane through which the nerve fibres pass to the retina. It is thus evident that the light must come from the summit of the tentacle, and indeed from the invaginated portion away from the pigmented side; the ends of the retinal cells are therefore parallel to the rays of light, as we should expect. Whether the inner ends of the cells are really provided with rods, similar to those of *Pecten*, for example, I cannot say. Perhaps the fact that it was difficult to obtain clear pictures of just those parts where the rods should be, may be considered as favorable to the supposition that they are true retinophorae. There is a striking resemblance between these retinal elements and those of *Pecten*, and, until evidence shall be produced to the contrary, I propose to consider them as homologous, and consequently shall designate the large cells (*rf.*) as retinophorae, and the small ones (*g.c.*) as nervous cells, homologous with the inner ganglionic ones of *Pecten*. Whether there is a central nerve fibre in the former, or not, I was unable to determine; this is a point of considerable importance for, if it is so, we should then have good reason for supposing that the cells in question are formed by the fusion of two cells, just as they are in so many other cases. The cellular body (*l*), which we shall speak of as a lens, — although it is probable that it combines in itself another function besides that of concentrating the light, — is composed of large characteristic cells, which, however, are not confined to this region alone, but extend thence in a double row, nearly half the length of the tentacle; they then break up into irregularly scattered cells, which have not lost, meantime, any of their characteristic color or appearance.

The nuclei of the hypodermis invariably contain nucleoli, with the exception possibly of those which are so constricted that it is impossible to determine whether nucleoli are present or not. The nuclei of the pigmented band are situated close to the inner ends of the cells and are distinguished by absorbing staining fluids more deeply and evenly than those of the unpigmented portions.

It has been known since Will's time, that the ends of the tentacles can be in-, or e-vaginated at pleasure. The former process is accomplished by the contraction of longitudinal muscular fibres, the thickened, nucleated, ends of which form a muscular ring attached to the inner surface of the hypodermis at the apex of the tentacle. By the contraction of these muscles only that part of the apex away from the eye will be invaginated. Even in the most extended natural condition, the tip of the tentacles is never convex, but on the contrary, slightly concave, as represented in fig. 112.

Still further contraction draws the pigmented band over the opening of the eye in such a manner as to prevent the access of light to it. Will was the one, who, in this case as in so many others, gave us the first description of these structures, and correctly considered them as visual organs. His description of their external characters is perfectly correct, as far as it goes; to this account nothing has been added up to the present day.

Carrière has also examined these structures and asserts that they are not eyes. Although he is careful not to call them luminous organs, one can see that he is inclined to lay stress upon the luminosity of some of the cells. He says, for instance, p. 97. »Augen jedoch sind es nicht und desshalb kann ich an dieser Stelle keine eingehendere Beschreibung der leuchtenden Zellen des Epithels und der Tentakelspitze geben. Ich glaubte nun Leuchtorgane vor mir zu haben. Schließt man aber das Licht gänzlich ab, so erlischt der Glanz und es findet hier somit keine selbständige Lichtentwicklung statt.«

Sharp has been less successful than Carrière in finding the eyes of *Cardium*: he declares that none are present in either *C. edule*, *C. muricatum*, or *C. magnum*; this, however, is probably due to the fact that he only examined specimens preserved in alcohol, which quickly dissolves the red pigment; one may then easily fail to see the lens and retina situated below the epithelium. But they are not so easily overlooked in *C. edule*, where one side of the eye is covered with brown pigment, not soluble in alcohol.

If we start with the supposition that all eyes are modifications of hypodermic cells, against which there can be, I think, no very serious objection, then it is natural to expect that, the farther the organ has become removed from the seat of its origin, the older it is, and the more changes it has undergone. But we also find, that those organs, which are phylogenetically the oldest, or which have passed through the greatest number of intermediate changes, are either highly developed, or were so once. In the present instance, the changes necessary to evolve such an organ from simple hypodermic cells must have been radical and numerous, and it is not easy to imagine any plausible method by which such a process could have taken place. But, in spite of the fact that it is so highly differentiated as regards what must have been its original condition, it is still an extremely simple organ, whose functional power must be of a very low order. I consider, therefore, that during the long and complicated series of changes necessary for the evolution of such an organ, it at one time probably reached a much higher structural, as well as functional condition, and that the present, very simple organ is due to degeneration.

Cardium tuberculatum.

In this species, the pigmented band at the summit of the tentacles is absent, and the brilliant lustre, so characteristic of *C. edule*, is almost entirely wanting. But, with a careful examination, one easily sees two rows of large, ova-like cells, closely packed, and extending from the tip of the tentacle, where they unite in the median spherical mass above the retina, nearly to its base. These cells contain diffuse coloring matter which gives them their reddish tinge. The same form and general arrangement of the tentacles obtain here as in *C. edule*, but cilia or sense hairs, I have not been able to detect.

The tentacles of *C. tuberculatum* are very sensitive to the amount and intensity of light, while, on the other hand, irritation by contact, and shocks or movements of the water caused by a sharp tap upon the glass in which they are contained, apparently produce no effect upon them. This is just the opposite to what is found in *Pecten*, where the tentacles are extremely sensitive to tactile impression, or to coarse vibrations, irritation of one causing immediate contraction of all the others, or even of the whole mantle. But, in *Pecten*, the tentacles are richly supplied with sense hair papillae, while this is not the case with *Cardium*, where, however, the sensitiveness to light is highly developed; for variations in the intensity of the latter, caused by shadows, produce lively movements of the tentacles, which may result in violent contractions of the whole animal. After repeated experiments, the irritating effect seems to be diminished, so that, finally, even quite deep and sudden shadows may produce only restless or uneasy movements of the tentacles, or perhaps no effect at all.

Cardita sulcata.

In fresh specimens, the only material I have examined, may be seen the orange-red mantle edge, near the oral end of which are five or six large pigment spots, dark brown or nearly black in the centre, but fainter near the periphery. In these pigmented areas, over which the cuticula is specially thickened, one may see numerous, scattered ommatidia, consisting of four or five dark-colored cells arranged around a single, central one, two of which are often situated close together. The latter may be found on the edge of the dark spots, as well as in the reddish colored area, surrounded, in the latter instance, by pigmented cells of an orange-red color, instead of black. Over the pigmented areas, the cuticula was especially thickened, but not faceted.

No experiment was made to test the sensitiveness of these animals to light, but I cannot doubt they have this property, since the diffuse ommatidia they certainly possess, appear to be as highly developed as those of *Avicula*, which, in comparison with the complexity of its organs, has this sensibility developed to a truly wonderful degree.

No statement, that I am aware of, has ever been made concerning the eyes of this genus of Molluscs.

It is not unworthy of remark, that two genera so closely allied as *Cardium* and *Cardita* should have eyes so different from each other.

Haliotis.

It was intended, in studying the eyes of this Mollusc, simply to test my observations on *Arca*, concerning the nerve endings in the retinidia, and the double structure of the retinophorae.

Among the many authors, who have described, in more or less detail, the eyes of Molluscs, three have given special attention to this genus. There is no room for a great difference of opinion as to the coarser anatomy of the eye. It is principally concerning the more minute, histological structure that I desire to speak, and to which I have given most attention. There is hardly any difference of moment between the eyes of *Haliotis*, and the invaginated ones found in *Arca*. The former may be considered as pigmented pits in the thickened hypodermis, with a specially thick cuticular covering, the outer and inner layers of which have become highly differentiated to form, in the first instance, the vitreous body and the lens, and, in the second, the richly innervated layer of rods. The so-called retinal cells consist of two elements, exactly homologous with the pigmented cover cells and the retinophorae of *Arca*. The pigmented cells are extremely long and narrow (figs. 68 and 62), their inner third or half being reduced to a slender hyaline stalk, or bacillus. The length of the cells varies greatly, those opposite the opening of the cup being the longest. The nuclei form a gentle swelling in about the middle of the cells, they may, however, be situated at different levels, so that it might easily be imagined there were two nuclei in each cell. Such, however, is not the case, as it may easily be seen that the outer ends of the isolated pigment cells are completely filled with intensely black pigment with which they seem to terminate; the clear, central axis of CARRIÈRE has no existence. In special preparations, the cell is seen to be sharply constricted at its outer end into a colorless rod, narrow at the base, and continued outwards until it terminates in an expanded end (fig. 62 *rh*). The pigment contained in these cells usually consists of fine, dark granules which often fuse to form large, round balls, equal in diameter to the width of the cell.

The bacilli (figs. 68 and 62 *bc.*) terminate at their inner ends in several fine fibres, which appear to rest upon a very delicate basal membrane. Several of these cells, the exact number I have been unable to determine, surround a single, colorless one with a large basal nucleus; the colorless ones are the so-called »Stützzellen«, or secrete-cells, as some have considered them, but they will here be called the retinophorae, since they are homologous with the similarly named cells in the eyes of *Arca* and *Pecten*; although, as I have already remarked in the introduction, the pigment cells likewise support retinidia, still the colorless cells alone perform this function in the more highly developed forms. Just as in *Arca* and *Pecten*, the retinophorae of *Haliotis* are formed by the fusion of two cells, one nucleus of which retains its original characteristics, and may be readily seen situated at the base of the cell. The other nucleus may, in many cases, become so degenerate as to entirely escape notice; but still, in carefully stained specimens, it at times appears as clearly defined as in ordinary cells, although it is usually seen as a homogeneous, faintly stained, oval body (figs. 66 and 67 *n. rf.*²) at the outer end of the cell, in the centre of a gentle swelling. Between the two nuclei, the cells are often constricted to a narrow neck, or even to a slender fibre; the outer part terminates in a narrowed portion filled with fine granules, which stain in haematoxylin, and give to this part a special prominence.

When seen in cross sections, this granular part projects a short distance beyond the ends of the pigment cells (fig. 58 *x*). In one instance, I found a very beautiful cell, the outer end of which terminated in two separate pieces (fig. 66) furnishing a most conclusive proof that the retinophora, with its two nuclei, was formed by the fusion of two cells. The cell contents consist of a clear, protoplasmic mass in which are imbedded many granules of various sizes, some of which are so refractive as to appear like pigment granules. The distinction between the pigmented cells and the colorless ones is not as sharp as in *Arca*, for I found several that I was in doubt whether to call pigment cells or retinophorae. The inner ends of the latter terminate in a relatively large, varicose nerve fibre, into which they are so gradually transformed that it is difficult to tell where the cells end and the fibres begin. One may follow the fibre in its course through the centre of the cell, passing to one side of the large basal nucleus, until it reaches the apex, where it issues again and passes outwards between the double rods of the retinophorae. Other nerve fibres follow the wall of the cell to its outer extremity, where they appear to terminate. The fibres often hang freely from the cells, so that one sees they are provided with numerous extraordinarily fine fibrils (fig. 66) exactly similar to those found in *Arca*. But the most conclusive proof that nerve endings occur here similar to those in *Arca*, was found by treating the rods in such a manner as to dissolve the cuticular substance of the rods, leaving the mass of nerve fibres perfectly free and intact. To do this, the eyes were hardened in 2% bichromate of potash, for 24 hours, and then removed to dilute glycerine, 1 part to 4 parts of distilled water; a further treatment with strong glycerine followed, after which they were washed in distilled water. Small pieces may then be placed in acetate of potash or water, separated with needles, and examined with a high magnifying power. Although I have not always been equally successful, some most brilliant preparations were obtained, in which could be seen half a dozen or more nerve fibres extending along the wall of the cell, over the outer ends of which they projected in long festoons, whose length often exceeded that of the cells themselves. The principal fibres were quite large and perfectly distinct, with very few side branches; but towards the extremity, they broke up into many smaller branches, which continued to subdivide more and more rapidly, until they at last ended in myriads of the finest fibrils, not terminating freely, but uniting with each other to form a perfect network of continuous fibrillae. In some cells, all the fibres, with their mass of terminal fibrillae, remained so united as to retain the shape of the rod before the cuticular substance was dissolved; in other cases, the large branches had become separated from each other, and were turned and twisted in all directions; fig. 63 is only one out of hundreds of similar cells, each provided with the long festoons of nerve fibres, the ultimate ramifications of which, with all their confusing complexity, could be seen infinitely more clearly in the original preparations, than I have been able to indicate in the figure, where only one of the fibres is entirely drawn. By selecting a small and well isolated portion of the retinidium, it will be seen to consist of innumerable, equally large branches, which become continuous with each other in all directions to form an inextricable network of fibrillae (fig. 61). Although nearly perfect, isolated retinidia are often obtained, they are usually united into larger or smaller groups in such a manner that there can be no doubt that, at the extremity at least, the individual retinidia are connected with each other by fibrils, in the same manner as the various nerve branches of the same cell. The bases of the rods are reduced to slender stalks, separated from each other by clear spaces through which the nerve fibres of the colorless cells pass outwards to form a similar network of fibrillae which unite with those described above. In preparations of isolated cells, from whose rods the cuticular substance has not been dissolved, I have never been able to find retinophorae with rods at their outer end: the latter was always continued outwards as one, or several fibres, that soon divided up into smaller branches, and terminated in the same manner as those of the surrounding pigment cells. It is probable that the rods of the colorless cells are so inconsistant as to lose their shape when the surrounding cells are removed, or that they are dissolved in the processes of maceration. The retinidial layer of the cuticula does not entirely fill the cavity of the eye; it passes quite gradually into a clear, nerveless, viscid fluid, which more than fills the remaining space and consequently projects somewhat over the pupil of the eye. This outer portion, often very irregularly shaped, is always harder than the inner part, or vitreous body (fig. 58). I have a series of sections, in which the surface of the vitreous body has become hardened into a lens shaped portion, situated over the opening of the eye, and almost entirely outside of it (fig. 58 *l*). This lens is conspicuous on account of the difference between its index of refraction and that of the vitreous body, and especially on account of the fact that its periphery alone stains deeply in haematoxylin. The vitreous body, the lens, and the retinidial layer, at the edge of the optic cup merge into each other, and by means of a gradual series of changes pass into the cuticula of the hypodermic cells surrounding the optic cup. The entire gelatinous mass, filling the cavity of the latter, may be reduced to a single, but highly modified, cuticular layer, in which the inner stratum, filled with the nervous fibres, constitutes the retinidial cuticula, while the vitreous body, and the irregular outer thickening, or lens, represent the corneal cuticula, homologous with the delicate corneal membrane in the compound eyes of Arca, as well as the corneal membrane of the invaginate forms. The retinidial layer is homologous with the similarly called layer in the invaginated eyes of *Arca*, or the retinidia taken collectively of the faceted eyes.

It is evident, therefore, that the colorless cells must be considered as essential elements of the retina, both morphologically and physiologically, even though, in the present instance, they play a relatively subordinate part; or rather it would be better to say that the pigmented cells, with their retinidia, have gained an unusual ascendency. This, however, is necessarily the case, owing to the small specialization of the retina, — the hypodermic characteristics of which are but slightly modified, — together with the equally poor functional development of the organ. In the phylogenetic development, accompanied by the specialization of certain cells in different directions and the acquisition of higher functional powers, it will be found that the colorless cells, with their retinidia, continue to gain the ascendency, until they constitute the essential and least variable elements, while the pigmented cells become more and more subordinate to secondary functions.

On the upper side of each tentacle of *Haliotis*, is a dark pigmented band, which, in the large head tentacle, is sunken into a furrow, in many places so deep that its lips may nearly close to form a tube. The floor of the furrow consists of thick, columnar cells filled with a dark brown or black pigment. The cuticula is not especially developed; neither could any colorless cells be seen in the sections. The similarity of these pigmented bands with those on the sipho and mantle edge of the Lamellibranchiata is at once evident; whether the resemblance is more than a superficial one, and whether a similarity in function is also present, can only be shown by actual experiment.

It was BABUCHIN, who in 1866[1] published a paper which, for accuracy of observation, has hardly been excelled by subsequent authors favored with much better means of study. He fully recognized that the retina was composed of groups of pigmented cells, surrounding a central, colorless one with a large nucleus. He likewise appears to have seen the intercellular nerve fibres, but erroneously considered them to be foldings in the cell wall. Also the important facts, that the colorless cells were continuous at their inner ends with a single fibre, while the pigmented ones ended in four or five, did not escape his notice. As far as the structure of the retina is concerned, no new acquisitions have been made since his time, except to extend some of his observations to other genera. In the majority of cases, subsequent authors have failed to recognize certain essential facts which he seems to have fully appreciated.

HENSEN failed to find in *Pterotrachea* the so-called colorless cells of BABUCHIN. He distinguished three kinds of cells, one of which, with the large, round nucleus, was probably one of the colorless cells in question, to whose surface, pigment was accidentally attached. One might likewise infer from his description, that the pigment cells were differentiated into two rows, as in *Arca*. His observations are not, however, sufficiently complete to determine with certainty whether his rods are formed by the combined products of the pigmented and colorless cells, or whether both bodies produce comparatively independent structures, as in *Haliotis*.

The researches of SIMROTH (30), are drawn out to an interminable length, and are accompanied by numerous careful drawings of histological rubbish, from which he has been unable to cull any new facts

---

[1] Up to this date the knowledge recorded concerning the structure of the retina is of such a rudimentary nature, that it will not be necessary for us to consider it.

or ideas, and indeed has failed to see what was so clearly pointed out for him in the much earlier work of Babuchin. In some inexplicable manner, he has attributed the omnipresent »Plättchenstructur« to the bodies of the colorless cells, while he has entirely overlooked the rods themselves.

Fraisse (36) considered that the colorless cells from the eyes of *Patella* and *Fissurella* (he failed to recognize them in *Haliotis* act as supports for the pigmented cells; he also sees in them the organs which secrete the vitreous body and lens. This idea has taken firm root in the minds of subsequent authors, who have compared them with the gland cells found generally distributed in the Molluscan hypodermis. More recently, however, Hilger (40) has recognized that they play an important part in the formation of the rods.

That the colorless cells are something more than mere gland cells is sufficiently proved by the complex structure which I have shown that they possess, and the homology that may be pointed out between them and cells which undoubtedly play the most important roll in the more highly developed eyes of *Arca* and *Pecten*. Fraisse noticed the fibres in the lens, as he called it, and although, at first, he is in doubt whether to call them rods, he finally concludes that, in all probability, they are artificially produced by the coagulation of the lens. He believes, moreover, that the lens is first secreted by the support cells, and after it has gained a sufficient size the vitreous body is produced. It seems to me that he has reversed the order, and that the lens is simply a part of the vitreous body hardened by exposure to the water, as in *Haliotis*, or by coagulation, as in the closed eyes of *Fissurella*.

I, however, agree with him in considering the lens and vitreous body as cuticular structures, but cannot consider, as he does, that they are secreted by the colorless cells alone; the cuticular substance is rather a modification of the walls of both pigmented and colorless cells, and shows various degrees of density and of vitality, according as it is more or less intimately connected with the cells to which it owes its origin.

The »Stäbchenzellen« of Carrière are so named because they contain a colorless axis surrounded by pigment: the former he calls the rod, and the pigment cells, the rod cells, which he considers to be undoubtedly the essential elements of the retina. He adopts Fraisse's terminology, and considers with him that the colorless cells are secrete cells, homologous with those large gland cells found in the general hypodermis. The retinidial layer, he has overlooked, having confused it with the vitreous body. His conception of an eye must be something altogether unique. for, after having described. in the eyes of *Patella*, the rods, which he erroneously considers as a vitreous body, and the retineum. — having the same structure as in other Mollusca, — he informs us that the organ in question is no eye at all, but simply a pigmented hollow in the epidermis! Then, immediately afterwards, he speaks of the pigmented cells as »Sinneszellen« or »Sehzellen«, and considers the thickened cuticula, secreted by the colorless cells, as being specially adapted to protect the very delicate ends of the rods. We should be pleased to know what a pigmented hollow, provided with a true retina. and containing delicate seeing cells, is, if it is not an eye. He evidently considers that these organs have too large an opening to be entitled to be called eyes, for he does not hesitate to apply that name to an exactly similar structure in *Haliotis*, the opening of which is of more modest dimensions! In the latter genus, he has mistaken the retinidial layer for the vitreous body, which, in his preparations, seems to have entirely disappeared, with the exception of the lens-like thickening covering the opening of the optic cup. The colorless elements are not secrete-cells, neither do the pigment cells contain any colorless axis which, when continued beyond the limits of the pigment, forms the rods. The fibres, supposed to be secreted by the colorless cells. instead of being simply formless cuticular secretions to be transformed into the vitreous body, are rods, similar to those of the pigment cells, and supplied in the same manner with nerve fibres.

HILGER. who has recently made a valuable contribution to our knowledge of the retina in various forms of Mollusca, has found that the colorless cells are generally, and probably universally present in the retineal layer. He has abandoned the old method of considering them as secrete, or support cells, and, recognizing the part they play in the construction of the rods, calls them the rod cells, although it is difficult to understand why, for, according to his figures, they contribute much less than the pigment cells to the composition of the rods. He has considered the retina of *Haliotis* in less detail than that of other forms with which I am unacquainted. I believe, however, that he is wrong in supposing that the rods of the several pigment cells, surrounding the prolongation of a central colorless one, unite to form a single rod. It seems to me much more probable that the same condition. — similar to that found in *Haliotis*, as regards the structure of the retinidial layer, — prevails throughout all the Mollusca with equally simple forms of eyes: or, in other words, that the pigmented, as well as the colorless cells produce independent rods, whose nerve fibres unite to form one complex retinidial layer. His so-called »Stäbchenmantel« is composed of the rods of the pigment cells, while the axial portion is the rod of the colorless one. It is true, that the rods in the eye of *Haliotis* do not seem to have reached a very high degree of specialization, as compared with those of *Fissurella* and *Helix*, but this is a difference in degree not in kind; moreover it would be impossible to compare a rod, as described by HILGER, with any similar structure known. The sharp, diagrammatic outlines with which he separates the rods suggest that possibly the material was not prepared in the best manner. He is surely in error in saying that the pigment cells end in one or more nerve fibres, since they end abruptly in root-like fibres, resting upon the connective tissue membrane. The incorrectness of his conception, that the rods are formed by the united activities of the colorless and pigmented cells, is proved by the difficulties he encounters in attempting to compare these rods with those of Heteropods, as described by SCHULTZE: for in the latter case, they are formed simply by the retinophorae, the central nerve fibre of which constitutes the so-called axis of the rod: while in the former instance, the axis is not a single fibre, but the double rod of the retinophorae, the sheath being formed by the rods of the pigment cells: therefore, in the Heteropods, it is evident that the rods of the pigment cells have entirely disappeared, while those of the double colorless ones with the central nerve fibre, have increased proportionately. We have an exactly parallel case occurring in a single genus of Molluscs; for in *Arca* the optic cups contain a retinidial layer, in which the rods of the pigment cells and the retinophorae play a nearly equal part, while, by a gradual series of transformations that may be followed step by step, a much higher type of visual organs is produced, in which the rods of the retinophorae, — or colorless cells, — are alone functional, while the pigmented ones have become subordinated to secondary purposes. It appears, from the description given by HENSEN of *Pterotrachea*, that the pigmented cells may be divided into two rows, as in the faceted eyes of *Arca*. It seems, therefore, that in the majority of Gasteropods, essentially the same condition found in *Haliotis* prevails in the structure of the retinidial layer, to which the pigmented, as well as the colorless cells contribute their more or less independent rods. In *Haliotis*, the ultimate fibrils of the retina terminalia have assumed no special direction; this, I believe, may be accounted for by the fact that no definite relation exists between the course of the rods, arranged radiately around the wall of the optic cup, and the direction of the rays of light entering it. In the simpler forms of Molluscan eyes, the relation existing between the rods of the pigmented and colorless cells has not been determined, nor, whether, as I believe, the ultimate fibrillae of the rods assume a direction more and more at right angles to the rays of light which impinge upon them. It is, however, certain that in those more complex eyes, in which the amount and direction of light is regulated by accessory organs, as in *Pecten*, Heteropods and Cephalopods, the rods are best developed at that point where the greatest number of nearly parallel rays impinge upon the retina, and, also, that in these very rods the transverse fibrillae attain the most perfect uniformity of direction. In proportion as the accessory organs become more and more complete, and consequently the functional power of the eyes; the greater advantages possessed by the double rods and their central fibres for uniform and economic distribution of parallel, transverse fibres, are seized upon, and, in proportion as the double rods become more and more developed, those of the pigment cells decrease and finally disappear. Consequently one finds that, in the most specialized eyes, only the true retinophorae have retained their rods in which the distribution of the transverse fibrillae has reached the highest perfection.

BÜTSCHLI '41) finds reason to believe that the colorless cells are the essential ones, and hence doubts GRENACHER's assertion that the colorless cells or »Limitanszellen« of the Cephalopod eye are not sensitive to light, and he would compare them with the colorless, sensitive cells in Gasteropods[1]. The reasoning is most fallaceous. It is perfectly well shown by the very article which he is discussing (HILGER's), that the pigmented, as well as the colorless cells contribute to form the rods, which are the homologues of the similarly named structures in all other eyes. It is equally evident that the so-called rods, and the cells which bear them, are the essential elements of the retina; hence it follows that the presence or absence of pigment cannot, in this case, serve at all as a criterion. Therefore, in attempting to discover the homology between the retinal elements of Cephalopods and Gastero-

---

[1] It does not appear as certain as it might, that the »Limitanszellen« do not contain any pigment. It would not be very surprising if the so-called »Sockel« of the retinal cells should turn out to be composed of several minute, pigment-bearing cells, and that the retinophorae, or retinal cells, were entirely colorless.

pods, it is simply necessary to know what are the rods, and by what cells they are produced, whether by the pigmented, or colorless ones, or by both. The presence or absence of pigment is a factor altogether too uncertain to be, alone, of any value; for, as I have shown in *Haliotis*, the double cells, or those which are usually colorless, may sometimes contain a small quantity of pigment, while in *Pecten* both elements are perfectly devoid of pigment. Still another factor must not be neglected, and that is that in the Cephalopods the pigment between the rods and around their axial nerve fibre is something entirely unique. The presence of pigment around the axial nerve fibre is of great theoretical importance, for, if pigment may be produced by a nerve fibre within the rod, there is no reason why the external fibres of the rod, arising from the limiting or ganglionic cells, may not also produce pigment. Moreover, the manner in which the axial nerve is protected from the light proves that it cannot be the percipient element, while, on the other hand, the access of light to the walls of the rods containing the retinidial cross fibrillae shows that there, as in other Mollusca, is the true seat of the light-sensitive elements.

GRENACHER (39) inconsistently speaks of the half of each rod as a rhabdomere, which, according to his definition, should be the product of a single cell. The so-called rhabdoms found by GRENACHER in the Cephalopods have absolutely no morphological signification. They are simply due to a deceptive, but economic arrangement, so that the broad sides of four different rods are adjacent to each other. The integrity of the individual rods, which are similar to those of *Pecten*, is in no wise affected by this arrangement. It is impossible to find any points of resemblance between such a rhabdom and that of any other animal. He has hastened to apply his name rhabdom to these accidental groups of rods, regardless of the consequences. When a person applies terms, necessarily restricted in meaning, to widely different objects, one is led to believe that there must be some resemblance between the objects in question, and possibly some morphological relationship. But in the present case (p. 251), he is neither able to find any resemblance between his rhabdoms in Cephalopods and Arthropods, nor is he willing to admit that any morphological value could be attached to such a resemblance, provided it existed.

Without further discussion of the views either of GRENACHER or of BÜTSCHLI, I may be permitted to draw comparisons between the retina of Cephalopods and that of other Mollusca, based upon my own researches. The whole question hinges upon the nature of the so-called

»retinal cells«. They are homologous with the retinophorae of *Pecten* and other Mollusca (the colorless cells of Gasteropod eyes); this is sufficiently well shown by the presence of the axial nerve fibre, and the double nature of the rods. It should also be indicated by the presence of two nuclei, one of which GRENACHER has probably overlooked. The »Limitauszellen« are ganglionic cells exactly similar to, and homologous with, the ganglionic cells, especially those of the inner layer, of the eye of *Pecten*. Consequently they represent modified pigment cells of the hypodermis, and are homologous with the retinulae of the Gasteropod ommatidia. Their prolongations form the external, nervous network of the rods. The limiting membrane corresponds with the corneal layer of the cuticula, and probably protects loops of the axial fibre, similar to those of *Pecten*.

Chapter II. Crustacea and Insects.

Penaeus.

The great impetus that modern Zoological science has received from comparative anatomy, has not been due so much to more subtle or able comparisons, as to a more perfect knowledge of the structure of single forms. It would not be too much to say that a perfect acquaintance with the anatomy of a single, typical Arthropod eye, with its various stages of structural and functional development, would furnish us with a key to many of the most difficult problems concerning the comparative anatomy and phylogenetic development of the visual organs, not only in Arthropods, but in other Invertebrates, as well as Vertebrates. In proportion as our knowledge of individual forms is less perfect, or built upon false foundations, so will our deduction from these false premises not merely be wrong in the same proportion, but exaggerated a thousand fold with every step, and finally entangle us in such a labyrinth of false deductions, that future progress would be well nigh impossible. We must expect a certain amount of structural uniformity in those organs which have to carry, by the same means, the same forms of energy to similar perceptive centres, and that the greatest uniformity should prevail in the most essential parts. My studies upon the nerve endings in the Mollusca have induced me to believe that a uniformity of structure prevails in the essential elements of all eyes. How far that has proved true will be seen in the following pages. A mere accident led me to choose Arthropods as most convenient for testing this supposition. I entered upon this subject with that respect for the researches of GRENACHER (which have been so steadily gaining in general acceptancy since their publication) that one must feel for honest work, whenever brought in contact with it. But my first observations, conducted under other methods, raised suspicions that, at least in that case, GRENACHER's explanations would not work, and against my desire I was drawn away from my intended course into a boundless field of observation, with the feeling that neither time, nor existing circumstances, would allow me to treat the subject in a satisfactory manner. The evidence against GRENACHER's theory appeared so over-whelming, that I could not resist the temptation of making a few observations, with the double object of testing my own conception of the structure of the ommatidia, and of studying the nerve endings there. The limits of this paper would not allow me to carry my observations any farther in this direction, but I hope in the near future to extend them, in order, if possible, to clear up many difficulties, which I am at present unable to explain. They are difficulties, however, which lie in those places where the least satisfactory work has been done, and it is not improbable that they too will disappear, as I have seen others do, upon a more careful study. The favorable conditions, offered by the eyes of *Penaeus*, have been utilized in order to obtain as complete a knowledge as possible of one form, which might then serve as a type for comparison with the eyes of other genera.

In *Penaeus*, the cornea is divided into square facets, the outer surfaces of which show mere traces of convexity. Beneath a thin, structureless and refractive, outer layer, is a thicker, less dense, and laminated one (Pl. 31, fig. 69 c^2). Below the cornea is a thin, continuous layer — the corneal hypodermis — to which the corneal cuticula owes its origin. Each facet rests upon two flattened, oblong cells, reduced in the centre to a delicate membrane. In the thickened, abaxial edges, are the faint, oval nuclei, so arranged that those of the adjacent facets are situated near each other, on either side of the dividing line (Pl. 31, figs. 69 and 76). It is not difficult to obtain examples in which the entire ommatidial hypodermis has been removed, leaving the corneal layer intact, so that the number and arrangement of the nuclei, as shown in fig. 76, and the median division between the two cells may be easily observed. The delicate outlines of these very thin cells, filled with granular protoplasm, are visible by contrast with the structureless, underlying cuticula. The division between each pair of cells is only indicated by a very faint line, while the cells belonging to neighboring facets are separated from each other by a clear, narrow space. In the centre of each facet, is a dark spot, or impression, from which a fine chitinous-like fibre often projects (fig. 75 x). One might easily overlook the nuclei of the cuticular cells, as they do not absorb coloring fluids to any great extent, neither have they a high index of refraction. They are usually oval, and perfectly homogeneous, often showing no trace whatever of that granular structure so characteristic of nuclei in general; but occasionally they are granular, and stain so deeply that there can be no doubt of their nuclear nature. By boiling a piece of the cuticula a short time in caustic potash, all the less resistant parts are dissolved, and the corneal facets alone left intact, their dark boundary lines being widened at the corners to form figures like those represented in the plate (fig. 75 $d.f.$). In the centre of each facet, is a small, round impression, usually the most striking one, while in the middle of each side, are similar markings looking like the ends of fine fibres, or the impressions where fibres had been attached. A series of extraordinarily faint, parallel lines, coinciding with the divisions between two corneal cells, separates each facet into halves. The impressions (fig. 75 y) indicate where the outer ends of the ommatidial cells were attached to the corneal membrane, which has at those points fused with the cuticula, upon which impressions of the ommatidial cells are thus produced, or fragments of their outer ends left hanging. When the treatment with caustic potash has been carried to excess, all markings disappear, except the contours of the facets.

Beneath the corneal cell layer is the infinitely thicker, ommateal hypodermis, composed of numerous ommatidia corresponding in number with the corneal facets. Each ommatidium consists of a conical group of 19 or 20 very long cells, each one of which extends from the corneal hypodermis to the basal membrane. They are arranged in four circles around a central axis, all the nuclei of each group being placed at the same niveau, in specially enlarged or pigmented portions, thus forming as many zones, at varying heights, as there are circles of cells. The innermost group consists of four colorless cells — the retinophorae — united to form an inverted pyramid, whose base abuts against the corneal hypodermis, while the apex rests upon the basal membrane. The bases of the pyramids are square, but, passing inward, the corners become bevelled, thus giving to a cross section an octagonal outline (figs. 79 and 80). Still farther inward, the corners are rounded, giving rise to a tube, decreasing in diameter towards the inner end until it is reduced to a slender, hollow stalk — the style — which, enlarging rapidly, becomes transformed into a solid, pyramidal thickening — the pedicel; the latter rests upon the basal membrane by a delicate stalk, divided at its inner extremity into three legs, formed by the diverging ends of the four retinophorae, two of which have united. The rounded, outer ends of the retinophorae are provided with peculiar, protoplasmic thickenings in which the nuclei are situated (fig. 69 *n.rf.*). They may be seen in cross sections, but more easily in macerated pieces of cornea to which the ends of the retinophorae, with their nuclei, remain attached. The latter are coarsely granular, oval bodies in which there are vacuoles, often so large as to transform the nucleus into a mere shell (fig. 76). In these preparations, one finds an instructive variety of figures, giving an accurate idea of the relation of the various parts. When most of the cell substance has been removed, it is easy to see the four nuclei of the retinophorae, located at the four corners of the square, together with the two smaller nuclei of the corneal cells, situated at its sides (fig. 76). The protoplasm is often torn away from the centre of the square, leaving an irregular, round space of varying dimensions, from the middle of which projects quite a large fibre, often surrounded by a group of smaller ones fig. 76).

Below the nuclei, the cells are filled with a mass of less consistent, finely granular protoplasm; then follow the conical, four cornered crystalline cones which are nearly half as long as the ommatidia themselves (fig. 73 *c.c.*). Each cone forms a square pyramid, the four quarters being produced by the thickened, axial walls of the retinophorae. Its outer end is quite firm and consistent, and is composed of a refractive, nearly homogeneous substance, which, towards the inner end, becomes softer and more granular, having at the apex a tendency to break up into fragments. Its diameter is only a trifle smaller than that of the calyx, which it almost completely fills, and with whose abaxial walls its faces are nearly parallel. Nearer the centre of the eye, almost at the inner end of the crystalline cone, the opposite halves of the calycal wall develop sickle-shaped, granular thickenings, which increase in size as the diameter of the retinophorae diminishes, so that the enclosed space becomes, at first, oval and, finally, round (figs. 80, 81 and 82 *x*). The narrowing apex of the pyramid, formed by the four retinophorae, is finally reduced to a slender, tube-like stalk, or style, *st.*; during this process, the granular thickenings become again reduced to thin, structureless walls, which, farther on, are supplied with four, minute and refractive, inner ridges (figs. 81—84 . As we progress still farther towards the basal membrane, the tube becomes square, the four ridges having developed into four rectangular thickenings, which nearly fill the central canal (fig. 84). Still the changes are not completed, for, farther on, the square tube becomes transformed into an oval one; two of the ridges at the ends of the small diameter constantly decrease in thickness, until that part of the wall is reduced to a thin membrane, while the remainder, surrounding the now circular opening, retains its original thickness (figs. 85—88). After a slight, final change, by which the tube with its central canal is increased in diameter, we have reached that expanded solid portion, or pedicel, usually spoken of as the rhabdom (figs. 93 and 72 *pd.*). The axial walls, in the middle of the four retinophorae, have disappeared: while the abaxial ones, having so completely fused with each other as to leave no trace of a former division, form a slender tube, the style.

In the pedicel, the abaxial walls have become so thick as to entirely obliterate the central canal, while the divisions between the four component segments are again visible (figs. 93—95). The base of the style expands suddenly, but gracefully, into the large, pyramidal, outer end of the pedicel, which, continued inward as a gradually narrowing oblong column, contracts, shortly before reaching the basal membrane, into the smaller, inverted pyramid, whose apex is drawn out into an extremely slender stalk (fig. 72 *st.pd.*). Near the basal membrane, the latter diverges into three legs composed of the attenuated, inner ends of the four retinophorae, two of which have united with each other. Each leg of the stalk is divided at its inner end into several fibres by which it is united to the basal membrane (figs. 72 and 108). This fact is of great importance, for it proves that the segments of the so-called rhabdom of GRENACHER are not secretions of the retinulae, but the inner ends of the retinophorae (or crystalline cone cells of GRENACHER), which terminate in the same root-like fibres, seen in nearly all hypodermic cells.

The complicated structure of the pedicels only became intelligible to me after the study of wax figures, which I was obliged to construct, provided with lines similar to those of the pedicels, and which were combined with each other, until imaginary sections gave approximately the same figures seen in actual cross sections of the pedicels.

The pedicel is a columnar, hyaline body, capped at each end with a pyramid. Just before the style is transformed into the pedicel, it is seen to be composed of a number of pieces which gradually grow shorter and shorter, until they are converted into a number of very thin plates constituting the outer pyramid of the pedicel. The plates, however, again increase in thickness, until, at the opposite end, they are again converted into blocks, 10 or 12 times as thick as the outer lamellae (figs. 72 and 74). The pedicel is oblong in section, and for convenience we shall speak of the long and short diameters as the primary and secondary axes, and the line coinciding with the axial nerve as the median, or optic axis, either of the pedicel, or ommatidium. The plates are of two kinds, alternating with each other: primary ones, composed of fibres, or marked with lines parallel to the primary, or long axis; and secondary plates of the same composition, but with the lines at right angles to those of the first, or parallel to the secondary axis.

The primary plates are lamellae which have been reduced to thin membranes along the secondary axis, while the two extremities have been transformed into oval, or diamond-shaped figures, the short diameters of which are equal to the original thickness of the plate (fig. 103).

The secondary plates are lamellae which retain their original thickness along the secondary axis, as well as along the faces forming the broad wall of the pedicel, while the ends are hollowed to receive the oval ends of the primary plates (fig. 104).

In a median longitudinal section (fig. 72), it will be seen that both kinds of plates are thinnest and most numerous at the outer end of the pedicel; toward the inner end, however, they increase in thickness, especially the secondary ones. The latter, figs. 104 and 105, may be regarded as compound, each one being composed of eight pieces. The zigzag line divides the plate into two, while the two double wedges of each half are again divided, by a horizontal plane passing through the middle of each plate, into four pieces.

I am inclined to think that, in the living condition, these plates form sharp-lined and geometrical figures, but in sections, or macerated preparations, they are usually somewhat rounded.

Each one of the primary plates is, at one end, indented by a fold of the scalloped retinula (figs. 72 and 93, *1*).

Surrounding the retinophorae, are seven, oddly shaped retinulae, four of which are nearly black, while the remaining three are filled with light brown pigment. They attain their greatest size at the base of the style, where the nearly spherical nuclei are situated. The inner ends are reduced to narrow bands, closely applied to, and surrounding, in irregular order, the pedicel. The nuclei, and consequently the most expanded parts of the cells, are situated at different levels so that, in a series of cross sections, one first sees, in the outer ones, the nuclei of the three brown pigment cells, all placed on one side of the style, the nuclei of the large median cell being the first to appear (figs. 74. 89 and 90). These three cells *1, 2, 3*) then become greatly reduced in size, while the outer ends of the two black ones (*6, 7*) gain the ascendency; their axial walls are compressed to thin edges resting upon the style, while, near the expanded abaxial faces, are situated the nuclei (figs. 91 and 92). In the next sections, cells (*6* and *7*) have nearly disappeared and the nuclei of the similarly shaped ones (5 and 7) appear (fig. 92). The relation of these cells is represented in a somewhat diagrammatic way in fig. 74.

In the following sections, the uniformity in size and pigmentation of the cells becomes gradually established, but they may still be easily recognized by their arrangement. In nearly all the figures, consecutive sections of the ommatidia, as well as of the same cells, are placed in the same direction, and uniformly lettered. In the largest portion of the pedicels (which are much more closely arranged than is represented in fig. 93), one may occasionally notice that the three cells of one half of the pedicel are thinner and contain less pigment, than the four of the other half. The arrangement shown in fig. 93 is very constant and characteristic, deviations from it being rare and of little importance. In following the sections still farther towards the basal membrane, the pedicel is seen to be less oblong and finally nearly round, while the retinulae, which have become proportionally larger, still afford the means of determining, by their shape and arrangement, the direction of the secondary axes of the pedicel (figs. 93—96). The latter is finally reduced to an extremely fine, and almost indistinguishable, central chord, completely enveloped in the seven retinulae, which, in the following sections, combine to form a butterfly-shaped figure, where the four black cells form the wings, and the other three, the body and tail (figs. 99—100). The median one (figs. 97—100, *1*), at this point, much exceeds its two neighboring cells in size, a fact which, later on, furnishes us with the means of determining their arrangement upon the basal membrane.

The outer parts of the retinulae seem to terminate with the knob-like swellings containing the nuclei; but this is, in reality, not so, for they are continued outwards as extremely delicate membranes, similar to those already described for the retinulae of *Arca*. At the base of the style, and especially at that point where it becomes continuous with the pedicel, the membrane is so closely applied to the former that it is with difficulty observed (figs. 83 and 84); but farther toward the exterior, the united terminal membranes of each group of retinulae form a delicate s h e a t h loosely surrounding the style, from which it is often separated by a clear and narrow area. As the styles expand into the closely packed, octagonal calyces, it is no longer possible to distinguish the s h e a t h, between the adjacent walls of the former, which are so closely placed that their walls have apparently fused to form one line. But the smaller faces of the calyces enclose quadrilateral areas, left for the passage of other elements, and in each of them a delicate membranous tube may be distinguished (figs. 79—81 *rt.s.*).

From theoretical considerations, it is probable that continuations of the membrane exist between the walls of the calyces, but are invisible for reasons already suggested. It is also probable that the sac-like membrane, in the open spaces between the calyces, is formed by the f u s i o n o f p a r t s o f f o u r a d j a c e n t s h e a t h s, producing the closed tubes seen in cross section (figs. 79—81), and which would, accordingly, consist of parts of the terminal membranes of seven retinulae, belonging to four different ommatidia. This fact will become more intelligible when we consider the outer ends of the membranes and their arrangement around the ommatidia.

Just beneath the inner edge of the pigmented band (fig. 69 *pg.c.*), the square spaces have attained their greatest size, and it is here that the circular membrane is most clearly seen (fig. 79 *rt.s.*); beyond this point, towards the exterior, the spaces become completely filled with the pigmented cells, and it is then a matter of the greatest difficulty to distinguish the membranous sheath in cross section. In the following sections, through that part of the ommatidium between the pigmented band and the corneal facets, the sheath may once more be distinguished, in the same form as before. Drawings of the sections have not been given, since the relation of the parts is sufficiently well represented in those macerated specimens, in which the outer ends of the retinophorae and various portions of the surrounding pigment cells, as well as the sheath of the calyx, remain attached to the inner surface of the cornea (figs. 76 and 77). In such preparations, all combinations of the above mentioned parts, in various degrees of clearness, are to be found, and by studying them, one may arrive at a tolerably complete conception of the existing conditions. In fig. 76, is represented a surface view of the corneal facets with the hypodermis and inner ends of the ommatidia still attached. Those portions of the calycal sheath which, by the fusion of corresponding parts from adjacent ommatidia, form the membranous tubes at the corners of the squares (fig. 76 $rt.s.$) — are exactly similar to those seen in the deeper parts of the eye. Here we have the evidence for the above made assertion that each tube is composed of parts of the membranous ends of seven retinulae belonging to four different ommatidia; for one may see that, as the tube approaches the facets, its walls thicken, and, when it finally abuts against the corneal membrane, are resolved into seven hyaline thickenings, so arranged as to form the regular, four-armed figures shown in the drawing (fig.76, I and fig.77). By careful examination of many specimens, some of which have been treated with caustic potash, a series of forms may be found, varying from those in which the tubular membrane projects some distance away from the cornea, to those having four arms extending outwards as thin membranes (fig. 77 $rt.s.$), and still others, in which these radiating membranes have become so extended as to be continuous with corresponding ones from adjacent tubes. In those treated with caustic potash, all the more delicate membranes are dissolved, their thickened extremities alone remaining. One then sees that the centre of the tubes is reduced to a small opening, while each of the radiating membranes has resolved itself into two, doubly wedge-shaped thickenings, seven or eight of which are arranged (fig. 77 IV) around a point which lies directly beneath a place where the corners of four adjacent facets touch each other. Of these eight radiating thickenings, two in each group always face the same square, and — since they unite with those forming the remaining sides of the same — the central retinophorae are completely and immediately surrounded by the outer ends of the retinulae, $1—7$, thus justifying our conclusion that, morphologically, the latter are the most intimately connected with the retinophorae. It has been said that the ends of seven retinulae constitute one of the four-armed figures described above, and, if this is so, it is evident that one of the pairs, and in fact a pair separated by an open angle (as e. g. s^1 and s^2, II, fig. 77), must be formed, not by two pieces, but by one only. Although it is not difficult under favorable circumstances to observe the dividing spaces between the segments, yet it is by no means easy to determine satisfactorily, whether two of the pieces in each group are fused to form one, as necessarily should be the case provided these figures are formed by the ends of seven retinulae. There is, however, one other supposition possible, and that is that the median, scalloped retinula (*l*) is really a double cell, a not improbable condition when we consider its large size, its median position compared with the paired arrangement of the two opposite ones, and its peculiar shape, which probably is connected with the performance of some special function differing from that of the other retinulae. This supposition would be changed almost to a certainty, if it could be shown that, for each ommatidium, there were eight segments in the tubes instead of seven. But as I have said the difficulties in the way of accurate observation were too great for the decision of this question.

The seven retinulae surrounding the pedicel are divided into two groups composed of four black and three brown cells. The median one of the three latter is remarkable on account of its greater size, and peculiar shape. At the beginning of the laminated structure of the pedicel, the axial wall of this cell becomes scalloped, each fold projecting into the end of a primary plate (fig. 72). I can form no conjecture as to the meaning of this remarkable structure. If my memory does not fail me, the same condition prevails in *Galathea*. The structure was then unknown to me, and I failed to give sufficient attention to, or to make a note of it.

The **pigmented collar** of the retinophorae is formed by a third circle of four cells arranged in two pairs, the darker ones forming the inner, and the lighter ones the outer circle of the collar. Each one of the inner cells is triangular in shape, the apex being directed outwards, and the thickened base inwards. Both halves of the cell are likewise triangular, but lie in planes at right angles to each other, the line of union being thickened to form a deeply pigmented ridge (fig. 69), smallest anteriorly, and increasing in size posteriorly, until it is continued beyond the base of the cell as a pigmented rod (fig. 78), which, after losing its pigment, is continued still farther inward, to the basal membrane, as a slender, colorless rod, or **bacillus** (figs. 79—100, *bc*). In cross sections of the collar, the halves of the pigment cells are seen to diminish in thickness at their edges, so that at the intermediate corners there is hardly any pigment at all; but the calyces are so closely packed that the thickest part of one pigment cell lies against the thinnest part of the other, the result being that each calyx seems to be surrounded by a uniformly thick band of pigment, which is better developed toward the inner edge of the collar than in the opposite direction.

The outer circle of collar cells has the same shape as the inner, but its arrangement is different, since here the bases and thickest parts of the triangles are turned outwards instead of inwards (fig. 69). The four cells of the collar are so arranged that the triangular spaces, left between the two inner cells, are exactly filled by the two outer ones, thus forming a continuous, pigmented band around the calyx. The outer edges of the cells contain, instead of pigment, a mass of refractive granules, which in transmitted light appear nearly colorless, but in reflected light are of a faint yellowish-white color, and perfectly opaque. The granules produce the same effect as those to be described in the cells at the bases of the ommatidia.

The collar cells are continued, as four delicate fibres, outwards to the surface of the ommatidium where they produce four minute impressions at each corner of a corneal facet, or, in case the ends of the retinulae have remained undisturbed, they are seen as four fibres in the centre of each tube (fig. 76). It may be well to call attention here to the uncertainty of obtaining these impressions, for in many instances, I have seen no trace of them; this is due, I think, to the fact that the inner chitinous layer of which the cornea is composed may be removed, and, consequently, all trace of the delicate impressions be lost. In cross section through any part of the calyx, the bacilli of the collar cells, of which those belonging to the inner row are the largest, may constantly be seen at their respective corners (fig. 79—81 bc.), an arrangement maintained as far as the outer ends of the style, when the smaller bacilli gradually change their position until each is united with one of the larger ones, which have meantime retained the same direction, in order to form two pairs, one on each side of the style (figs. 81 and 82). On the level of the calyces, the bacilli are situated within the membranous tubes formed by the ends of the retinulae (fig. 71—81). In passing between the pedicels, they are continued along the median line of their broader sides, between the paired lateral cells (*2, 4* and *3, 5*).

Just before the basal membrane is reached, the two pairs of bacilli approach each other at that side of the pedicel opposite the median, scalloped cell, and there become fastened to the diagonal bar of the basal membrane squares, by means of the characteristic, root-like fibres (figs. 99, 101 and 110 bc^1 and bc^2). A much better idea of the bacilli, or cell stalks (which only differ in the amount of development from those of the outer row of cover cells in *Arca*, or the inner ends of the pigment cells in the retina of *Haliotis*), may be obtained by studying macerated preparations, in which the entire bacilli are isolated. In such cases they are seen to be elongated, hyaline fibres. with node-like swellings at various intervals (fig. 111). These bacilli, unless the position and arrangement had been accurately determined, might be mistaken for the so-called rhabdom of GRENACHER, for which in the present instance we have absolutely no equivalent. That no doubt as to the nature of the rods can for a moment be entertained, is shown by their root-like, characteristic ends, and the ease with which. in cross, or longitudinal sections, as well as in macerated preparations', one may demonstrate their continuity with the pigment cells at the outer ends of the ommatidia. Moreover the size of these rods is so great that they form one of the most prominent, as well as easily understood objects in macerated preparations; they furnish us with a striking proof of the accuracy of previous studies upon this subject, which have failed to reveal the presence of such prominent and simple structures! This cannot be due to a difference in the species studied since, in all other Crustacea, as well as in several types of Insect eyes, I have found that the bacilli play an equally important part.

In the spaces between the diminished inner ends of the ommatidia, is a third group of cells, the boundaries of which cannot be distinguished, and therefore it is difficult to determine the number belonging to each ommatidium. The nuclei are arranged at various niveaux around the inner ends of the pedicels, seldom far removed from the basal membrane (fig. 73 *y*). The protoplasm of these cells forms a thick sheath around the inner ends of the retinulae, and completely fills the intervening spaces. These cells contain a mass of yellowish, fat-like crystals which, by reflected light, appear perfectly white and opaque, forming, along the inner surface of the ommateum, a narrow and intensely white band, perfectly visible to the naked eye. The crystals, which are very similar to those formed by certain fats, are insoluble in absolute alcohol, clove oil, creosote, chloroform, or ether. But a very dilute solution of caustic potash dissolves them at once, with the formation of a p u r p l e s o l u t i o n. I thought, at first, that the color came from dissolved pigment, but soon found that that was not the case, for, after a short time, it was noticed that the formation of the purple solution, instantly produced by the addition of very weak caustic potash, issued only from those parts where the crystals were situated, and further, that in a short time all the white crystals had disappeared, while the pigment remained unaffected. Moreover the latter was only dissolved by subsequent treatment with much stronger caustic potash, then producing a brown, instead of a purple solution. As already remarked, there is a smaller deposit of similar crystals in the outer ring of the pigmented collar of the calyx. On observing these crystals under the microscope, I unconsciously recalled to mind similar crystals, so commonly found in embryo insects, and which in *Blatta* I considered to be crystals of uric acid. Whether there is more than a superficial resemblance between the two substances or not, I was unable to determine. When treated with caustic potash, one often sees, in the spaces between adjacent corneal facets, four groups of fibres, or impressions of the same (fig. 75 y). They are probably the outer ends of the basal cells just described, although I have been unable to trace any connection between the structures in question. This supposition, if correct, would fix the number of these cells at four, a number which agrees very well with that which appears to be present.

The basal membrane in *Penaeus* has reached an extremely high stage of complication, and supplies us with facts which lead to very valuable results; at the same time, it may serve as a type, from which similar structures in other genera will probably not vary greatly. Our knowledge of the so-called basal membrane may be summarized in the oft repeated statement that it is a membrane provided with holes for the passage of nerve fibres (the »durchlöcherte« membrane of the Germans. No attempt to determine the relation between the holes of the membranes and the superimposed ommatidia has yet been made. The fact, that only in this manner one can obtain a definite knowledge of the innervation of the ommatidium, and, at the same time, valuable facts concerning their general morphology, has led me to consider this subject in some detail. The facts have been obtained in two ways: by tangential sections, and by isolating the membrane by means of maceration. In both cases it is necessary to dissolve the innumerable, fat-like crystals, described above, with dilute caustic potash.

We will consider first, the structure of the membrane, second, the arrangement of the ommateal cells upon it, and, third, the bundles of nerve fibres by which it is penetrated.

The basal membrane consists of a mass of connective tissue fibres, in certain places so compactly fused as to form hyaline, and apparently structureless masses, connected with each other by a network of fine fibres. Their shape is nearly that of regular Greek crosses, the inner surface being smooth and compact in structure (fig. 107), — while toward the outer surface their fibrous nature is more clearly seen. The general shape and combination of the crosses which form the membrane cannot be better described than by referring to the drawings (figs. 106, 108 and 110). Throughout the entire membrane, the arrangement and direction of the pieces is precisely the same. The inner faces of the arms of the crosses are continuous with each other by means of a delicate hyaline membrane (fig. 107), while the faces directed towards the enclosed squares are united by a series of fibres extending from the inner to the outer surfaces of the crosses. From the centre of the inner surface of each cross, a group of fibres projects inwards, and unites with the connective tissue cells underlying the basal membrane (fig. 107, *c. t.f.*). The enclosed squares are bridged by a bundle of diagonal fibres (figs. 106 and 110) which begin at the inner corner of the squares, as a single, round bar, and, after breaking up into two brush-like bundles, extend outwards to the opposite corner, there becoming attached along the four lines *a, b, c, d* (fig. 110). These diagonal fibres, which maintain the same direction in all the squares, are of service in orienting the arrangement of the ommatidial cells upon the membrane. For convenience, we will call the vertical plane passing through these fibres the diagonal plane of the eye; it coincides also with the long diameter of the pedicel, but its relation to the body, I have not determined. The inner openings of the squares are not rectangular, but rounded, and reduced in size by the formation of a circular membrane, thickest at the corners. If now, we study a series of very thin, cross sections of the inner ends of the ommatidia, we shall be able to determine the position that each cell occupies upon the basal membrane. Beyond the base of the pedicel, and after the retinulae have formed the butterfly-shaped figure around the central and almost imperceptible stalk (figs. 99 and 100), the retinulae suddenly separate, and the central thread, increasing in size, soon dissolves into two groups of fibres (figs. 106 and 110 *rf.*, which become attached to the inner surface of the cross. One group is formed of two separate bundles, while the other is apparently composed of two similar ones, so closely placed as to form one figure, the configuration of which still indicates its dual composition. These four bundles, — of which one may discern the impression upon the crosses in macerated specimens, — are the four inner ends of the retinophorae, and the fibres are their root-like terminations.

If one follows the retinulae in the same manner, it will be seen that after the separation indicated in (fig. 101), the four cells, *4, 6, 5, 7*, unite to form two pairs, each one of which occupies one angle of the cross, on opposite sides of the diagonal plane (fig. 106). The three remaining retinulae occupy that intervening angle from which the diagonal bar arises, so that two cells are placed on one side of it, and the remaining one on the other. The bases of all seven retinulae rest upon the thickenings of the circular membrane filling the inner corners of the enclosed squares (fig. 110). It now remains to indicate the position occupied by the inner ends of the four bacilli belonging to the cells constituting the pigmented collar of the calyx. We have seen that, on a level with the pedicel, they formed two pairs arranged on either side of its broad face, between the black retinulae on the one hand, and the brown on the other (figs. 89—93). After passing the pedicels, the bacilli come to lie outside of the cell group formed by the narrowed, inner ends of the ommatidia (figs. 95—100), and still nearer the basal membrane they approach each other until finally, they end, in the characteristic manner, on the stronger inner fibres of the diagonal bundles, in the angle opposite that occupied by the three brown retinulae $1, 2, 3$ (figs. 106 and 110).

No traces of the inner ends of the basal cells have been found. A diagram, representing these conditions, and lettered to correspond with those of the sections at other niveaux, will make this rather confusing series of changes more comprehensible. Thus we see that each connective tissue cross of the basal membrane furnishes the support for a single ommatidium, and that both these structures correspond in number. Moreover, that the distribution of the various circles of cells around their respective centres is determined by certain planes of division, the resulting arrangement being identical in all the units and in all the parts of the eye.

A knowledge of the basal membrane and of the arrangement of the cells upon it has prepared the way for a comprehension of the distribution of nerve fibres to the cells of the ommatidia. In longitudinal sections, one can easily see that a single, large, pigmented bundle of nerve fibres passes to each of the openings leading into the square spaces enclosed by the neighboring crosses: just before reaching the latter, it breaks up into four, smaller branches going to the four corners of the square. Each of these branches divides again into still smaller ones, which ascend along the inner ends of the cells: the number of bundles for each corner corresponds with the number of cells there. Thus each of the eleven cells, whose ends rest in the corners of the squares, is supplied with a small bundle of pigmented nerve fibres, all of which have arisen from a single branch. But it will be seen, by consulting the diagram, that the eleven nerve bundles of each square belong to four different ommatidia. It is also evident, that the eleven pigmented cells of each ommatidium rest in the corners of four different squares, and therefore must receive their nerve fibres from four different, main bundles. Besides the bundles of pigmented fibres, there are likewise four colorless ones, which, arising from as many main branches, ascend the four angles of the cross and extend along the outer surface of the four retinophorae (fig. 110 *n.f.*). Lastly, a single, minute, colorless branch enters the base of the cross just below the origin of the diagonal bar (fig. 108), and, describing a gentle curve, issues from the centre of the opposite surface, to be continued straight upward between the four retinophorae as the axial nerve fibre of the ommatidium. In macerated specimens, one may see, in the centre of the cross, the minute canal, from the round opening of which a small nerve fibre often projects. On the inner surface of the membrane, the canal opens into a triangular depression, situated on the very edge of the cross, at the apex of the angle formed by the two sides (fig. 107 *c.ax.f.*). On consulting the diagram (fig. 108), it will be seen that the axial nerve fibre comes from the left hand bundle, as does also a group of fibres for the outside of one of the four retinophorae, the remaining three of which are supplied from the three surrounding squares; consequently the retinophorae are provided externally with nerve fibres from four main branches passing through four different squares. The retinulae of each ommatidium are similarly supplied from three different branches, while the four bacilli of the pigment cells receive their nervous supply from one and the same bundle. The diagrammatic figure (fig. 108), represents a longitudinal section of the basal membrane, fig. 106, a tangential section of the same, and finally, fig. 109, sections through one of the nerve bundles just beneath the basal membrane; they are supposed to represent the cells of the same ommatidium with their nerve fibres, and consequently are designated with corresponding letters and figures, easily understood by referring to the explanation of plates. Thus, although the ommatidia, basal membrane crosses, and enclosed squares, as well as the principal nerve bundles, coincide in number, each ommatidium is supplied with nerve fibres from **four different bundles**, or, conversely, each main bundle, instead of supplying a corresponding ommatidium, divides into sixteen groups which supply the cells of four different ommatidia.

In macerated specimens, it is not a difficult matter to follow the nerve fibres of each cell along its entire length. One always finds several fine fibres twisted about the bacilli, on account of their greater size, more easily seen at the inner ends, where they may be observed in cross sections, or in the isolated cells (fig. 111). They may be followed out to the pigmented ends where, on account of their excessive fineness, they disappear. The nerve fibres of the retinulae cling closely to the wall of the cell, which they follow as far as the nucleated portion, where they become confused with those of the outer wall of the retinophorae. Those of the latter are the most important, and may be traced along the outer walls of the retinophorae, surrounding the style and pedicel with a number of longitudinal fibres continued outward over the surface of the calyx (fig. 71 *ex.n.f.*). The axial nerve extends from the base of the retinophorae, through the pedicel and the central canal of the style (figs. 70 *ax.f.*', into the calyx, between the four segments of the crystalline cone. In cross section, it is most easily seen at either end of the pedicel (fig. 94—96', or in the lower parts of the calyx. The conditions for the study of the ramifications of the axial fibres to form the retinidium in *Penaeus* are not favorable, and therefore my observations in this respect are not as complete as I desired. Still, one may see enough to be convinced that the same principle prevails here as in *Mantis*. Those parts of the calyx, not occupied by the crystalline cone, or by the lateral thickenings, seem to have been filled with a fluid, in which probably existed a network of nervous fibrils, similar to those forming the retinidium in *Arca* and *Haliotis*. One may find positive evidence of it, however, in the fact that the lateral thickenings are marked with extremely fine, and nearly straight, cross lines, which I consider to be parts of the retinidium, better preserved by being imbedded in the more compact substance of the lateral thickenings. Moreover, in the softer portions of the crystalline cone, the same structure may be seen (fig. 79 and 80 . It is therefore probable that the whole space enclosed by the outer walls of the four retinophorae, or the cavity of the calyx, is filled with a mass of radiating nerve fibres, which are better preserved in those places where the substance filling the calyx has hardened to form the lateral thickenings, or the centrally placed crystalline cones. It is also probable, from theoretical considerations, that the system of superficial fibres, distributed over the wall of the calyx, communicates with the cross branches from the axial nerve, just as in *Pecten* and *Arca*. In the outer ends of the crystalline cone, in that part which is densest and most hyaline, I have not been able to observe anything like cross lines or fibres.

Galathea, Palaemon and Pagurus.

After completing my observations upon Penaeus, I desired to make similar studies upon typical genera from the various families of Crustacea, but neither time, nor the limits of this paper (already longer than I originally intended), have allowed me to carry out the plan. Still, I have made a number of observations upon the eyes of the above named genera, concerning the most important points I desired to illustrate, and which, although by no means so complete as those upon *Penaeus*, still, as far as they go, fully confirm what I have already described for that genus. A more complete description of the ommatidia will be reserved for some future time.

In all three genera, one may easily demonstrate the presence of the corneal hypodermis, the general characters of which differ but little from those of *Penaeus*. In both *Palaemon* and *Pagurus* there are two peripherally placed nuclei for each quadrilateral facet (Pl. 31, fig. 115 *n.c.h.*). In *Galathea*, however, there is a remarkable modification of these cells to form, for each ommatidium, an iris with a slit-like contractile opening, the walls of which may be expanded by means of radiating, contractile fibres, attached to the periphery of the cells (Pl. 31, fig. 114). The iris is formed of the two corneal hypodermic cells, the very indistinct nuclei of which are situated so close together, that they often appear like a single oval body, placed exactly over the centre of the hexagonal facets, instead of on the periphery. The cell protoplasm is thickened into two opaque, triangular curtains enclosing a clear, slit-like space, in the centre of which are situated the two nuclei. When the closed iris is observed from below, in surface preparations, one sees simply the thickened edge of the adjacent cell walls enclosing a very narrow, central space. In an open iris, prepared in the same manner, the free edge of the triangular curtain, which otherwise projects inwards between the slightly expanded outer ends of the retinophorae, is seen to have been drawn towards the periphery of the cell, thus enlarging the central opening, or pupil, and also affording a better view of the shape of the curtain (fig. 114 *cu.*): the latter is composed of a granular protoplasm, filled with what appear to be vacuoles of varying size. The edge of the curtain is continuous with many fine, radiating, protoplasmic fibres, which, at their opposite extremities, unite with a thickened, peripheral ring of protoplasm, *x*.

In surface preparations, made as described for *Penaeus*, the iris of each facet may be seen in various stages of expansion and contraction. The two nuclei, placed in the centre of the opening, are extremely transparent and refractive, and these facts together whit their lenticular shape might lead one to consider them as minute lenses. The curtain of the iris, in the living condition, is probably filled with fat globules, which, being readily soluble in alcohol, produce the vacuolated appearance described above; they would tend to make that part of the iris opaque, thus facilitating its function of modifying the intensity of the light.

In *Galathea*, as well as in *Pagurus* and *Palaemon*, I have succeeded in isolating, by maceration, the style of the retinophorae, which was continuous, at one end, with the four segments of the calyx, and, at the other, with the four rows of plates constituting the pedicel. In the centre of the style, the four hyaline stalks of the retinophorae are inseparably united to form, as in *Penaeus*, a tube, which near the pedicel has again the tendency to divide into four segments (fig. 117, Pl. 31). There can be no doubt that the calyx, style and pedicel (or the Krystallkegelzellen and rhabdoms of GRENACHER), are continuous parts of the four retinophorae, a fact that is fatal to GRENACHER'S theory that the Krystallkegelzellen (or what corresponds to my calyx of the retinophorae) are homologons with the cells of the vitreous body in Spiders and Myriapods. There are besides several other insurmountable objections to this theory, rendering it no longer tenable. The real homologues of the vitreous cells of Myriapods, Spiders and Hexapod ocelli, are those of the corneal hypodermis, which I have been able to detect in all the genera that I have examined, and which without doubt must be considered to be universally present!

For example, I have found the corneal hypodermis present in *Musca, Mantis, Branchipus, Penaeus, Palaemon, Pagurus* and *Galathea*.

The number of the retinulae in *Palaemon, Galathea*, and *Pagurus* is seven, the same as in *Penaeus*, but the nucleated portions, instead of being situated close to the inner end of the style, are extended outwards as far as the neck of the calyx. The four outer pigment cells form a dense black circle, just above the former, and are continued outwards toward the cornea, as well as in the opposite direction, as slender pigmented rods, which in the latter case become reduced to the colorless and hyaline bacilli, and are continued, as such, up to the basal membrane.

The calyx of *Galathea* is very favorable for the study of the nerve fibrillae which there form the retinidium. For this purpose, I have prepared the cells by the same method used to dissolve the cuticular substance of the rods in *Haliotis*. It also gave very good results here, but did not dissolve the crystalline cone. In such preparations, one could follow the external, longitudinal nerve fibres surrounding the style, as well as the central, axial fibres (Pl. 31, figs. 131 and 132) up to the calyx, where the former became continued into the centre of the crystalline cone, while the latter, spreading out over the wall of the calyx. form a complete network of nerve fibrillae: the latter branch, in pretty regular order, at right angles from the larger longitudinal ones, and then unite to form a continuous network of superficial fibres (figs. 129 and 130).

One finds in *Galathea* the same abaxial thickenings, (four), of the calycal wall, as in *Penaeus*, and can readily distinguish in them the cross fibrillae, which have exactly the same appearance as those in the rods of *Pecten*. In cross sections, it can, in some cases, be seen where these fibres are continued across the cavity of the calyx to the crystalline cone. It is extremely difficult to prepare the crystalline cone in such a manner that the radiating cross striae can be seen. In some cases, the cones remain perfectly transparent and apparently structureless: in others. one may succeed in detecting the striae, especially towards the inner ends of the cones, which there appear to be less dense. In *Pagurus*, however. I have succeeded in obtaining the clearest insight into the structure of the crystalline cones. Here they are less hyaline, and the striae may be seen without special difficulty.

In all these genera the pedicels are composed of two sets of plates. the fibres in one of which are at right angles to those of the other. The plates themselves appear to fit into each other in the same manner as those of *Penaeus*.

In the last named genus. the division of the corneal facets into halves. produced by the impression of the two underlying cells, was so faintly marked that one might be tempted to doubt its meaning, if, in other cases, there did not exist such positive evidence to the contrary. In *Galathea*, the division of the facets is so plain. and corresponds so exactly with the outlines of the corneal cells. that there can be no doubt that the latter, and not the Krystallkegelzellen, as GRENACHER believes, give rise to the facets of the cornea. Indeed I have observed two instances in which a facet was composed of two perfectly distinct parts, each one of which corresponded with the underlying corneal cells (Pl. 31. fig. 116, *a*. In fig. 114, the divisions are represented as extending from one angle of the facet to the opposite one. This however is very exceptional. for in by far the majority of cases it extends from the middle of one wall, to a corresponding point in the opposite one (fig. 116). This line of division, whatever its direction may be. compared with the periphery of the facets, always lies directly over the adjacent, median walls of the two corneal cells.

Branchipus and Orchestia.

I have had the pleasure of examining some well preserved eyes of *Branchipus Grubii*, prepared during my stay in Leipzig. The four nuclei of the retinophorae are located at the outer ends of the cells, over which they form a kind of cap, situated in a thickening similar to that found in a corresponding position in the eye of *Penaeus*. The corneal hypodermis is well developed and consists of a layer of indefinitely arranged cells upon the inner surface of the unfaceted cornea. The style of the retinophorae forms a spindle-shaped tube, largest near the outer ends of the retinulae, and decreasing in diameter towards either extremity; the outer end becomes directly continuous with the calyx, while the slender inner one rests upon the basal membrane. The tube, within which may be seen the axial nerve fibre, is laterally flattened, the two narrow walls being much thicker than the broad ones. The cross nerve fibres within the calyx, together with the superficial ones upon the walls of the same, may be seen here just the same as in *Galathea*, *Penaeus* etc. from which they do not differ to any noticeable extent. The four lateral thickenings seen in the calyx of *Galathea*, and the outer row of pigmented cover cells (and of course the bacilli, or their stalk-like ends), are absent in *Branchipus*.

In *Orchestia*, I have also seen in macerated specimens the same nervous network upon the surface of the calyx, although I was unable to detect cross striae in the crystalline cones. Along the wall of the calyx, which is almost completely filled by the crystalline cone, may be detected several comparatively large, longitudinal fibres, from which a great number of irregular, smaller branches arise.

A valuable confirmation of my opinion, that the corneal hypodermis is the very much modified and reduced layer of similarly named cells in the eyes of Myriapods and Spiders, was found on examining some sections of embryo lobsters which were just ready to escape from the chorion. Here the cells formed a broad and very distinct layer, separated from the underlying ommatidia by an extremely delicate membrane. An exactly similar condition was found in the eyes of larval *Penaeus*, or an allied genus. In both cases, the development of the larval cuticular hypodermis was much greater than in the adult, where it is reduced to an almost unrecognizable thinness. Moreover, the nuclei of these cells stain more deeply, and consequently are more easily recognized, in the larval, than in the adult condition. These two facts indicate that the cuticular hypodermis must have once constituted a more important and conspicuous part of the eye than at present.

Mantis religiosa.

The thick cuticular covering of the eye is divided into hexagonal, biconvex facets, the inner surface being more strongly arched than the outer. They are divided into a hard, homogeneous. outer layer (fig. 118 c'), and a thicker, less refractive, inner one, composed of a great number of thin, superimposed layers having the same curves as the outer surfaces of the facets. The latter are separated from each other by a thin layer of chitinous substance, the refractive index of which is different from that of the facets (fig. 118). On the periphery of the inner surface of the latter, are two small nuclei $c.h.$, around each of which is a rather large, triangular space, filled with protoplasm, diminishing quite rapidly in thickness towards the centre of the corresponding facet. I have only been able to study these nuclei in sections, since the fresh material at my command was not sufficient for maceration. It is only by the latter method, by which one may isolate large portions of the corneal cuticula with their underlying nuclei. that an adequate knowledge can be obtained of the number and arrangement of these cells, to which the corneal facets owe their origin, and which form a continuous and distinct layer, — the corneal hypodermis, — between the cuticula and the ommateum. The latter is composed of a number of ommatidia, each one of which, in turn, consists of four central retinophorae surrounded by several rows of pigment cells. The outer ends of the retinophorae are greatly enlarged to form the calyx, which contains the retinidium. The two inner thirds are reduced to a narrow tube, the style, which nearly corresponds with the so-called rhabdom of GRENACHER.

The calyx is surrounded by a layer of yellowish brown pigment cells, the nuclei of which are so arranged that it is difficult to determine their number. but they appear to form two, rather indistinct rows. In longitudinal sections, it is only occasionally that one sees isolated, oval nuclei high up, between the retinophorae, as in fig. 118, pg^1. But in the large space, formed by the constriction of the inner ends of the calyces are several large nuclei, varying considerably in size, and undoubtedly belonging to the yellowish brown pigment cells. These cells do not show any distinct constrictions, and it is therefore difficult to determine their exact number or shape. Judging from the nuclei, there are at least six brown pigment cells for each ommatidium. Two prominent, black pigment cells completely surround the neck of the calyx. In longitudinal sections, or in isolated preparations, it is seen that their expanded and deeply pigmented inner extremity ends squarely, and contains a round nucleus; in the opposite direction they become thin and narrow, and the pigment, which is diminished in quantity, finally disappears (fig. 118, $pg.^3$). The style of the retinophorae is completely enclosed by seven retinulae, whose outer ends, in which the nuclei are situated, are completely impregnated with nearly black pigment, while, towards the inner ends, the axial faces alone are colored in this manner. Three of these cells are longer and more deeply pigmented than the others, so that a cross section of the ommateum, just below the calyx, shows only the ends of these three cells arranged as in fig. 123; at the very ends they are broad and thin, increasing in thickness, inwards. All seven retinulae form a long double cone, whose greatest diameter is in the part where there is the most pigment.

The spaces between the inner ends of the ommatidia are occupied by irregular, slightly pigmented cells, containing oval, and distinctly visible nuclei (fig. 118, y).

Numerous, fine, tracheal branches, tr, are found between the ommatidia.

The ommatidial layer of the eye rests upon an enormously thickened, connective tissue, basal membrane, which forms a thick, sieve-like layer permeated by canals, corresponding in number with the ommatidia, and through each of which passes a bundle of pigmented nerve fibres. The outer surface of the basal membrane, upon which rest the inner ends of the ommatidia, is well supplied with pigment, which obscures its finer structure. The inner surface is thickened and forms a sieve-like membrane, which stains deeply in haematoxylin, and might easily be mistaken for a true basal membrane (fig. 127, $a. c.$). The latter is composed of more compactly united, connective tissue fibres, and is sharply defined on its outer surface, while on its inner, the fibres of which it is composed become continuous with those irregularly encircling the numerous »nerve channels«. Towards the periphery of the eye, this massive membrane, which contains many nuclei, becomes thinner, and, finally, at the beginning of the ordinary hypodermis disappears. The rounded outer ends of the retinophorae, where the four large, oval nuclei are situated, contain a very thin, watery fluid; anything equivalent to a crystalline cone being absent. The walls of the calyx are finely striped, as though covered with quite regularly arranged fibres (fig. 118).

The calyx is divided into four chambers by the inner walls of the four retinophorae (fig. 119); near its inner end two of the walls disappear, and consequently the retinidium is divided into halves, the plane of division passing through the two pigmented cells, $pg.$[3] (fig. 121). Finally, these walls also disappear, at that point where the calyx is transformed into the style (fig. 122). Although the axial walls of the retinophorae have disappeared, the abaxial ones, which form the calyx, continue as a closed and narrow tube, the style, as far as the basal membrane. The same method of innervation is to be found here as in the Mollusca and Crustacea; each cell is provided with a number of nerve fibres, extending its whole length, and closely applied to its outer surface. By the concrescence of the retinophorae, the nerve fibres of the adjacent walls did not disappear, but came to lie in the centre of the group; as the union became more intimate, the inner walls disappeared entirely, and the nerve fibres became as completely enclosed by the united cell walls as though they had developed within a single cell. With a good oil immersion, it may be seen, without special difficulty, in properly prepared material, that the axial bundle of nerve fibres thus formed occupies the centres of the narrow tubes produced by the united stalks of the four retinophorae fig. 128). The conditions for observation are so unfavorable at the inner end of the style, that the narrow tube with its central fibre is with difficulty distinguishable; but at the outer end, the tube is considerably enlarged, and the axial nerve bundle is seen to consist of four distinct fibres, which themselves are probably composed of numerous smaller ones (fig. 124). Just beyond the narrow neck of the calyx (fig. 128), the four bundles of nerve fibres break up into innumerable branches, which follow the median partition for a short distance and then separate to form four groups, each one of which passes through the middle of one of the four chambers of the calyx (figs. 121 and 119). From each of these fibres, are given off innumerable horizontal fibrillae, which fuse and interlace with each other to form a complete nervous network, distinguishable only in the most carefully prepared material. The best method of preparation is the one I have already described for *Pecten*, i. e. treatment for about half an hour in chromic acid, $\frac{1}{5}\%$, at $45°$ Centigrade. The following day, one may pick to pieces with needles, and examine in acetate of potash. By this method, the most beautiful results are obtained, for it very often happens that the whole retinidium may be isolated as a spongy-like core, in which the longitudinal fibres with their cross branches may be seen with perfect ease. It is not within my power to give, by means of drawings, an adequate idea of the marvellous complexity, yet at the same time wonderful clearness and simplicity, of this structure, which at once furnishes such a complete proof that the seat of vision is located at that place, as it has seldom been the lot of a student to experience, in an equally difficult subject. Sections of another eye, prepared at the same time in this manner, show essentially the same structure, except that many of the finest fibrillae have become so strongly varicose as to disguise their real nature; under unfavorable optical conditions, a mass of fine granules are seen, with comparatively few, distinctly visible, cross fibres. But even then a careful examination would not fail to disclose the same general structure that is so plainly visible in the dissected eyes. However indistinct the cross fibrillae, at times, may be, the four central bundles always remain visible. In cross sections of the hollow style, may be seen, with a distinctness that leaves no doubt in the mind, very fine fibres radiating from the axial bundle towards the periphery (figs. 128, 124 and 125). The effect is similar to that seen in cross sections of the retinidia of *Pecten*.

If a cross section of the retinidium of *Mantis* be compared with one of *Penaeus*, *Arca*, or *Galathea*, a slight difference will be observed: In the last three, the axial nerve bundle remains exactly in the central axis, between the adjacent walls of the four cells. In *Mantis*, there are four bundles, one inside of each cell; this can only be explained by the fact that, at the inner end of the calyx and indeed throughout the whole length of the style, the axial walls of the four cells have disappeared, and thus the way was left open for the fibres to pass into the centre of each cell; this is evidently a clear gain in the distribution of the horizontal fibrillae, and may possibly account for the absence of a crystalline cone. The wall of the style is surrounded by six nerve fibres, which appear in cross sections as so many small dots (figs. 125 and 124). They may be followed as far as the neck of the calyx, where they disappear, breaking up into numerous smaller branches, continuous with those inside the calyx by means of minute cross fibrillae. Towards the outer end of the ommatidium, the retinulae are easily seen to consist of seven distinct cells, closely surrounding the style; towards the inner ends, the space enclosed by the pigmented axial faces of the retinulae, remains about the same, while the enclosed style with the six nerve fibres becomes smaller and thus gives rise to a pigmentless area between the style and the retinulae (fig. 125). Whether that is the normal condition, or an artificial product of the reagents used, I am unable to say. The retinidium, besides being enclosed in the calyx, is also surrounded by a somewhat thicker and structureless membrane, the retinidial sheath, formed by the united outer ends of the seven retinulae, which are continued outwards to the surface of the ommatidial layer as thin cell walls. The abaxial face of each retinula is provided with a number of longitudinal nerve fibres connected with each other by numerous, minute, circular ones (fig. 118). Around the retinulae are several bacilli, the number of which for each ommatidinm I was unable to determine with certainty, but I have counted eight in several instances, and think that that is the normal number. They are much larger than the nerve fibres and are undoubtedly the inner, stalk-like ends of the outer pigment cells, with which they should correspond in number. They are round, colorless and refractive rods, surrounded by nerve fibres; the inner ends, which rest on the basal membrane, expand into several root-like fibres, a proof that they are the modified inner ends of hypodermic cells. The nerve fibres surrounding each bacillus, supply the outer pigmented ends of the same. The bacilli may be followed in longitudinal sections as far as the outer ends of the retinulae, but, occasionally, one is seen to extend as far as the inner row of nuclei of the brown cells (fig. 118, *b. pg¹*): they probably belong to those pigmented cells, the nuclei of which may be seen between the outer ends of the calyces.

Through each canal in the basal membrane, passes a bundle of nerve fibres which are pigmented towards their outer ends. Whether the same breaking up of the nervous bundles to supply four different ommatidia takes place here, as in *Penaeus*, or not, I am unable to say, since the material at my disposal was neither sufficiently abundant, nor favorable for the observation of such minute details. At all events, the fibres, or groups of fibres, may easily be seen passing to the individual cells which constitute the ommatidia; they may then be followed along the whole length of the same, either in cross or longitudinal sections, or in the dissected and isolated cells.

Chapter III. General Remarks on the Mollusca.

The term ommateum was first introduced by LANKESTER to designate all the soft parts of the Arthropod eye, with the exception of the cuticular lens. CARRIÈRE adopted this term, and added that of ommatidium, to designate the individual eyes of which the Arthropod ommateum is composed. According to my own reseaches, the structure and morphological signification of the latter term is entirely different from that ascribed to it by my predecessors. Two difficulties have presented themselves, either new terms must be invented to designate what I consider to be the real unit of the Arthropod, or in fact of all eyes, or the meaning of the old, must be extended to suit my conception of the structure. I have chosen the latter course, the less of the two evils.

By the term ommatidium, I shall designate those constructive elements of all eyes consisting of single (?, or compound, colorless cells the retinophorae, surrounded by one or more circles of pigmented ones, or retinulae.

A typical Molluscan ommatidium consists of a double, colorless and, in some cases, gland-like cell, the retinophora, containing two nuclei and an axial nerve fibre. The external surface of the retinophora is provided with nerve fibres, which at the outer ends of the cells break up into numerous fibrillae directly continuous with similar ones from the axial nerve. This network of cross fibrillae, the retinidium, is usually supported by a cuticular secretion, or rod, of the retinophora. The latter, except in the retinated types, always contains a number of refractive globules which serve as a kind of mirror, or argentinula, for each rod, so that the rays of light are reflected back again, passing a second time through the retinidium. The retinophorae are surrounded by a circle of pigmented cells, which may also be provided with nervous retia terminalia imbedded in a cuticular secretion; but these cells are in all cases single and contain no axial fibres. In the simplest condition, the terminal nerve fibrillae of the retinophorae, of the pigment cells, or retinulae, and of the adjacent, unmodified epithelial cells, form a continuous nervous network.

The retinophorae, in all the varied stages of their modification, are distinguished by their pointed inner ends drawn out into the axial nerve fibre, and by the presence of two nuclei; one is faint and difficult to observe, while the other is large and oval, stains sharply but not deeply, and always contains a nucleolus.

The retinulae end in several root-like fibres resting upon the basal membrane. Their nuclei are comparatively small, stain deeply but not so clearly and sharply as those of the retinophorae, and, as far as I have observed, never contain nucleoli.

The retinulae may be transformed into ganglionic cells, which, in the early stages, migrate inwards leaving the retineum, with which they remain in connection by a nerve fibre, or, in the later stages, they may be converted »in situ« into ganglionic cells which never leave the retina (Pl. 32. figs. 139 and 140).

Animals provided with the simplest ommatidia may possess an extraordinary sensitiveness to changes in the intensity of light, as witness *Avicula*. An epithelium provided with such ommatidia is seldom, or never, perfectly smooth; it is thrown into innumerable folds which usually run at right angles to the course of the greatest amount of light. The folds serve a double purpose; first, of increasing the light sensitive surface, and second, of bringing the ultimate nerve fibrillae, which are in general tangential to the surface, as nearly as possible at right angles to the rays of light coming from various directions.

Here, then, we have the conditions which shall determine the ultimate structure of the incipient visual organ. In the folded portions of the ommatidial surface, a double advantage is gained: first, a protection for the retia terminalia supported by the cuticula; and, second, a partial exclusion of lateral rays of light, so that both the retinidia of the pigmented, as well as of the colorless cells, may become functional. In the convex type of eyes, the pigmented cells lose their terminal nerve fibrillae, and serve solely to surround the radiating retinidia of the retinophorae in such a manner that each one shall receive only the vertical rays of light. In all convex eyes, the so-called faceted structure is a necessary consequence of the law that the perfection of a visual organ depends upon the degree to which lateral rays of light are excluded from the retinidia, and upon the degree to which the ultimate fibrillae of the latter have become perpendicular to the rays of light. In convex eyes with radiately arranged ommatidia, the protection of the retinidia from lateral rays can only be accomplished by the isolation of the individual retinidia, a function to which the pigmented retinulae have become subordinate; in the same proportion, the retinophorae become the more essential elements. The rapidity with which the latter assume the supremacy is, without doubt, due to their axial nerve fibres, so well adapted to the most economic distribution, over a given area, of radiating fibrillae. To this may also be added their refractive and granular contents, acting as mirrors, which reflect the light that has once passed the retinidia, and cause it to pass a second time through the retinidial fibrillae.

The absence of pigment in the retinophorae, even when its presence would not interfere with the accession of light to the retinidia, is a fact worthy of consideration. That it must have an importance hardly exceeded by that of the nerve fibres themselves, is shown by the constant[1] absence of granular pigment in all retinophorae, from the simplest isolated ones, to the most specialized.

It is not impossible that the retinophorae originated from simple gland cells, which had the advantage over the pigmented ones in that the rays of light would be reflected outwards again, by the colorless and refractive contents underlying the retia terminalia: pigment would absorb, not reflect, light. But I am inclined to regard the refractive globules as being secondarily acquired by the colorless cells, since in the Coelenterata they are absent. The remarkable constancy with which similar gland-like cells are associated with the sense hair papillae of the Mollusca, the sense organs of the lateral line, and organs of taste in Vertebrates, indicates that these gland-like cells have something more than a casual connection with organs of special sense.

In the invaginated forms, the shape of the eye determines, to a certain degree, the direction of the rays of light, and we should expect to find in the simplest eyes of this type that both retinulae and retinophorae contribute nearly equal parts to the formation of the retinidia: and, indeed, such is invariably the case in the simpler forms of Molluscan eyes. According as these invaginate eyes become more highly developed, — a process accompanied by the narrowing of the pupil together with the addition of some refractive body, as the lens, — the direction of the rays of light becomes definitely fixed, and the fibrillae of the retinidia assume a more perfect radial arrangement, in overlying planes, around the larger nerves fibres.

In the simplest Molluscan eyes, the arrangement of the fibrillae is not of great moment so that both retinophorae and retinulae may produce rods; but in the more perfect organs, as those of Cephalopods, Heteropods and *Pecten*, the retinophorae, owing to the advantageous arrangement of their axial nerves, alone develop rods.

The visual organs of the Mollusca may be divided, according to the arrangement and modification of the ommatidia, into four types: the diffuse, the invaginate, the faceted, and the pseudo-lenticulate type, representing the three modifications of light sensitive surfaces, i. e., a retineum, ommateum and a retina.

The Mollusca is the most interesting group of animals we know of, as far as visual organs are concerned, since it contains all types of

---

[1] In Cephalopods, *Nautilus* and *Sepia*, there appears to be an exception, in that the so-called sense cells are somewhat pigmented.

such structures known to exist. Even in one genus, as *Arca*, one finds innumerable examples of the diffuse, the invaginate, and the evaginate, or compound eye.

The isolated ommatidia, constituting the diffuse form, seem to be present in nearly all of the Lamellibranchiata, regardless of whether other and more perfect eyes are present or not. In the Gasteropods, their presence has never been demonstrated, but from the rudimentary character of some of their eyes (*Patella, Helix, Haliotis*, etc.), there can be no doubt, that in the well developed pigmented areas of these animals, there are also isolated ommatidia similar to those of the Lamellibranchiata.

The chromatophores of the Cephalopods offer striking resemblances to the isolated ommatidia. BLANCHARD (70) has shown that they develop as single, colorless cells surrounded by pigmented ones. If we suppose that these embryonic organs are ommatidia, and that the colored cells, or retinulae, should assume the features so characteristic of the pigment cells in certain Coelenterata, Crustacea, and embryo fishes, i. e. amoeboid arms and contractility, the ommatidia would then be transformed into chromatophores. Their original function as ommatidia, and consequently the intimate relation they bore to the light, would prepare the way for their transformation into their present condition. In the Lamellibranchiata, the isolated ommatidia are found principally in those pigmented areas exposed to the direct rays of light, that is, on the edge of the mantle and tip of the sipho. In the former region, on the branchial side of the ophthalmic fold, the ommatidia tend to form into groups, covered with a slightly thickened cuticula, on the surface of rounded summits or elongated ridges, or upon the floor of shallow grooves or circular pits. Although in these cases the cuticula shows no traces of a division for each underlying cell, it may be divided into two continuous layers: a very thin, structureless, outer one, or corneal cuticula, and a thicker, less compact, inner one, the retinidial cuticula, filled with the fibrillae of the retia terminalia (Pl. 32, fig. 130).

In general, the ommatidia seem to be scattered about indefinitely over the pigmented surface of the mantle, but the irregular folds in the epithelium offer certain advantages which are seized upon by the ommatidia, causing them to develop more rapidly in those regions with the most folds.

The invaginated eyes of *Arca* may easily be proven to have originated from the pigmented furrows, or pits. Did the faceted, or evaginate eyes, originate from the pigmented summits and ridges, or by a modification of the invaginate eyes? Although I would not entirely exclude the former possibility, I have only found evidence in favor of the latter. As far as we know, only *Arca*, *Pectunculus*, and possibly the ancestral forms of *Pecten*, were supplied with evaginated, or faceted eyes, while all other Mollusca possess only the invaginate types. We may mention the following facts in favor of the supposition that the faceted eyes are modifications of the invaginated ones. The latter are found in all stages of development, large or small, deep or shallow, round, oval, or elongated. If now the faceted eyes were formed from the summits and ridges separating the pits and grooves, we should expect to find a series of intermediate forms, parallel with those of the invaginate ones. But this is not the case, for the faceted eyes are usually of a large and constant form, sunken in pits more or less shallow according to the development of the eye. It is very rarely that one finds small faceted eyes composed of two or three ommatidia. Moreover there is a tendency on the posterior portions of the mantle to produce intermediate forms between the faceted and invaginated types. Finally the faceted eyes are only found in *Arca*, *Pectunculus* and probably the ancestral forms of *Pecten*, while all other Molluscs are provided only with the invaginate types. These facts render it probable that the latter are the simplest and ancestral forms, from which the faceted ones have arisen by an evagination of the pits, accompanied by the degeneration of the pigment cells into protective ones, while the retinidia of the retinophorae have developed in a corresponding degree (Pl. 32, figs. 132 and 133). The faceted structure of these convex eyes is, as we have already said, a necessary result of the radial arrangement of the retinidia, upon whose fibrillae it is necessary for the rays of light to act at right angles.

In the shallow grooves on the mantle edge and at the base of the siphonal tentacle of Lamellibranchiata, as we have already remarked, the cuticula forms a continuous layer, the inner surface of which, the retinidial cuticula, is filled with a thin stratum of tangential nerve fibres, the retia terminalia. In the deeper grooves, or in the less developed invaginate eyes, the cuticula is considerably thicker, and its inner layer shows a tendency to form, over each cell, a cuticular cylinder, or rod, containing the terminal fibrillae of the nerves surrounding each cell. As the divisions between these cuticular cylinders become more and more marked, so also the nerve fibres in them assume a more constant relation, giving rise to the retinal rods, each of which contains a specialized portion of the retia terminalia, the retinidium. The corneal cuticula remains as a thin, structureless membrane covering the outer ends of the rods (Pl. 32, fig. 132). These organs constitute the simplest invaginate eyes, such as are found in *Arca*, *Patella* etc. An advance in the structure of such an eye is made by an increase in the depth of the optic cup and in the size of the retinidia, accompanied by a reduction in the size of the opening, or pupil of the eye. What seems to have been an incidental result of the deepening of the optic cup was an increase in the thickness of the corneal cuticula, which may be followed in its growth in various genera of Gasteropods until, finally, it completely fills the optic cup. A discussion of the effect which a constant increase in the thickness of this refractive substance until it entirely fills the cavity of the eye would have upon the rays of light entering the pupil, would lead us too far into physiological grounds, for this paper. The general result would be, first, to increase the number of direct and reflected rays of light falling upon the floor of the optic cup; second, to exclude the outer walls more and more from the light, until finally only direct rays fall upon the inner wall of the cup. Either a central, or external part of the enlarged corneal cuticula, or vitreous body, becomes hardened into a rounded, or lenticular body to form the lens.

According as the inner wall of the optic cup becomes more exposed to rays of light whose direction is more and more fixed and constant, so a corresponding change in the structure of the rods will appear, in that they become more sharply and regularly defined, the fibrillae of their contained retinidia showing a more perfect cross arrangement, and consequently being more perfectly at right angles to the rays of light. The more complete the arrangement of the retinidial fibrillae, just so much greater will be the effect of this uniformity in direction upon the cuticular substance of the rods supporting the fibres, until, finally, the so-called lamination of the rods, due to the perfectly radial arrangement of the retinidial fibrillae, is produced. My own observations only extend over those Gasteropod Mollusca (*Haliotis* and *Patella*) in which the eye is very imperfectly developed. In the higher forms, the observations as yet made are too incomplete to allow a definite conclusion concerning the structure of the rods and their origin. According to HILGER, they consist of a sheath and core, formed respectively by the pigmented and colorless cells. A rod of that composition has no resemblance to any similar structure of which we know, and cannot be compared in any way with the rods of other Mollusca. I believe that HILGER has formed a false conception of the rods in Gasteropods. It seems much more probable, from my own studies and from what I can gather from his, that both pigmented and colorless cells form independent rods, and that what he has described as a single one is really the product of an entire ommatidium: the core and sheath of his rod being due to the arrangement of the cells composing the ommatidium. The rod of the retinophora, or colorless cell, forms the core of HILGER'S rod, while those of the surrounding pigment cells form the sheath.

Whether there are Gasteropod eyes in which only the retinophorae bear retinidia, while the pigment cells are modified for other purposes, is not known at present. In the Heteropods, however, according to HENSEN, it looks as though the retinulae were reduced to very thin pigmented cells at the outer ends of the retinophorae: the latter alone appear to develop rods.

In the Cephalopods, as we have already pointed out, the retinophorae (retinal cells) alone produce double rods, which may be compared directly with the double rods of *Arca*, *Pecten*, etc. The retinulae have become transformed into cells homologous with the ganglionic ones of *Pecten*. In the latter case, the inversion of the rods necessitates the absence of pigment in these cells, while in the Cephalopods, where the original direction of the rods is retained, no such change is necessary.

The pseudo-lentic eyes of *Arca* must be regarded as small aggregations of ommatidia on a nearly level surface, the retinidial cuticula of which has become thickened into a lens-shaped body richly supplied with nerve fibrillae, — in fact exactly what would be produced by pulling an invaginate eye out flat. One might consider them as incipient invaginate eyes, the retinal cuticula of which has increased in thickness more rapidly than the ommateal layer has become invaginate.

The retinated type of eyes is confined, as far as we know at present, to *Pecten*, whose retina is characterised by the great development of the retinophorae and their rods, and the complete absence of pigment from the retinulae. The sensitive layer of the Cephalopod eye must be regarded as a retineum in which the retinulae have ceased to produce rods, some being modified to form the colorless ganglionic cells (»sockel« cells of GRENACHER). The eyes of Cephalopods are remarkable on account of their complicated dioptric apparatus, rather than for any great specialization of the sensitive layer.

Before making any comparisons between the retina of *Pecten* and that of Cephalopods, I will attempt to explain my idea of the origin of the eye of *Pecten*. An incomplete knowledge of the anatomy and development of these eyes has deterred all my predecessors from making any attempt to solve this apparently hopeless problem. They have contented themselves with the statement that we must look to the development for the solution. I thought so too, and after a careful, and, I believe, in the main successful study of the development, was much disappointed to find that the solution did not appear any easier than before. Instead of developing from invaginations, as I had expected would be the case, they were formed from knob-like papillae. I left the matter for a while, and turned my attention towards other genera of Lamellibranchiata in hopes of finding some clew to the subject. After studying the eyes of *Arca*, I came to the conclusion that the solution could be found there, if anywhere. Although the following explanation may not rest upon sufficient evidence, still, as far as it goes, it is good. Development has shown that, in the young *Pecten*, the branchial side of the ophthalmic fold is covered with a number of small pigmented pits exactly similar to the invaginated eyes of *Arca*. There are also small pigmented papillae consisting of a few ommatidia, which in the larvae are exceptionally large and well developed, but which in the later stages degenerate or disappear. These facts indicate that the ophthalmic fold, in the ancestors of the present *Pecten*, was provided with many invaginated eyes, together with innumerable, well developed and isolated ommatidia, a condition which could best be compared with that in *Arca* of to-day. A most remarkable agreement is to be found between the paired arrangement of the eyes of *Pecten* and the faceted ones of *Arca*. In neither genera is the sequence of the pairs constant; usually two large eyes are separated by one or two small ones. We have seen that the largest eyes of *Arca* are arranged along a pigmented line on the summit of the ophthalmic fold, and that on the branchial side of this fold were many smaller eyes in various stages of development. Now in the larvae of *Pecten* a similar condition prevails. There is a pigment furrow at the base of the ophthalmic fold from which the large permanent eyes develop, while on the branchial side of the fold are numerous small and transitional invaginate eyes. We may suppose that, in the ancestral *Pectens*, there were many highly developed, invaginate eyes along the pigmented furrow. There is in all Mollusca a tendency for such cup-like eyes to form closed sacs, but in all cases, except *Pecten*, the posterior wall becomes the most highly developed, and gives rise, finally, to the retina. If we suppose that in *Pecten* the vesicle, formed by the closure of a primitive optic cup, becomes somewhat flattened, then those ommatidia on the edge of the vesicle would be turned inward, retaining meantime their rods Pl. 32. fig. 150); those ommatidia on the anterior wall, which in such cases are usually short and functionless, would, with the folding in of the cup, lose their pigment, so that light could still penetrate to the posterior wall of the vesicle. By a continued ingrowth of the ommatidia on the periphery of the outer wall towards the centre of the eye. the inverted ommatidia of the anterior wall would become expressly adapted to the function of vision, while those on the floor of the optic vesicle would gradually become functionless, or modified in other directions. In the primitive optic cup, the retinophorae were probably surrounded, as often happens, by a double circle of pigment cells. an outer and an inner one. After the closing of the cup, this arrangement appears to have been partly retained, the outer row of ganglionic cells being the product of the modified basal row of retinulae, while the inner ganglionic cells are the modified outer ones (Pl. 32. fig. 151). A similar condition must have obtained in the floor of the optic cup, which now forms the inner wall of the optic vesicle, whose layers, if they are homologous with those of the retina. should be in the inverse order. In this case the structureless and non-cellular rete-vitrosum would be homologous with the layer of rods; a continuation of this comparison would make the argentea, composed of flattened and colorless granules, homologous with the retinophorae with which it agrees in the secretion of the hyaline layer, and in the presence of the colorless and refractive globules, so characteristic of the retinophorae in general. Lastly, the tapetum, composed of pigmented cells. would be homologous with the entire ganglionic layer; both therefore represent modifications of pigment cells. or retinulae. After the closure of the optic cup, the modifications of the surrounding connective tissue necessary to form the lens and pseudo-cornea. present no morphological difficulty. The basal membrane of the primitive optic cup would, with the formation of the optic vesicle, form the ommateal sac, from the thickening of whose anterior and posterior walls would be formed the septum and sclerotica, both of which are double layered.

There is still the greatest difficulty to solve, namely: why is it that *Pecten* and *Arca* are so richly supplied with highly developed eyes, when there seems to be no more necessity for them here than in any other Mollusc? The innumerable eyes of *Chiton* and *Onchidium* undoubtedly owe their origin to the same laws governing the development of the eyes of *Arca* and *Pecten*. The material, upon which SEMPER made his observations concerning the eyes of *Onchidium*, was undoubtedly in a very poor state of preservation, as may be easily seen from the figures. The most doubtful of all his statements is, that the inverted retinal layer is penetrated by the optic nerve. It is very probable that, in *Chiton* and *Onchidium*, the whole surface of the epithelium is filled with isolated ommatidia, from which, in the younger specimens, the eyes are being constantly formed by the aggregation of ommatidia into groups, which subsequently become invaginated.

The following suggestion, although it does not strike at the root of the real difficulties, may possibly direct attention towards a phase of the question which has not, heretofore, been considered. For instance, in almost every Mollusca I have examined, the epithelium was found to consist, together with other elements, of colorless gland-like cells and pigmented ones. In certain instances, we notice a tendency of the pigment cells to form a circle around each colorless one, giving rise to ommatidia irregularly scattered over large areas. Now there is, moreover, a tendency for the ommatidia to collect into larger or smaller groups; but this tendency acts at one place nearly as well as at another, so that innumerable groups of ommatidia will be formed at the same time over wide areas. The development of these groups into simple grooves and pits, and finally into fully developed eyes, is a very simple process, and may easily be observed. But what is the motive power? We must necessarily assume, that, up to a certain stage, the formation of ommatidia and their collection into groups was of some advantage to the animal (see chapter V). If, now, we assume that the conditions for the growth of these organs were exceptionally favorable, a powerful impetus would be given which would carry them to a degree of development far exceeding the necessity of the animal. After a time many of the organs thus made would degenerate and disappear. This degeneration of many young eyes of *Pecten*, and of the faceted eyes in full grown *Arcas*, may be considered as steps towards the reduction in number of the numerous eyes thus unnecessarily produced. There is, however, still another factor of great importance, which I shall discuss more fully in another place, and that is the change of functions undergone by the ommatidia. Two well developed eyes are, under most circumstances, enough for any animal. But, if it could be shown that the eyes originated from organs having other functions, so that an increase in their number and perfection would be of corresponding advantage to the animal, then the presence of a great number of these highly developed organs would offer no difficulty. If we suppose that these structures could, by a progressive series of changes, be transformed into rudimentary eyes, the function of one not being lost until after that of the other had been acquired, then we could account for the presence of an unnecessary number of eyes in any one animal.

As we hope to show more clearly in the last chapter, the so-called eyes of *Pecten*, *Arca*, *Onchidium* and *Chiton* are highly developed heliophags, or organs for the absorption of energy from the sunlight. The more light concentrated upon the energy-receiving surface, the more benefit the animal would derive from the light. An increase in the number of these organs would also be a great benefit, provided the animals were nocturnal, or lived in dark places. It is, therefore, on this supposition, not strange that some animals should have a great many such organs in a high stage of development, for every additional organ, or every step toward a more perfect structure, would be of a corresponding advantage to the animal: we can therefore offer some reasonable explanation for the great number of such organs present. This, however, would be impossible on the supposition that they were mere eyes, for it would be very difficult to offer any explanation of the use *Arca* could make of two highly developed eyes, to say nothing of the 1200 such organs that it possesses! The same reasoning would apply to *Pecten*, with from 60—100 highly developed eyes, and *Onchidium* or *Chiton* with several thousand eyes each. But if it is impossible to offer any plausible suggestion as to the present function of these eyes, how is it possible to account for their first appearance, and for the innumerable intermediate stages through which they must necessarily have passed before reaching their present condition? These difficulties are obviated by supposing that they were, or are, heliophags; we can then account for their great number and high development according to the theory of natural selection. But we know from experiment, that *Arca* can see — in the ordinary sense — that is, even a very small object will cause muscular contraction. A heliophag absorbs light energy, and therefore the most perfect forms have lenses or refractive bodies for concentrating the light, or are constructed in the most advantageous way for its reception: but these are just the conditions that an eye has to fulfil, so that the most perfect heliophag could at the same time be an eye. Heliophags, like those of *Arca* and *Avicula*, receive a constant stream of energy, but if this stream is broken by the intervention of any object, a special irritation will be produced giving rise to muscular contractions. The heliophags of *Arca* are so perfectly constructed and so sensitive, that the slightest change in the light received causes an irritation sufficient to produce strong muscular contractions; it is, therefore, a heliophag of a high stage of development, and might very properly be called an eye.

If the heliophag became so sensitive that the slightest changes in the amount of light caused muscular contractions, we would have the first steps towards the formation of an eye. If, by association, and by the high development of the heliophag, certain light combinations i. e. images of certain objects, caused contraction, and others, equally intense, not, then the heliophag would have all the essential characteristics of an eye, but would not necessarily have lost its primitive function of absorbing energy.

The so-called eyes of *Pecten*, *Arca*, *Chiton*, and *Onchidium* represent various stages of transition from heliophags to true eyes, but in all probability with their primitive functions still unimpaired.

Nerve Endings.

In order to comprehend more fully the nature of the nerve endings in the retinal layer, it is necessary to study the similar process on the unmodified epithelium. Sections show that in the Mollusca indifferent epithelial cells are usually very high and narrow, being constricted in the middle, and ending at the base in several root-like fibres attached to the basal membrane. In certain regions, notably on the ophthaimic fold, the cells are deeply pigmented at the outer ends; they are covered by a cuticula varying in thickness, and divisible into two layers, a thin, refractive outer, and an inner one passing insensibly into the outer ends of the cells. When these cells have been successfully isolated, one may see, in nearly all, several nerve fibres extending along the wall of the cells towards their outer ends. These fibres generally cling quite firmly to the sides of the cell, but examples may be found in which they have been separated from the whole length of the wall, remaining attached only at the outer extremity (Pl. 30, figs. 50 and 53). I have seen cases in which, to one cell, as many as five or six such fibres, several times as long as the cell, were attached. In sections of the mantle edge preserved either in chromic acid, or picro-chromic osmic acid (FOL) and mounted in acetate of potash, a perfect network of fibrillae, the general trend of which is parallel to the surface, may be seen beneath, or in the inner layer of the cuticula. This nervous network, the rete terminale, seems to be present in greater or less perfection throughout the whole hypodermis of the mantle edge, but is especially well developed either near the eyes or in the pigmented portions. In some cases, large and unbranching nerve fibres pass directly to the outer cuticular layer, where they seem to terminate in one or more minute, stiff, sense hairs (Pl. 30, fig. 64 *n.f.* and Pl. 32, fig. 153 *d*). These larger nerve fibres expand, a short distance below the basal membrane, into small bipolar vesicles containing a nucleus. These structures are young ganglionic cells formed by the elongation of the slender sense hair cells in the following manner: the nucleated basal expansion wanders into the underlying tissue, while the external end becomes reduced a fibre, still extending to the outer surface of the epithelium, and terminating in one or more sense hairs. The outer end of the fibre then gives rise to minute cross fibrillae, which either adhere to the wall of the neighboring sense cell, or unite with similar fibrillae from older nerve fibres; lastly, the tuft of sense hairs disappears, and the conversion of the sense cell into a bipolar ganglionic one is complete (fig. 153 *e* and *f*). Subsequently the body of the bipolar cell gives rise to numerous secondary fibres which unite with those from other cells, and so convert the bipolar cell into a multipolar one, whose primitive outer end still retains its original position between the epithelial cells, and extends into the cuticular layer. This process of nerve formation may occur at any part of the mantle edge, and is not confined to the larval stage, but takes place also in the nearly full grown individual. Here then is the explanation of the universal intercellular nerve endings in the Mollusca, and unless degeneration of the outer ends of the nerves has taken place, they should always extend into the cuticula. In no case do nerves from the central nervous system unite directly with the sense cells of the epidermis. All the nerve-ends in the hypodermis mark approximately the places where ganglionic cells originated. The latter alone are directly united on the one hand with the hypodermis, and on the other with the central nervous system. These facts must give a certain bias to all our suppositions concerning nerve endings in the hypodermis, for it is evident that, unless great secondary changes have taken place, the nerves must terminate between the cells, and probably extend to their very outer ends; while, if we suppose that the nerves from the central nervous system grow towards the ectoderm and there unite with the cells, there is a possibility of a greater variety of nerve endings, which we must always bear in mind in making any supposition.

There are numerous sense cells in the skin of the Mollusca, which apparently terminate in a single fibre, which certainly does not extend along the walls of the cells. The latter pass so gradually into these fibres that it is impossible to determine the limits of either. This, then, appears to be an exception to the intercellular method of nerve endings. Does the nerve fibre stand in direct communication with the central nerve system? I think not. It seems to me that we have exactly the same condition here as has been described by Hertwig for the Coelenterates: that is, there are two classes of cells in the Mollusca, constituting the greater part of the hypodermis; the myo-epithelial, and the neuro-epithelial cells. The former consist of the ordinary epithelial cells. ending in radiating, root-like fibres, the union of which gives rise to the basal membrane, which is probably homologous with the sub-epithelial layer of myo-epithelial fibres of the Coelenterates. The sense hair cells, which terminate in a single fibre. would then be homologous with the neuro-epithelial cells of the Coelenterates. The inward prolongations of the sense cells in the Mollusca are not then nerve fibres, arising either from the nervous system, or from peripheral ganglionic cells, but are simply nervous prolongations of the sense cells themselves and are probably united as their inner ends with a contractile one which originated near the sense cell, and which during its inward growth has drawn the nervous fibre of the latter after it. The sense cells are provided with inter-cellular nerve fibres, in the same manner as the ordinary epithelial cells.

The central nervous system is simply a large group of ganglionic cells, which originally arose in the same manner as the peripheral ganglionic cells do now; the invagination of the whole surface of the hypodermis to form a nervous system is a secondary process. The union of the central nervous system with the ganglia of remote sense organs takes place in exactly the same manner as the various ganglionic cells of a single sense organ became united with each other. The conversion of ordinary hypodermic cells into ganglionic ones could not be better illustrated than by the cells of the outer ganglionic layer in the eye of *Pecten* (Pl. 29. fig. 33).

Therefore in the origin of any sense organ from a group of hypodermic cells, the increase in number of nervous cells arising from that point goes hand in hand with the increasing sensitiveness of the organ, and finally gives rise to a subjacent layer of ganglionic cells united on the one hand with the central nervous system, and on the other with the sensitive cells, between which the ganglionic ones have arisen. The only difference between the so-called sense cells and the ganglionic ones is that the former retain to a greater degree their power of receiving stimuli directly from the stimulating agents, while the latter, with increased sensibility, receive only those stimuli which have acted upon the former, and conduct them to the central nervous system. We should, therefore, expect to find, and do find even in highly developed sense organs, many transitional stages between sensory, and ganglionic cells.

In the ontogenetic development of the higher sense organs, we no more find a repetition of the phylogenetic process, than is found in the central nervous system. There is an invagination, or thickening, of the place in question, with a separation »en masse« of the ganglionic and sense cells, and a subsequent outgrowth from the nervous centre to join the sense ganglion. These two processes, the separation of the ganglionic cells and their union with the central nervous system, are easily studied in those organs which are widely separated from the latter. But when the two structures originate from the same place, as in the eyes and brains of Arthropods, the origin of the brain and the optic ganglion, and their union with each other, may, ontogenetically, form a single process. The united ganglionic cells, which have arisen with the sense cells, form the optic ganglion (Cephalopods, Worms, and Arthropods). The optic ganglion may be united with the eye by a primary, ganglionic optic nerve, and with the brain by a secondary optic nerve, or outgrowth of the central nervous system. But, if the eye and brain are closely united, then the optic ganglion will fuse with the latter, and the secondary optic nerve disappear.

Chapter IV. General Remarks upon the Arthropods.

Our studies have shown that the eyes of Arthropods, like those of Molluscs, consist of ommatidia, the structure of which is dependent upon the shape of the eye.

The compound Arthropod eye consists of a double layer of cells; the ommateum, and the corneal hypodermis; the latter has been invariably overlooked by GRENACHER; the ease with which it may be demonstrated in such different genera of both Insects and Crustacea as *Mantis*, *Musca*, *Penaeus*, *Orchestia*, *Branchipus*, *Galathea*, *Pagurus* and *Palaemon* renders it highly probable, even if not beyond all doubt, that it occurs in all faceted eyes. Wherever the corneal hypodermis is present, the corresponding configuration of its cells and of the corneal facets, or when these are absent the corneal markings, prove that to this layer the corneal cuticula owes its origin. In the absence of positive evidence, it would be unreasonable to suppose that in other compound eyes the cornea was due to a different source. We are therefore compelled to admit that the corneal hypodermis is universally present in the compound Arthropod eye, and always gives rise to the corneal facets. It is probable that the corneal cells may in some cases be regarded as more than simple constructive elements: their radiating fibres and their general shape in *Galathea* render it almost certain that they play a physiological part in regulating the amount of light, and therefore acting as a sort of iris.

The general structure of the ommatidia remains about the same as in the Mollusca; there is a tendency, however, towards an increase in the number of retinophorae, which reach four, or very rarely five, in the compound eye, while in certain aberrant forms, as *Limulus*, they may increase to as many as 8 or 10.

In the Mollusca, we have seen that a natural result of the evaginate, convex arrangement of the ommatidia is an expansion of the outer ends of the latter, and a reduction of the retinulae to protective purposes. An exactly similar series of changes follows the evagination of the Arthropod eye. The retinophorae of each ommatidium have increased to four equivalent cells, showing no trace of the subordination of one, accompanied by the predominance of others, as is the case in Mollusca. The terminal, cuticular secretions, or rods, by a series of changes to be shortly enumerated, have been transferred to the axial faces of the outer ends of the retinophorae; they there unite to form the crystalline cones, to accommodate which the outer ends of the retinophorae are enlarged into a cup-like expansion, the calyx, while their inner ends are reduced to a slender tube, or style, serving at once as a support for the calyx, and as a protective canal for the axial nerve.

The compound eye of *Arca* is extremely valuable for comparison with that of Arthropods: firstly, because it is very simple, and may be traced back to an invaginate eye in which the retinulae also played primary roles: it is therefore easy to determine what conditions are essential, and what are the results of a simple modification in form; secondly, by a comparison of the Molluscan and Arthropod compound eye, between which there is not the slightest genetic relationship, we may possibly arrive at some conclusion as to what elements of the Arthropod eye are essential, and what secondary to vision; or in other words, what characters may be regarded as morphological, and what analogous.

A primitive ommatidium may be regarded as a colorless (single? or compound) cell, provided with a terminal rod and an underlying reflective part, and surrounded by a circle of pigment cells. When the colorless cell, or retinophora, of an evaginate eye assumes a more important part, the pigment cells become modified into circles, one surrounding the rod, and another the reflective part; e. g. *Arca*. An analogous condition prevails in Arthropods, where the retinulae are modified into two principal circles; an outer one of comparatively light-colored cells, surrounding the calyx, and an inner row surrounding the reflective part, or pedicel; other pigment cells may be present, but they show a less constant and uniform arrangement.

A layer of irregular cells is quite widely present in the compound Arthropod eye, around the bases of the ommatidia, just above the basal membrane. They contain little or no pigment, but are often filled with highly refractive crystals, milk-white in reflected, yellowish or colorless in transmitted, light: they are often so refractive that when seen in the latter manner they may appear nearly black. The outer row of retinulae may be divided into secondary circles, of which the very outer one often contains crystals similar to those over the basal membrane (*Penaeus*). The middle row of retinulae, the retinulae of GRENACHER, are most constant in number and shape, seven being usually present; four, and less often six, cells surround the calyx.

The style of the retinophorae consists of a structureless tube which towards its inner end often breaks up into numerous, striated, refractive plates, the striae running at right angles with each other in alternating plates of different refrangibility. The faces of the plates are never parallel with each other. The frequent absence of the pedicels in those Arthropods that can see well, together with the absence of nerve fibrillae, indicates that they are not essential structures. It appears that the pedicel is more frequent in nocturnal, than in diurnal, Insects. I must confess that I am very loath to make any statement about the style and pedicel, except that they are not concerned directly with vision; but the facts enumerated point in a certain direction, and, in the absence of any proof to the contrary, we must not hesitate to point out what that direction is, knowing perfectly well that the evidence is likely to turn in this, or that direction, with the accession of new facts.

The facts then to be considered are the following: (1) in the Molluscs, one finds in the retinophorae, beneath the rods, a reflecting surface composed of refractive granules; (2) in the compound eye of *Arca*, the reflective granules are surrounded by a special circle of retinulae; (3) in the absence of the granules, a special reflecting membrane, the argentea, is developed, serving the same purpose (*Pecten*); (4) behind the latter is a layer of red pigment, the light from which may pass through the argentea to the rods; (5) the argentea consists of colorless, refractive plates, the angles of whose faces are so arranged as to cause the reflection of incident, and interference of transmitted light. If now we consider, for the sake of argument, that the pedicel is a reflector, we have the following points of comparison with similar structures in the Mollusca: (1) A continuous argentea being absent we have instead, at the base of each retinophora, a collection of refractive plates, whose structure renders it highly probable that they have the same optical properties as those of the argentea in *Pecten* and *Cardium*; (2) the plates are formed by the retinophorae under the rods, as in *Arca*, and not by the retinulae; (3) they are surrounded by a special circle of retinulae, as in *Arca*; (4) in the absence of a red tapetum, the coloring matter is lodged in the plates themselves: they therefore possess the combined functions of argentea and tapetum; (5) the red light from the plates passes through the styles to the crystalline cones, as is shown by examining with the naked eye the red light issuing from the eyes of nocturnal Lepidoptera, in which the pedicels and their red color is specially developed.

The argentea is to intensify the effect of the light, and is therefore best developed in those eyes where it is necessary to obtain a great quantity of light, or in nocturnal, or deep sea animals, which need to economize the light. The presence of the pedicels in nocturnal Lepidoptera indicates a similar function.

The most characteristic thing about the Arthropod eye is its convexity, which has its advantages in an economic arrangement of the peripheral ends of the retinophorae. This arrangement is favored by the hard, chitinous skeleton of the eye, affording a protection for the otherwise exposed soft parts. The ommateal layer, although divided with great distinctness into several zones, consists (excluding nerve fibres) in the strongest sense of the word of a single layer, since each cell extends from the basal membrane to the corneal cells. The great thickness of the ommateal layer is probably due to the additional strength and firmness thus obtained. The bacilli may be regarded as supports for the pigment cells, and the style, as a similar modification of the retinophorae, whose bacilli have fused to form a hollow tube for the protection of the axial nerve.

If we were asked to arrange a flat layer of cells in the most economic manner, of course with certain limitations, and without changing the size of the outer ends of the cells, we should have to arrange them in a hemispherical mass, the inner ends being reduced in size to fibres. The problem has been solved in the same manner by the Arthropod eye. The greater the number of ommatidia, the greater is the curvature of the surface and the depth of the layer.

It cannot be said that GRENACHER, or any of his predecessors, perhaps with the exception of SCHULTZE who has represented the fibrous markings on the style and calyx, have succeeded in demonstrating anything like nerve endings in the Arthropod eye. To assume, having seen nerve bundles penetrate the basal membrane, that they terminate in this or that place, is a pure supposition and of absolutely no value, until one at least is able to draw some reasonable comparison between the presumable nerve end cells and those in the retina of some other group, where it is known what the sensitive cells really are. That both these criteria have been wanting in the Arthropods is well known. My observations have shown that it is only in the most simple forms of ommatidia that the retinulae produce rods. In all other cases they are the product of the colorless cells or retinophorae. In Arthropods it is the same: the colorless cells with their various parts are the essential elements, the pigment cells, or retinulae of GRENACHER, having nothing to do with the formation of the so-called rhabdom. One might discuss the subject, and offer objections to GRENACHER's theory, indefinitely, and never come to any more decisive conclusion. GRENACHER's whole work hinges upon the supposition that the rhabdoms are secreted by the retinulae which, according to him, form a layer of cells, distinct from those of the crystalline cones. I believe we have proved that the inward continuations of the crystalline cone cells constitute the »rhabdoms«. in whose formation the retinulae take no part whatever. If this observation alone is correct, the entire results of GRENACHER's work must fall to the ground.

If the retinulae are not the essential elements, what then are? They are the crystalline cone cells, which, morphologically, must be the essential elements, when compared with those in the Mollusca and simple eyes of Arthropods. But besides the morphological necessity for considering them as the essential elements, we have, in addition, a physiological one, since we have proved that in them the nerves terminate. forming that system of cross fibrillae. so characteristic of the Molluscan rods. called a retinidium. There is a third reason for considering the crystalline cone cells as essential elements. for upon their retinidia there is a constant effort to throw the greatest amount of light, often in the form of a perfect image. The structure of the retinidium coincides with that of the Mollusca, in that it consists of successive layers of cross fibrillae, radiating from one or more axial fibres, and uniting with nerves on the outer wall of the calyx. The fibrillae of the retinidium may be supported, as in the rods of Molluscs, in a firm chitinous secretion, the crystalline cone: or the secretion may be fluid, or so inconsistant as to be destroyed or dissolved by reagents. as in *Mantis* and *Musca*. The facts we have enumerated furnish us with entirely new data for comparison. and without further consideration for the present of GRENACHER's views, we will see in what direction they lead us.

It is, of course, no longer possible to compare the vitreous cells of the simple eyes with the crystalline cone cells. or retinophorae. of the compound eye. The undoubted homologue of the vitreous cells, however, is to be found in the corneal hypodermis of the compound eyes: the position and function of both layers point to this conclusion. There is no course open except to compare the two remaining layers with each other. Let us take. for instance, one of the lateral eyes of *Scorpio*, and it will be found, according to GRABER and LANKESTER, that the ommateum consists of ommatidia each one composed of five central, colorless cells. or retinophorae. bearing on their axial faces a cuticular secretion. or rod. The retinophorae are surrounded by two or three circles of pigment cells, or retinulae. Here then the colorless cells secrete the rods, while the pigment cells play only secondary parts. It is exactly the same in the compound eye: the axial faces of the colorless cells secrete rods which fuse to form a »rhabdom«, the crystalline cone. In some of the simple eyes of Spiders, exactly the same condition prevails, except that the retinophorae are double like those of Molluscs, instead of fivefold like those of Scorpions. This comparison will be made much clearer by referring to the diagrammatic figures on Pl. 32.

Although there appears to be no doubt about the homologies of the compound eyes in Insects and Crustacea, the most difficult problem has not been solved, and that is the relation of the compound eyes to the stemma, and the ocelli of the Myriapods and Spiders. First let us consider the structure of the median, and lateral eyes of Myriapods and Spiders. The question here is, are the lateral eyes double layered like the median ones? Opinions, unfortunately, seem to differ on this point. I believe that both are double layered, and hence morphologically identical organs. If it can be proved in a single instance that, in the lateral eyes of Spiders, or in any of the ocelli of the Myriapods, such as *Lithobius* or *Julus*, a vitreous layer is present, giving rise to the cuticular lens, it is highly probable in the absence of positive evidence to the contrary, that it is always present. We need go no farther than GRENACHER's (59) own paper to find this evidence; any one must be hopelessly prejudiced not to see that, in Pl. 20, figs. 2, 3, 4, 5 and 9 of his paper, a nucleated layer must exist between the retina and the lens. But if the corneal lens is formed by a distinct hypodermic layer in one instance, how are we to explain the formation of a lens in the very same, or nearly related, animals without the hypodermis? The simplest and only advisable course is to suppose that it likewise exists in the other forms, but has been overlooked. That such errors of observation are to be expected, will be evident by recalling the conspicuous elements, i. e. the bacilli and the corneal hypodermis, which have escaped notice in the compound Arthropod eye, where the difficulties of observation are far less than in the simple ones. Moreover we have the assurance of GRABER that all ocelli possess a vitreous layer. In spite of the torrents of abuse that GRENACHER has showered upon GRABER for his discovery and misinterpretation of a few extra nuclei in the retina of Myriapods, Spiders and Scorpions, it is tolerably certain, that if GRABER has made some unfortunate interpretations, he has also made several accurate and valuable observations concerning structures which have entirely escaped GRENACHER. A person who admits that his observations are full of gaps and errors, and who invites criticism with the assurance that it will be thankfully received, should, it seems to me, treat those kind enough to respond to the call, with consideration, for persons treated otherwise are liable to take offence, and may find more mistakes than was anticipated.

There seems to be very little to choose between the »flüchtige Streifzüge« of GRABER, and the »eingehenderen und genaueren Studien« of GRENACHER. The former has helped out his observations with too much theory, the latter has helped his theory with too little observation. Now since the doctors disagree, it is only left us to choose our own course, picking out, when possible, those facts which seem to point in the right direction. Therefore, in the absence of all positive evidence to the contrary, and possessing a few facts in the affirmative, we will conclude for the present that all the ocelli of Myriapods and Spiders possess a vitreous layer. But the ocelli of Hexapods are undoubtedly homologous with the simple ocelli of Myriapods and Spiders, therefore, they likewise must possess a vitreous layer. Here, also, we have confirmatory evidence, since GRENACHER and CIACCIO have figured the ocelli of *Musca*, and CARRIÈRE, of *Polistes gallica*, with a vitreous layer which we may assume is always present.

But what is the relation between the compound and simple eyes? The evidence and the probability is very strongly in favor of the supposition that all ocelli and compound eyes are diploblastic; the vitreous layer of one, being homologous with the corneal hypodermis of the other. The compound eye must have originated in one of two ways: 1) by the fusion of many ocelli, or (2) by the modification of a single ocellus.

Let us first form some idea of what the primitive Arthropod eye was like, that we may see in what direction subsequent modification tended to lead it. It is very probable that the ancestral Arthropods, like many Annelids of today, were provided with numerous invaginate eyes situated upon both sides of the head. By the deepening of the cup and ingrowth of the lips, a closed optic vesicle was formed: the entire organ consisted of three layers[1] (Pl. 32, fig. 141); (1) the thick inner wall of the optic vesicle, the retineum; (2) the outer wall, or vitreous layer, secreting the vitreous body; (3) the corneal hypodermis, producing the corneal lens, when one was present.

The central eyes of *Scorpio* (LANKESTER, Pl. 32, fig. 145) and those

---

[1] We shall not consider the connective tissue fibres which may intervene between the corneal hypodermis and vitreous layer, as a distinct layer.

of certain Spiders (GRENACHER) seem to be formed of three layers: the middle fibrous one probably represents the outer wall of an optic vesicle together with the connective tissue layer. In *Peripatus* all four layers are present (Pl. 32, fig. 142). In these primitive eyes, it is probable that the retinulae were reduced to cover cells, while the retinophorae alone gave rise to the rods. Judging from the structure of the cells and rods as seen in the simplest larval ocelli, i. e. *Phryganea*, it is probable that the retinophorae were very similar to those of the Mollusca and Worms (Alciopidae), i. e. composed of double cells and double rods (Pl. 32. fig. 141); from such a simple retina, or retineum, the more modified Arthropod ocelli have originated. The modification was in two directions: (1) an increase in the number of optic vesicles, accompanied by a reduction in the number of ommatidia, which at the same time acquired additional size and complexity; and (2), a decrease in the number of vesicles, accompanied by an increase in the number and complexity of the ommatidia. That the optic vesicles may vary in number is sufficiently shown by the Mollusca and Worms. Changes in the number of eyes are always accompanied by variations in structure. The lateral ocelli of *Limulus* may be regarded as optic vesicles whose inner wall has been reduced to an ommateum containing but one ommatidium. A comparison with an ommatidium of the ancestral eye will show how far the specialization has been carried: one sees that the retinophorae of each ommatidium have been increased to 10 in number, while upon their axial faces are formed the rods. The changes, then, undergone by the lateral eyes of *Limulus* were an increase in the number of ocelli, with a conversion of the ancestral retineum into an ommateum, the rods being transferred from the apices of the retinophorae to their axial faces. The number of ommatidia was then reduced to one, while their retinophorae were increased from two, to ten. In the central eye, the reduction in the number of ommatidia has not proceeded so far, there being about 20 according to LANKESTER; neither, as we should expect, is the specialization of the individual ommatidium so great, since each one possesses only six or seven retinophorae.

If we seek for some other form, in which the series of changes supposed to have been undergone by *Limulus* has been less extensive, we shall find it in the Scorpions. Here, the lateral eyes have increased but little in number, while there is a correspondingly small decrease in the number and specialization of the ommatidia. The central eyes[1] only differ from the lateral ones in the larger number of ommatidia, and in the greater development of the vitreous layer: in both, the retinophorae of each ommatidium are only increased to five in number. Both *Limulus* and *Scorpio* must be regarded as diverging in the same direction from the ancestral form. *Limulus* being the more remote.

The Myriapods are characterised by the small number and uniformity of their ocelli. They in this respect approach more nearly the ancestral form. It is in no way clear what the structure of the ommatidia in the Myriapods, is. GRABER's observations are not complete enough, while GRENACHER seems to have been more intent upon making pretty drawings, than upon elucidating the actual structure of the retina. The observations of both authors are so widely different that it is difficult to select what seems to be the most probable. It would be of great value, in determining the relative position of the Myriapod eye, to show whether the rods are terminal. that is forming a retineum, or axial, forming an ommateum similar to those of Scorpions and Spiders. If the former should prove true, as seems probable, then the eyes of Myriapods would be the most nearly related to the presumed, ancestral form. Whether the lateral, horizontal rods are normal is not certain: it might be supposed that they were really situated on the floor, and assume their horizontal position by a lateral collapse of the vesicle, caused in some way by the reagents: or it is possible that they are not rods at all. but simple stratifications of the vitreous body.

The comparatively small number of eyes in Spiders indicate that they have in that respect not departed very much from the ancestral form. But the most interesting fact connected with them is the differentiation of the ommatidia in the anterior and posterior ocelli. In all the ocelli. here. as in Myriapods, there is an undoubted vitreous layer present. In many anterior ocelli the rods are apical, that is. retain their primitive. terminal position. forming a retineum. In the larger, posterior eyes, there is a tendency for the rods to become axial, forming an ommateum. That this type of retina has not departed far from the original condition, is shown by the primitive double rods. and consequently, the double retinophorae. The manner in which a double.

---

[1] Of course it must be recollected that both LANKESTER and GRENACHER deny the existence of a vitreous layer in the lateral eyes of Scorpions and *Limulus*, while GRABER states that in the former such a layer is present; for theoretical reasons I am obliged to assume that this layer is always present.

apical rod like that of *Pecten, Area,* or *Phryganea,* may be transformed into an axial cone, like that of the posterior eye of Spiders, is shown in the diagram (Pl. 32. figs. 132—138).

In the simpler eyes, where the retineum still exists, the retinophorae seem to be formed of double cells; only one nucleus is well developed, the other is probably reduced in size and distinctness, as in Molluscs and in Worms. With the development of axial rods in Spiders, one or two nucleus may be found at the outer end of the cells, above the rod, as in the compound eye; in other cases it seems to be below. In spite of the interesting modification of the ommatidia in the anterior and posterior ocelli, there can be no doubt that they represent different phases of morphologically identical structures; the posterior eyes being simply a higher modification of the anterior ones.

In the Hexapoda, we have the most difficult question to deal with; the divergence of structure in the two kinds of eyes is so great that doubt arises as to their morphological identity. The compound eyes whether formed by one modified ocellus, or by the fusion of many, have progressed wonderfully in structure and functional powers. The simple eyes, however, have remained nearly the same; and the presence of a vitreous layer, and of the terminal rods, shows at once their identity with the anterior ocelli of Spiders, and their very slight departure from the ancestral form. But what are the compound eyes? A group of united ocelli, or a modification of a single ocellus? Three classes of facts must be considered in answering the first of these questions: (1) are there any existing stages of such a fusion to be found in the possible, existing ancestors of the Insecta? (2) are there any traces in the perfected eye itself of any ancestral fusion? (3) does embryology give any evidence on this point? On the other hand, the same inquiries may be made concerning a supposed progressive modification of a single ocellus into a compound eye. These two suppositions seem to be the only permissible ones.

First, then: are there any existing stages in the ancestors of the Insects, showing a tendency for the ocelli to fuse into compound eyes? First let us decide upon the possible ancestral forms. There are *Limulus*, Scorpions, Myriapods and Spiders. The first two may be excluded, since we have shown that they diverge from the ancestral forms in a direction diametrically opposite to that of other Arthropods. There are then remaining Myriapods and Spiders as possible ancestors of the Insecta.

What, now, would be the indications that a fusion of the ocelli, to form a compound eye like that of Insecta, was taking place? We should expect an increase in the number of ocelli, accompanied by a reduction of each retinenm to a single ommatidium with axial rods. There does not appear to be any evidence of this kind in either of these groups. The ocelli are not numerous; they remain perfectly distinct, each one surrounded by its basal membrane, and provided with a single optic nerve; the retineum shows no traces of reduction to a single ommatidium: and the rods are apical. In Spiders there is much less evidence of such changes than in Myriapods. In the latter group, *Scutigera* promises to give a solution to this problem. Whether its systematic position is beyond doubt, remains to be seen. The observations of GRENACHER alone are too uncertain to decide the question, and besides it would be exactly as difficult to suppose, with our present knowledge of the subject, that the eye of *Scutigera* was formed by the union of many ocelli, as by the modification of a single one. Therefore, in spite of the interest that must centre upon a more accurate knowledge of its structure, we must leave it for the present, and be satisfied with more definite evidence.

2) Is there any evidence in the compound eye itself, that it was formed by the fusion of ocelli? If such had been the case, we should expect to find around each ommatidium some trace of the connective tissue capsule which formerly surrounded the ocellus. In some of the simpler compound eyes, where we may suppose that the modifications of the ocelli have been less extensive, we should surely expect to find some indication of this membranous capsule, a structure which, by its almost universal presence in the isolated eyes, could not be so quickly disposed of in the aggregate condition. Around each ommatidium there is, however, not the slightest trace of any capsule arising from the basal membrane, nor is there any infolding of the same, which might be interpreted as a remnant of the basal membrane belonging to a primitive ocellus! But even if we suppose that such infoldings once existed and have now disappeared, we surely ought to find some trace of the original arrangement of the ommatidial cells in isolated groups. The circular arrangement of the retinulae around the retinophorae is a very ancient one; and, as we have seen, the position of the cell-ends upon the basal membrane is very constant, and furnishes a valuable key to the relation of the circles of retinulae to the retinophorae. If, then, each ommatidium is to be regarded as the remnant of an ocellus, the position of the cell-ends, which furnish us with the safest evidence, should show

some traces of their primitive arrangement upon restricted areas of the compound basal membrane. But our studies upon the basal membrane of *Penaeus* have shown just the opposite of what we should expect, provided the supposition was correct, for we have proved that the inner ends of cells belonging to neighboring ommatidia, instead of forming isolated groups, intermingle with each other in such a way that, unless one followed the cells from each ommatidium inward, it would be impossible to say whether they belonged to the same, or different ommatidia! We have, moreover, seen that in the Spiders and Myriapods each ocellus receives a special nerve branch. Now if each ommatidium represents an ocellus, it should also receive a single nerve branch, going to its cells alone. But this is not the case, for I have shown that in *Penaeus*, although the number of nerve bundles is equal to the number of ommatidia, each nerve bundle breaks up into several smaller ones going to four different ommatidia!

As far as the third question goes — Does Embryology show any evidence of fusion? we are not in possession of any very important evidence. Neither my own observations, which in this direction have been very scanty, nor those of others, have shown any indications that the compound eye was formed by the fusion of ocelli.

We have now to ask the same question concerning the progressive development of a single ocellus into the compound eye, and then, by weighing the evidence for, or against each supposition, we may be able to arrive at some conclusion.

Do we find any evidence in the ancestors of the Insecta of transitional stages between a simple and a compound eye? In Myriapods the answer is short: all eyes are alike, and are the simplest form of simple eyes. In Spiders, the anterior ocelli retain their primitive, undifferentiated condition, and the percipient elements form a retineum; but in the posterior eyes the ommatidia have undergone a series of changes towards a higher form. But what are the changes necessary to convert a primitive ocellus into a compound eye? In order to simplify matters, let us first determine what the simplest condition of the compound eye is. The presence of the corneal facets in certain higher forms, only, of Insects and Crustacea indicates that they are of late origin; moreover the presence of a thick corneal hypodermis, and the absence of corneal facets in such animals as *Branchipus*, the Isopods, Amphipods and many Insects, show this condition to be a primitive one. The retinophorae are usually four in number, but we have seen in *Penaeus* and *Galathea* that one of the planes of division is more distinct than the others, and that the inner ends of the cells show traces of a paired arrangement. We interpret these facts as indicating that the present, quadruple retinophorae were originally double; and in fact we do find certain Crustacea, the Amphipods and Isopods, in which the paired arrangement is a permanent condition. The majority of these simpler eyes form flattened, or slightly protuberant, surfaces containing but few ommatidia. An eye with the following features could, then, be considered as one of the least specialized and primitive forms of the compound eye: a facetless cornea; a thick corneal hypodermis; a small number of short ommatidia containing double retinophorae provided with two, large, axial rods which form a nearly terminal crystalline cone; SEMPER's nuclei may be above or beneath (*Musca*, HICKSON) the retinidia; and finally, the entire ommateum forms a nearly flat surface. How, then, does such an eye compare with the lateral ones of Spiders? It seems to me that the resemblances are so striking that they hardly require enumeration. In Spiders, the terminal rods have become axial, forming a double refractive body homologous with the crystalline cone; in some cases, one or two (?) nuclei have shifted their position so as to lie above the rods. That the apical position of the nuclei, above the rods, in the compound eye, presents no morphological difficulty, is shown by the frequency with which their position is changed in Spiders, sometimes being above, and sometimes below the rods. In the simplest ocelli with terminal rods, the retinulae form a single, or probably, at most, a double zone; with the formation of an ommateum by the development of axial rods, the retinulae show a strong tendency to form two or three zones surrounding corresponding parts of the retinophorae. GRENACHER has not described any nuclei in the retina of Spiders, except those of the retinophorae; but we may be sure that the pigment is deposited in distinct cells, just as in Scorpions and *Limulus*, whose nuclei have been overlooked by GRENACHER and misinterpreted by GRABER. In Spiders, as has been shown by LANKASTER and BOURNE for *Scorpio* and *Limulus*, the outer and middle nuclei of GRABER must be referred to an outer and middle (and inner? row of pigment cells, or retinulae! Then each ommatidium of the middle eye of Spiders would consist of a double retinophora with axial rods surrounded by two or three circles of retinulae (Pl. 32, figs. 137 and 146). Such an ommatidium agrees, in all essential respects, with an ommatidium of a compound eye like that of *Gammarus*. The only change necessary to convert a lateral eye of Spiders into a compound one, would be to reduce the thick lens to a thin cuticular layer, and decrease the depth of the ommateal cup; or, vice versa, to change an eye like that of *Gammarus* into an ocellus, we have only to increase the thin corneal cuticula into a thickened cuticular lens.

To recapitulate: we have answered, as nearly as possible, the six questions proposed above. To the question: Does 1) comparative anatomy, (2) histology or (3) embryology give any evidence of a present, or past, fusion of ocelli to form a compound eye, we are obliged to answer, no; even a very thorough study has proved that just those features are absent that ought to be present, provided any fusion had taken place! (1) We find no traces in the possible ancestors of the Insects and Crustacea of a union of ocelli, that could lead up to the present compound eye. (2) We find no evidence in embryology, or in the simple forms of compound eyes, of any fusion of elements: the faceted cornea, which on this supposition, i. e. that of fusion, should represent the primitive condition and should therefore be found in the lowest types, is on the contrary a highly specialized condition only found in the higher forms, and is entirely absent in the lowest. (3) Careful study has failed to reveal the presence of any structural peculiarity, such as envelopes for the ommatidia, arrangement of their cells, structure of the basal membrane, or of innervation, which could in any way be interpreted in favor of such a supposition. In fact the evidence is all against such a mode of thinking.

On the other hand, our questions concerning the supposition that a compound eye is formed by the progressive modification of a single ocellus have received the following answers: (1) we do find stages in the Spiders where a single ocellus has developed into an organ that only insignificant changes would suffice to convert into a compound eye like that of Amphipods and Isopods; (2) embryology shows that the very thin and degenerate (shown by faint staining of nuclei) corneal hypodermis of the more specialized compound eye, assumes, in the larval stages, a greater proportional development, rendering its homology with the important corneal, or vitreous layer of the ocellus more intelligible; (3) we find a complete identity in all essential parts between the ommatidia of a compound eye and those of an ocellus.

When to all this evidence against the first supposition we add that obtained by comparing all the fundamental changes necessary for the conversion of a group of ocelli like those of the Myriapods into a compound eye like that of Insects and Crustacea, and the disappearance of all evidence of such a change, — with the slight modifications necessary to convert an ocellus like the lateral one of Spiders into a similar organ. the evidence in favor of the latter supposition is so strong that there is no course left but to adopt it.

We have, therefore, arrived at the following conclusions: (1) that the ancestral forms of all Arthropods were probably provided with a small number of eyes placed on each side of the head: (2) these eyes consisted of closed optic vesicles, formed by invaginations lying close beneath the hypodermis, which formed a continuous layer over them; (3) the deep wall of the vesicle formed a retineum, similar to that of Worms and certain Mollusca, composed of colorless, double retinophorae, bearing terminal rods and containing an axial nerve fibre: each retinophora was surrounded by circles of rodless pigment cells: (4 the outer wall of the optic vesicle secretes a cuticular, vitreous body, similar to that found in the optic vesicle of Worms 'Alciopidae' and Molluscs *Fissurella* etc): (5) the hypodermis overlying the optic vesicle (corneal hypodermis) gave rise to a lenticular thickening of the cuticula, the lens. Such a primitive form, which closely resembles typical Molluscan. and Worm eyes, has undergone no great modification in the simpler ocelli. In general, the modification has been in two directions: (1 an increase in the number of ocelli, accompanied by a decrease in the number of their ommatidia: this is in turn accompanied by an increased complexity of the ommatidia; and (2 , a decrease in the number of ocelli accompanied by an increase in the number and complexity of the ommatidia. The condition of the lateral eyes of *Limulus* indicates that the development of axial rods. in place of the terminal ones, was the first step in the modification of the ommatidia. Afterwards, came a decrease in the number of ommatidia with an increase in the number of retinophorae.

According to this description, then. the median eyes represent a less modified condition of the archaic eyes, than the lateral ones. The eyes of *Limulus* represent the extreme modification, in this direction, of the ancestral one, while those of *Scorpio* have progressed in the same direction, but have stopped at an intermediate point. LANKESTER regards the lateral eye of *Limulus* as a »monostichous, polymeniscus« eye. and therefore a modification of a single ocellus into a compound eye. I am, on the contrary. as has already been said. inclined to regard it as a group of ocelli, whose ommatea are reduced to single, complex ommatidia. This is therefore just the opposite to what takes place in the higher Arthropods, where a compound eye is due to the modification of a single ocellus. I am conscious that the opponents of the latter view might see here a contradiction, and could urge with some plausibility that, if the lateral eye of *Limulus* is due to an aggregation of many ocelli, it furnishes just the illustration desired to show that the faceted eye was produced by a similar, but more extensive series of changes. But we have already given reasons for believing that the changes undergone by the eyes of *Limulus* would never lead up to a typical compound eye, — in fact their development has been in a diametrically opposite direction — and that the resemblance is of the most superficial and insignificant nature.

The condition represented by the eyes of *Limulus* and *Scorpio* is as far removed from the primitive type, as are the compound ones of Insects and Crustacea. But this condition is attained by a great reduction in the number of ommatidia without a corresponding increase in their functional powers. When we compare the direction of their development with that of the ocelli which give rise to the compound eyes, we must admit that, if the development of the latter is upward, towards organs of greater structural complexity and functional activity, then the former are tending in the opposite direction, downwards, towards greater structural simplicity and less perfect functional activity.

In the Myriapods, the eyes have remained nearly stationary: there has been no great change in the number of ocelli, or in the condition of the ommatidia, which retain their primitive characteristics, in that their rods are terminal and form a continuous layer, a retineum.

In the Spiders, most of the ocelli have likewise remained nearly stationary, the ommatidia forming a retineum; others, the posterior eyes, have undergone important changes, not so much on account of their extent, as direction. These changes carry such ocelli nearly to the level of typical compound eyes. The changes consist in the development of double, axial rods, terminal nuclei for the retinophorae, and two or three (? circles of retinulae, an outer (middle?), and inner one. The primitive, double retinophora is in direct contrast with the 5 and 10 fold retinophorae of *Scorpio* and *Limulus*. To change such an ocellus into a compound eye, we have only to reduce the corneal lens to a thin layer and flatten the ommateum. A necessary result of these changes would be a more perfect isolation of the retinophorae, and consequently a better development of the retinulae. A compound eye being once formed, it is further perfected by the development of a corneal facet, or lens, for each ommatidium; the number of retinophorae increases to four, and two well defined and constant circles of retinulae are developed, an outer row surrounding the cone, and an inner one, the stalk of the retinophorae, or the reflector when one is developed. The circles of retinulae may increase, in certain cases, to three or four.

It will be seen that, as far as the conversion of a so-called double layered ocellus, or stemma, into the compound eye is concerned, I agree more with LANKESTER than with GRENACHER; but there the resemblance ceases; LANKESTER has, in other respects, followed GRENACHER in regarding the crystalline cone cells as homologous with the corneal hypodermis of the simple eyes. In confirmation of his supposition, LANKESTER alleges that there is a tendency in the simple eyes to become retinulate; this is especially true in regard to Scorpious, and upon this fact he seems to base his conclusions. As we have shown, this statement is true not only of Limulus and Scorpions, but is likewise the case in all eyes, since all are formed of ommatidia showing a greater or less amount of segregation. The relation of simple eyes to compound is not shown by a greater or less degree of retinulation, since this is carried nearly to its extreme in such remote forms as *Limulus* and *Scorpio*, but by the position and number of the rods, which tend to become axial, giving rise to the crystalline cone of the compound eye.

LANKESTER has introduced a number of terms which we cannot accept. The term »nerve end cells«, if my observations are true, is not logical, since every cell is supplied with nerves; we can only distinguish the manner in which they terminate. If we reject the term »nerve end cells«, we must do the same for the term »perineural cells«. The primary division he would make into »monostichous« and »diplostichous« is no more appropriate than the terms simple and compound eyes, or ocelli and facetted eyes. It is, firstly, extremely doubtful whether a »monostichons« Arthropod eye exists; and, secondly, many of the so-called »diploblastic« ones are in reality three layered, as in Scorpions (GRABER), and Spiders (GRENACHER). All organs tend to vary in certain directions, dependent primarily upon the primitive structure of the organs in question. To know what those directions are we must know the structure of a few specialized forms, and how they differ from the primitive ones. I have endeavored to find these factors in order to found a new method of classification. I have shown, with a certain show of reason, what the original structure of the sensitive layer, and the general structure of the eye, was. It is supposed that the primitive Arthropod eye was formed of three layers (Pl. 32, fig. 141), and that all other forms are modifications of this type. Even if we admit that this supposition is true, our knowledge of these layers is too small to be used at present with any effect. Although not of primary importance, the evidence obtained from a study of these three layers may be used in conjunction with that obtained from a knowledge of the ommatidia, which must be regarded as the elements possessing the greatest classifying value. Upon them, I believe, must be founded the classification of all eyes, and not upon the number of layers, or upon the lens, or any similar part of equally small, physiological, or morphological value. LANKESTER'S term retinulate, signifying »an ommateum in which the nerve end cells are segregated to form definite groups, or retinulae«, is not admissible, since it is founded upon a wrong conception of the structural elements of the eye. All eyes are retinulate in this sense, since they consist of ommatidia formed of compound retinophorae surrounded by pigment, or ganglionic cells.

The term »vitreous body« is a bad one, since he uses it to designate a layer of cells, whereas the term has already been universally used to designate a non-cellular, vitreous secretion. Moreover he applies it to »the anterior cell wall of a diploblastic ommateum«: it is certain that in the compound eye this layer (the corneal hypodermis) does not secrete any vitreous body, but gives rise to the corneal facets alone. It is also extremely probable that the homologous layer in the stemma and ocelli, or the vitreous body (which ought to be called the corneal hypodermis), likewise gives rise to the corneal lens, but to no vitreous secretion; this function is performed by the outer wall of the primitive optic vesicle, or by the median of the three ectodermic layers. To this layer, which is entirely absent in the compound eye, I have given the name vitreous layer, and to that immediately underlying the corneal cuticula, that of corneal hypodermis; the latter cannot fail to be present in all Arthropod eyes, possibly with the exception of certain Crustacea, such as Copepods, Cladocera etc. which we have not included in any of our previous statements.

We cannot recognize the term »vitrella«, or »a group of cells of a vitreous body which has become segregated in correspondence with the segregation of the retinal body and of the lens«, since it is founded upon what we consider to be a false conception of the structure of the compound eye.

There is no necessity for regarding some eyes as »exochromic«, and others as »autochromic«, since there is no evidence to show that pigmented mesoderm cells have forced their way through the basal membrane into the eye; neither can it be shown, as any inducement for the supposition that there are two kinds of pigmentiferous cells in the eye, that they owe their origin to two different sources. LANKESTER moreover carries this supposition to an absurd degree, in stating that such mesodermic cells have wandered through the basal membrane, forcing their way between the retinulae, then through a second membrane, and finally between the crystalline cone cells, in order to surround them with pigmented ones in a manner to correspond to the arrangement of the retinulae around the rhabdoms.

Moreover the pigment cells are the most ancient elements in the eye, older even than the retinophorae, and their origin, as well as that of the retinophorae, is always ectodermic. It follows, then, that I cannot accept his division of eyes into exochromic, and autochromic, since according to my views such a division is not consequent.

It must be borne in mind that I have not attempted to draw any inference, founded upon the structure of the eyes, in regard to the genetic relationship of the different groups constituting the Arthropods. I have simply made what seemed to be a reasonable supposition as to the primitive Arthropod eyes, and have attempted to show how far, and in what direction, the eyes now known diverge from this ancestral form. Whether this evidence will be of any phylogenetic value, I am not prepared to say. A verdict can only be rendered after a careful study and comparison of all other evidence entitled to consideration.

A superficial examination of the eyes of Copepods and Cladocera shows at once a resemblance between the crystalline body, — not the cuticular lens which is sometimes developed, — and the crystalline cone of the compound eye. If this resemblance is more than a superficial one, we might attribute to them a similar function. Our knowledge of the structure of these eyes is too vague to allow of any speculations concerning them. But if it could be proved that the ommatidia were separated from the cuticula by a layer of cells, then there would be ground for believing that they represent modified invaginate eyes in which the retineum was reduced to one, or a small number, of ommatidia. On the other hand, it is possible that they may represent single, or small groups, of isolated ommatidia which, without separation from the primitive hypodermis, have reached their present condition.

Considering the fact that the retinophorae in Mollusca are double, and contain a highly developed, and an aborted, nucleus, we must admit that the possibility of regarding the phaosphere, found in *Euscorpius Italicus*, by LANKESTER, as an aborted nucleus, is not so remote as he would have us believe. I have omitted this factor in my deduction, for the sake of simplification: for, even if it were so, it would not materially alter the conclusions at which we have arrived.

It was not until I had definitely decided, by comparison, what must have been the character of the primitive Arthropod eye, that my attention was called to the eye of *Peripatus* as described by CARRIÈRE. This type of eye resembles so perfectly the presumed ancestral one that either might be regarded as the primitive form.

This conception, then, is of double value, firstly, because, according to it, all the various forms of Arthropod eyes (with the exceptions already mentioned) may be regarded as modifications of a single, primitive type, exactly like that found in the most primitive Arthropod; secondly, because the so-called Molluscan eye of *Peripatus* is no longer remarkable on account of its dissimilarity with other Arthropod eyes, but, in fact, is completely identical with what we have good reason for supposing is the primitive Arthropod eye.

In the Crustacea, the number of cephalic eyes is never so great as that often found in the Insecta, and in by far the majority of cases is limited to two. There is seldom more than a single, median, larval eye. probably representing a fusion of two paired ones, which are very rarely retained in the adult.

Euphausia is remarkable on account of its numerous, segmentally arranged eyes, or luminous organs, as SARS[1] considers them. Through the kindness of DR. PAUL MAYER, I have had the pleasure of examining some very carefully prepared sections of these organs. I hoped to give a more complete description of them, but that must be reserved for some future time.

SARS states that there is no reason to consider them as visual organs, since their structure is not like that of eyes in general. I cannot agree with him to this respect. I do not think SARS examined the eyes by means of sections, without which it would be extremely hazardous to form an opinion. The sections I had the pleasure of studying showed a complete agreement in essential characters with the visual organs of other animals. The lens is separated from the exterior by a double layer of cells, and is suspended in a well-developed

[1] Report on the Schizopoda collected by H. M. S. Challenger during the years 1873—1876. in: Challenger Reports Vol. 13, Part 37, p. 70—72, Pl. 12.

(muscular?) band. The retina is nearly hemispherical, and contains a deep row of large nuclei and a superficial layer of more numerous, smaller ones. According to SARS' description, this layer should contain bright red pigment, although in the preparations I examined the cells were colorless, the pigment having been extracted by the reagents. The cavity of the optic cup is almost completely filled with a mass of rods (SARS' »flabelliform bundle of fibres«), which are remarkable on account of the long, vertical, median rods, and the shorter, horizontal ones, on the side walls of the cup. Beneath the retina is an extraordinarily thick, (laminated) layer, or argentea, nearly hemispherical, and remarkable on account of the uniformity in the thickness of its peripheral and central parts. The great development of the lateral rods, and of the peripheral part of the argentea is a correlated and dependent condition, probably due to the great amount of lateral light reflected by the peripheral parts of the argentea upon the lateral rods. The vertical rods probably receive the direct vertical rays from the lens, and the same a second time after their reflection by the underlying argentea. The general tendency has been to regard these remarkable organs as eyes. on account of their evident similarity to them, though SARS has come to the conclusion that they are not eyes, but luminous organs. But let us consider what a luminous organ is, and how it originated. It certainly must be of some decided advantage to the animal, else it could never have originated. It is extremely improbable, if not impossible, to suppose that such highly complicated organs could have been developed by a series of gradual changes, for the purpose of frightening other animals. Besides luminosity is too common to suppose that it would affect any nocturnal animals — the only ones to be frightened by it. They could not serve as sexual attraction, since they are present in both males and females. It is extremely improbable that they could have originated as luminous organs, to be used as a help in capturing prey. It is only possible to suppose that their luminosity was a newly acquired property, originally, only a secondary, or incidental one. For instance, it would be very easy for an eye, with a well developed tapetum and lens, to be transformed into a luminous organ, provided the rods, or some other substance in the optic vesicle, as the vitreous body, should acquire highly phosphorescent properties: the lens and concave argentea would then act like a miniature dark-lantern, in which the phosphorescent substance is the light, the argentea, a concave reflector of the most perfect description, and the optic lens. the bull's eye lens of the lantern. If such a transformation took place, the rods and histological structure of the retina would necessarily undergo degeneration, and no longer function as sense organs; hence their nervous supply would almost entirely disappear, a condition which has, apparently, not been realized. But the difficulty in the way of such a supposition is to point out any purpose in such a change, or any adequate advantage to be gained by the animal; and then we have only doubled the difficulties, since we must still explain how so many accessory eyes were originally developed.

In fact, to suppose that the organs are luminous does not decrease, but on the contrary augments the difficulties to be met in treating this subject, therefore I cannot agree with SARS in considering them as luminous organs, but am compelled to regard them as accessory eyes. It seems to be beyond doubt that they are luminous; but still I desire to call attention to the fact that the proof does not as yet appear to be perfect. For instance, SARS has not said that the eyes are luminous in absolute darkness! It must be borne in mind that the presence of the brilliant argentea would, in certain positions, cause a sudden reflection of any bright object in the vicinity, and thus produce the brilliant flashings which SARS considers voluntary. But in spite of these facts, it appears that the rods, or fibres, are faintly luminous, even when isolated and crushed. But even this does not prove that the structures are luminous organs, since this property is a very common one, found in almost all conditions of matter, living or dead, and in the present instance it could very easily be an incidental property, having nothing at all to do with the use of the organs. I would also like to call attention to the presence of the bright red pigment so characteristic of certain forms of Invertebrate eyes i. e. Cœlenterata, Echinoderms, Molluscs and Worms.

If these bodies in *Euphausia* are not »luminous organs« — that is, if the luminosity is not an essential, but only a secondary and incidental property, — then they are, in all probability, visual organs, or eyes. But how can we explain the presence of so many eyes in this isolated group? It is probably due to one of two reasons, either they are deep sea, or nocturnal animals. But from the »Challenger Reports«, it is evident that they are found in great abundance on the surface, and seldom, or never, at any depth. They are, probably then, nocturnal, and this fact has led to a great development of ommatidia in certain regions, giving rise to the eyes as we now see them. The enormous development of the argentea is an evidence that they are constructed for an economy of light impressions, just as in *Pecten*, and in those nocturnal, or deep sea fishes, which are so universally supplied with reflecting surfaces.

I must anticipate the theoretical remarks to be given in the fifth chapter, in order to say that I regard these bodies as organs adapted for the absorption of light energy, rather than for the perception of objects. These accessory organs may with propriety be called eyes since, originally, all eyes had such a function, and may still have it even in the more highly perfected forms.

The careful and valuable studies of GROBBEN (55) upon the eyes of Phyllopod Crustacea, have shown that in this group the lateral eyes are overgrown by a double, membranous fold, in some cases enclosing the eye in a complete sac, which in other instances remains open. He regards these folds as protective, and considers that they are not developed in *Branchipus*; but the fact, as I have shown, that the latter genus is supplied with a corneal hypodermis, would indicate that a similar fold was present in the embryos. If this is so, we must suppose that the hypodermic folds over the Cladoceran eye represent the corneal hypodermis of the higher Crustacea, and that the folds have a deeper phylogenetic signification than has been supposed. The resemblance between this folding of the hypodermis, and the invagination to form what I have considered as the primitive Arthropod eye, is so striking that one cannot fail to notice it. But on the other hand the resemblance may be a superficial one, and we should not be warranted in regarding it as having a phylogenetic meaning, without a more accurate knowledge of the eye in this group of Crustacea.

Development.

I can see no reason for supposing that the development of the visual organs of Arthropods should be any different, in principle, from that of Molluscs. CARRIÈRE states, on the authority of KENNEL, that the eyes of *Peripatus* are formed by the modification of invaginated, and in the early stages, open-mouthed, optic cups. The strongest objection that can be urged against the supposition that all Arthropod eyes are modifications of primitive optic vesicles is that embryology gives no evidence of such an invagination. Although the embryological evidence is very scanty and entirely confined to the compound eyes, it is pretty certain that in most, if not all, compound eyes, there is no trace of an invagination; but this ought not to be an insurmountable objection, since such processes are often omitted. In *Pecten*, where it is pretty certain that the eyes were formed by the modification of invaginated cups, ontogeny gives no indication of such a process. If it is once agreed that the compound eye is a modified ocellus, then the safest course would be to study the development of the simplest and most primitive ocelli. It is needless to say that this has not, as yet, been done. Basing our supposition upon the facts obtained in the Mollusca, concerning the development of ganglionic cells in general, and of nerve branches, or nervous centres of sense organs in particular, we are compelled to apply the same principles to the Arthropod eye, and although we have no such embryological evidence, the same method of nerve endings i. e. intercellular nerves, — in the most primitive condition, reaching to the outer extremities of the cells, — furnishes very good reason for supposing that the ontogenetic and phylogenetic development of nerve cells must be essentially the same in the two groups under consideration. If, then, this is true, we can no more admit that, in Arthropods, the sense cells and their nerve ends are outgrowths from the brain, than in the Mollusca, unless we suppose a case analogous with that found in the Vertebrates, where a part of the brain, originally external, has become evaginated to form a retina with inverted rods. This supposition, however, will not apply to the Arthropod eye, even leaving other difficulties out of consideration, because the rods are not inverted.

The observations of BOBRETZKI are founded upon the supposition that the crystalline cone cells and the retinulae form two distinct layers, and he was therefore led to mistake the corneal hypodermis — not knowing of the existence of such a layer, — for the crystalline cone cells. I have myself had the opportunity of making sections of some young lobsters' eyes in a comparatively late stage of development, and found that the corneal hypodermis was then much more highly developed than in the later stages. This fact would also explain why BOBRETZKI has asserted that the outer ends of the crystalline cones are surrounded by four cells, believed by him to be identical with the nuclei of SEMPER BALFOUR, Vol. II, p. 397). If the development is the same here as in the Mollusca, the following must be the processes undergone: 1 a thickening of the cephalic hypodermis, giving rise by cell proliferation to two layers, an inner one, the brain, and an outer one forming the permanent hypodermis; that part of the brain arising from the seat of the future eye gave rise to the optic ganglion, which is never entirely separated from the seat of its origin: 2) that part of the hypodermis from which the optic ganglion originated again becomes thickened and divides into two distinct layers, the outer one forming the **corneal hypodermis**, and the inner, the **ommateal layer**, consisting of the retinophorae surrounded by their circles of retinulae. I must insist that, if the description I have given of the structure of the compound eye is correct, then **it is impossible for the sense cells**, either the so-called retinulae of GRENACHER with their rhabdoms, or the retinophorae, to have reached their present position, as outgrowths of the brain. This mistaken conception is undoubtedly due to the close proximity of the ommateal hypodermis to the brain, and to their common point of origin. The mesodermic ingrowth, between the inner, hypodermic, and the outer, neural layer did not, in all probability, give rise, as BOBRETZKI believes, to the pigmented cells and perforated membrane (the latter has no existence) between the crystalline cone cells and the retinulae, but to the often pigmented mesodermic cells between the basal membrane and the optic ganglion.

WEISMANN (49) and CARRIÈRE (19) have likewise shown that the **entire optic layer** arises from a hypodermic thickening, and not from any outgrowth of the brain.

Vision in the Compound Eye.

The facts which I hope have been made clear in the preceding pages necessitate a modification in the supposed process of seeing in the compound eye, as advocated by GRENACHER, — the so-called MÜLLER's Theory of Mosaic Vision.

The facts which bear on this point are the following:

(1) I have shown that the so-called rhabdom of GRENACHER has not, in any case examined by me, the structure he has ascribed to it.

(2) The rhabdom does not owe its origin to the pigment cells, or retinulae.

(3) What GRENACHER regards as a highly specialized rhabdom (or the pedicel), that should consequently possess the greatest sensibility as well as greatest number of nerve fibres, is, in fact, entirely devoid of those nerve fibrillae which we have shown to be the light percipient elements.

4 A more accurate knowledge of their structure (the rhabdoms) shows that they can in no way be regarded as homologous with

those bodies, or rods, known to be the percipient elements in other animals.

(5) According to GRENACHER's theory, the retinulae and rhabdoms must form a cell layer, distinct, in the strongest sense of the word, from that formed by the crystalline cone cells; that this is not so, can be proved by the most conclusive evidence, showing that the three circles of retinulae and the crystalline cone cells form a single layer.

(6) According to this theory, no adequate explanation can be given concerning the function of the corneal facets and crystalline cones.

(7) According to this theory, the crystalline cone cells must be homologous with the vitreous layer of the simple eye. It is then impossible to account for the crystalline cones, the presence of pigment cells, or the grouping of the crystalline cone cells in fours, — not the slightest trace of any of these structures being found in the vitreous layer of any simple eye.

(8) According to GRENACHER, the rods, or rhabdoms, are secreted, in the compound eye, by the retinulae, or pigmented cells; this is directly opposite to what is found in the immediate ancestors of Insects, and, in fact, in all the higher Mollusca and Worms, and probably in the Vertebrates as well, where it is the colorless cells alone which give rise to the rods.

(9) This theory entirely ignores the presence in all faceted eyes of a corneal hypodermis, a fact which alone is sufficient to upset the whole series of deductions upon which it is founded.

If these facts are sufficient to overthrow the theory of GRENACHER, they are none the less important in their bearing upon a new interpretation of the structure, morphological signification, and function, of the different elements in the compound eye. The changes these facts necessitated, concerning the origin and structure of the compound eye, have already been alluded to. According to what was then remarked, it follows that the network of cross fibrillae, or retinidium, contained in the calyx of the retinophorae, either with or without a crystalline cone, is the essential element of the compound eye; without considering a great many minor points which militate against all other suppositions, and in favor of this, we shall briefly enumerate the following facts: (1) the crystalline cones, and the cells which bear them, are homologous with the rods and retinophorae in the eyes of Molluscs, and in the ocelli of Arthropods: (2) a series of cross nerve fibrillae can be traced in the crystalline cone, or in the place where the cone should be when it is absent, exactly similar to those nerve endings in the rods, or percipient elements, of all other animals; (3) in those animals best able to see, the corneal facets are so constructed as to throw a perfect image upon the crystalline cone, or upon the centre of the calyx.

Hence, morphologically, the seat of vision ought to be in the crystalline cones, the necessary nerves are only to be found in the crystalline cones, and finally the most perfect optical conditions are obtained in the crystalline cones; therefore the crystalline cones are the percipient elements!

Accepting this conclusion, there can be but one supposition concerning the result. In those eyes with lenticulate facets, an inverted image of those objects lying within the axis of the ommatidia will be formed upon the crystalline cone. In such forms as *Musca* and *Mantis*, besides many others, there is absolutely nothing to prevent the formation of a perfect image. not upon one or two nerve fibres whose surface is in no wise proportional to the size of the image, but upon a complete and perfect series of fibrillae, whose extension in all three directions is sufficient to receive the whole of any image formed by the corneal lens.

The lack of focal accommodation in the lens is balanced by the depth of the retinidium.

We have already called attention to the fact that the corneal facets are the products of two or four hypodermic cells. The division between the product of each cell is far less distinct (in all but exceptional cases, reduced to almost nothing), than the division between the corresponding facets. These facts indicate that the latter divisions, by the great difference between their refractive index and that of the surrounding cuticula. serve to exclude more perfectly lateral rays of light from each crystalline cone. Even if we accept the conclusions of EXNER (61), GRENACHER, and others, that the crystalline cone would prevent the formation of an image, that very conclusion necessitates the supposition that in the crystalline cone there would be the greatest accumulation of rays of light! In by far the majority of cases, the shape, consistency and position of the cone is such as to offer no hindrance to the formation of an image. If we add to such cases those in which no crystalline cone is present and where there is undoubtedly a highly developed visual power, as in the Diptera, the number of cases in which it is even probable that the cone would prevent the formation of an image is very small. On the other hand, in the Flies, there is undoubtedly very sharp vision, and therefore, if the rhabdom is the percipient element, we ought to find the lens and cone highly perfected in order, according to EXNER's supposition, to bring as much light as possible into the extraordinarily small hole at the bottom of the calyx; the cone is, however, entirely absent, but the lens remains, and is well developed; but alone it must be a positive disadvantage, since, with it, only a single, central ray of light can possibly enter the rhabdom; all others, since the focus of the lens usually falls in the middle of the calyx, will fall at a sharp angle on the lateral walls of the calyx, never entering the rhabdom. If the calyx and lens were entirely absent, or were reduced to a thin layer, — a change that could be accomplished with the greatest ease, we may be sure, provided there was an advantage to be gained by it, — many more rays of light could gain access to the rhabdom. But as a matter of fact, only a single ray can, under existing circumstances, enter the rhabdom. Now let us consider the extraordinarily small number of rays, arising from an ordinary sized object, that could enter a corresponding number of rhabdoms, and the faint impressions that these single rays would produce, and we cannot fail to wonder how these imperfect means could, in so many cases, cause such perfect vision. On the other hand I presume the advocates of MÜLLER's theory of mosaic vision would discover, in the presence of the axial nerve fibres which I have shown to be so universally present in the style of the retinophora, a striking confirmation of their views. The presence of a single nerve element in the rods was regarded by the followers of MÜLLER, as the fact necessary for the complete confirmation of this theory. GRENACHER emphasized this point, but finding in many cases six or seven rods, or nerve elements, came to the conclusion that, since they were not large enough to receive any entire image, they must act as a single element, like the rod of a Vertebrate for instance; if he accepts the fact of an axial nerve fibre, a though his rhabdoms disappear, his theory may take a stronger hold than before.

But those, who, on these grounds, would still retain MÜLLER's theory, will have difficulties to contend with, besides those presented by the crystalline cone. Why for instance is it, if only a single ray of light penetrates the rhabdom, and consequently only extends over the axial nerve, that the rhabdom is, in the presumably most sensitive part, so much larger than is necessary: it should only be as large as the axial nerve, and surely not larger in one place than another. Then again the axial nerve, in other animals without doubt, is not the sensitive element, but only the radiating and infinitely smaller fibrillae. In Cephalopods, the axial nerve is entirely protected from the light by a coating of pigment granules. Moreover in all other animals, the rays of light act at right angles upon the fibrillae, and there is no reason to suppose that in Arthropods a different condition prevails; in fact we meet with insurmountable, physiological difficulties, in attempting to imagine the effect a ray of light will produce, acting parallel with a long and large nerve fibre.

Indeed the objections to MÜLLER's theory, as advocated by EXNER, GRENACHER and CARRIÈRE, and almost universally accepted by modern Zoologists, might, in the light of the facts given above, be multiplied indefinitely without coming to any more decisive conclusion. It will be sufficient, I believe, for the present, to allow the matter to rest until the observations, upon which my views are based, shall have been confirmed, or proved to be incorrect.

I must again warn against the interpretation given to results obtained by superficial, physiological experiments upon the Arthropod eye. Such results should be accepted with the greatest caution. The effect produced by any change in the amount of light, or by any object, depends upon the structural perfection of the visual organ, and upon the association of light impressions with the impressions received by other organs. To determine the functional perfection of a visual organ, we must know the entire life history of the animal. How far we are as yet from such a condition is only too evident. Let a person offer a dog a stone, and it would be a mere chance if the dog took any notice of it; this evidence alone would be sufficient to prove, to some people, that the dog was blind. Let our imaginary experimentor present him, after being fed, with a piece of meat, and if no notice were taken of it, he would be certain that the dog was blind. If, on the contrary, the dog had, by chance, been very hungry, the results would have been different, and any person would then come to the conclusion that the dog could not only see well, but could actually distinguish between things that were fit, or unfit to eat. This simple and perhaps unnecessary illustration will, I think, enforce the statement already made that, in such comparatively simple creatures as Insects and Arthropods, whose actions are almost entirely controlled by so-called instincts, it is impossible to judge of the effect certain objects will produce, without knowing the relation which they bear to the animal. In other words we should have to know the conditions governing the instincts of the animal. An instinct is a series of causes and effects which may be represented by a formula. Let x be any vibration, as sound, or light; $x.n'$. the nervous vibration caused by the first; and $n.m$..... the muscular contractions caused by the same; then, providing $x.n'$. always causes the same muscular contractions, all that is necessary to cause $x.n'$., $n.m$. is x; but the potentialities $x.n'$., $n.m$..... are inherited, while x is a constant, e x t e r n a l factor. The experimentor has the quantities n', the sense organ; n, the nerves; and m, the muscle, given; in order to produce the sequence $x.n'$., $n.m$....., he must select the factor x, and without a previous knowledge of the sequence to be produced, it will be a mere chance if he choose correctly.

If the sequence of muscular contractions, $n.m$....., produced by any external factor, is short, we have a reflex action. If the sequence is long and complicated, we have an instinct.

It has been said that in all those compound eyes with lenticulate facets, an inverted image of external objects will be thrown upon the crystalline cones, but it does not at all follow that an image is p e r - c e i v e d. As I have already remarked, an image is an incidental result of the concentration of light upon a given area. The perception of form is due to constant association with the sense of touch; it is not improbable that the perceptions in Arthropods may be due to a combination of the sense of sight with that of smell, hearing, or of motion. The perception must depend, also, upon the structure of the nerve centres to which the sensations are conducted, and upon the quality of the nerve fibrillae upon which the vibrations act. If the facts we have stated, in regard to the constant origin, up to certain limits, of ganglionic cells from sense organs, be true, then it follows that the nervous quality of their nerve fibrillae must be improved with age, or use.

The great mistake in discussing vision in compound eyes is to suppose that all have a similar degree of functional perfection, simply because they are similarly constructed. It is only necessary to direct attention to this point, in order to show how essential it is. So far as we know, the eye of an ant, as far as its structure goes, is nearly as well adapted for seeing, as that of a fly; but the latter sees exceptionally well, while, according to Sir J. LUBBOCK, it is extremely doubtful whether the former sees at all. The difference may be due, in a small degree, to the greater number of ommatidia in the eye of the fly. but it is probably due in a much greater degree to the difficulty of inventing satisfactory methods of experimentation.

It seems as though GRENACHER had sought refuge under the shadow of MÜLLER's genius for the propagation of some theory of vision that would go with his own observations. I must confess that I cannot see any evidence of extraordinary brilliancy in MÜLLER's celebrated Theory of Mosaic Vision; his genius has, however, been ample to protect, even up to the present day, his »geistige Lieblingskind« as GRENACHER calls it.

A necessary deduction from the theory of mosaic vision, and one which MÜLLER himself recognized, has, apparently, been forgotten by GRENACHER in his discussion of vision in the compound eye. MÜLLER says, as GRENACHER has quoted, »Die Insecten sehen weder nach dioptrischen noch nach katoptrischen Gesetzen, sondern bloß durch eine nähere Bestimmung der Beleuchtung!« I understand, by this rather loose expression, that Insects are only able to distinguish light from darkness, and it cannot be denied that it is a necessary deduction from MÜLLER's theory. But it is certain that many insects can perceive objects with great precision, therefore the theory cannot be true. If only a single ray of light from any part of a small object — say ten feet distant — entered each rhabdom, then the points of origin of these rays of light would be so minute, few, and far apart, that no perception of form would be possible. On the other hand, if we bring to our aid the crystalline cone and corneal facets, as has been done by EXNER, we would be no better off, since a widely divergent cone of light entering the corneal facet would, by repeated reflection, be concentrated as a confused mixture of light at the apex of the cone. giving absolutely no effect of form, while only comparatively great changes in the amount of light would be perceptible. Moreover a most important point has been neglected by the advocates of MÜLLER's theory, and more especially by EXNER, in attempting to explain the function of the crystalline cone. Even if we suppose with him that the latter concentrates at its inner end all the rays of light entering it. it is perfectly evident that the repeated reflection will not make the rays parallel. Now the inner end of the crystalline cone in its most perfect condition never reaches the outer end of the narrow pigmented tube in which the supposed rhabdoms are, therefore the rays of light will diverge from the apex of the cone at nearly the same angle at which they entered, no more rays of light gaining access to the rhabdom than if no crystalline cone was present!

If we make the most generous allowance possible for the theory of mosaic vision, so celebrated on account of its wonderful acuteness of conception, we are at best provided with organs that can only distinguish between light and darkness. But Exner, while admitting that there is probably no perception of form by the compound eye, considers that it is an organ very well adapted to perceive motion. We are not prepared to discuss to any extent what the conditions necessary for a motion-perceiving eye must be. It seems certain, however, that any organ perceiving simply light gradations could never distinguish motions of objects, except when they affected to a sensible degree the amount of light; therefore, in that case, there could be no perception of motion, but only a sensibility to the changes in the amount of light. It seems to be equally certain that to perceive motions of objects, it must be necessary for the light impressions produced by these objects to have some definition; but this is also just the condition essential to the perception of objects! It is extremely probable that the image of an object in motion is more irritant than that of one which is at rest. This is intelligible on the ground that all other sensations, either of touch, smell, hearing, or of slight electric shocks, are much more excitant when interrupted, than when continuous. We may consider that a moving object causes an image to be felt successively on various parts of the percipient surface, causing a vibration of images, so to speak; in an ear, for instance, sound produces a succession of impressions upon the same elements; in an eye the moving object produces a succession of impressions upon different elements. It has not been shown how the compound eye is especially adapted for seeing objects in motion; since having the percipient elements either in a continuous layer, like that of the Vertebrate eye, or isolated, as in Arthropods, cannot affect the principle of the action.

In conclusion, we may say that of two objects of equal luminosity, other conditions being likewise equal, the one in motion would produce a greater nervous irritation than the one at rest, simply because it would cause a succession of interrupted impressions; therefore the animal would be more likely to see the moving object than the one at rest. The transmission of these impressions from one retinidium to another would be as gradual in the compound eye as in that of a Vertebrate, since, (1) the image of any object is, in most cases, not confined to one crystalline cone, but to several: (2) the retinidium is formed by a set of nerves supplying not only one ommatidium, but several, so that a single impression produced in one would be liable to cause, by sympathy, an impression in the next.

An important, but fallacious argument in favor of MÜLLER's theory was elucidated by him, and strangely enough has been sufficient to support it until the present day. This argument is, briefly, the following: there appear to be but two suppositions possible: either the Insect must see an upright »mosaic image«, or a multitude of inverted ones; but it would be impossible for the animal to rectify all these inverted images in order to see well, therefore the former supposition must be the correct one! MÜLLER seems to have forgotten that according to his adopted theory there is no necessity of inverting the images: because, surely, if the insect could not invert the images, it would still be able to see infinitely better than one, which, according to his theory, was only able to distinguish the amount of light!

MÜLLER also ignored the fact that some Insects are provided with as many as forty simple eyes, the images formed by which must be inverted. Neglecting the last named fact, to which GRENACHER has also called attention, MÜLLER preferred to consider that all Insects, some of which he must have known were notoriously sharp-sighted, are only capable of distinguishing light from darkness, rather than suppose that they could rectify numerous inverted images! But it seems to me that a little consideration will show that there is no more difficulty in this process, than in that performed by Vertebrates. It is a great mistake to suppose that all animals with compound eyes see equally well, or that it is necessary for them to form an idea of a landscape. There is a great difference between the structure of an eye like that of an Ant and that of a Dragonfly, and there is undoubtedly as wide a gulf between their visual powers. But a landscape even could be seen and recognized by means of a compound eye, provided the inverted images were small and very numerous; it would consist of an upright picture, with its general features unchanged, composed of innumerable inverted images. But most of the objects brought into daily relation with insects are small, therefore their images would be formed only on one, or a very few crystalline cones, so that the erection of their inverted images would not present any physiological difficulties.

It would be absurd to assert that Insects or Crustacea could see in this or in that manner without giving specific cases. That, however, we are not prepared to do. But we may say with safety that there is nothing in the principal upon which the compound eye is constructed to prevent its possessor from seeing with clearness and precision, by means of inverted images, either a landscape or small neighboring objects. There seems to be no reason to deny that many Insects have developed at least one of these faculties to a special degree. On the other hand there seem to be many Arthopods, with well developed compound eyes, which are able to see, but not to perceive objects, or at least only a very few objects, — those with which they are brought into the closest relation. Then again there are probably many Insects which can only distinguish light from darkness. The difference in vision is due more to the powers of association than to variation in the structure of the eye.

Chapter V. General Remarks upon other Groups.

The knowledge we possess concerning the visual organs of Coelenterates is sufficient to warrant a comparison between the structure of their essential elements and those of Mollusca and Arthropods. As far as I know, there are no structures in the Coelenterata that might be regarded as isolated ommatidia, but that such organs do exist, or have existed once, is quite probable, since their eyes are formed on the same plan as those of the Mollusca, i. e. of collections of ommatidia which, in the less perfect condition, must have been irregularly scattered about. The sensitive layer, which appears to form a retineum, consists of colorless retinophorae, whether single or double is not known, surrounded by pigment cells, or retinulae. This structure is found in the sensitive layer of all the various forms of Coelenterate eyes. The only difference of any moment is that the retinophorae are much smaller, and in shape and general appearance resemble more closely ordinary sense cells than is the case in Mollusca, where the bright, refractive contents give them the appearance of gland cells. But in the Coelenterates anything similar to the rods of Molluscan eyes has not as yet been described. But I think we may safely conclude that what has been, heretofore, regarded as a vitreous body is, in reality, a cuticular thickening containing a highly specialized part of the retia terminalia. Such appears to be the case with the minute invaginate ocelli, described by CARRIÈRE, situated near the large lenticulate eyes of *Charybdaea marsupialis*, which can be compared with the invaginate eyes of *Arca* (Pl. 30, fig. 43). The vitreous layer in the large, lenticulate eyes of the same species is, in all probability, a layer of retinal rods.

In *Aurelia*, according to HERTWIG, the ocelli are very poorly defined, and are not provided with any special thickening of the cuticula. They probably represent only the simplest aggregation of ommatidia.

It is very probable that the so-called lens of the simple, non-invaginate ocelli is not a lens at all, but a lenticular thickening of the cuticula, filled with nerve fibres; or, in other words, it is composed of the cuticular secretions, or rods, of the ommatidial cells, and contains the retinidia. Such a condition could be compared directly with the pseudo-lenticulate eyes of *Arca* (Pl. 30, fig. 51). It is extremely improbable that a purely dioptric lens would be developed before the specialization of the rods. Another striking fact that deserves attention is the wide presence of red, and less often, black pigment, which when united give rise to shades of brown varying in color according as one or the other pigment prevails.

Another important point to be considered is the great number of imperfect eyes, and the presence of very highly developed ones, as in *Charybdaea*. This condition is exactly parallel to that found in *Arca*, and brings us a confirmation of our supposition that the evaginate eyes of *Arca* did not arise independently, but as modifications of the invaginate ones. If, for instance, both types of eyes were developed from an irregularly folded surface, the hollows forming into invaginate eyes, and the ridges into the evaginate ones, then we should expect to find as many transitional stages in the development of one form, as in that of the other, especially when there were a great many of both kinds in all stages of development. This, as we have seen in *Arca*, was not the case. In Coelenterates also, although there are many very simple invaginate eyes in all stages of development, there are no traces of the evaginate ones.

In the Worms, that uniformity in the structure of the sensitive layer, found in Mollusca and Coelenterates, does not appear to prevail. The eyes found in the Annelids are best understood; therefore they can be more readily compared with those found in the Mollusca and Arthropods. We shall speak of them alone.

CARRIÈRE has furnished us with the best observations concerning the eyes of Polychaetous Annelids. The same composition of the sensitive layer, and of the ommatidia, is to be seen here as in Mollusca. The colorless cells (Secretzellen of CARRIÈRE) are the retinophorae, and the pigmented ones, the retinulae. It is remarkable how a person can fail to be impressed with the similarity between the colorless cells of the Coelenterate retina, and similar ones in the retina of Molluscs, or Worms. It is evident that CARRIÈRE either failed to recognize this similarity, or regarded it as of no consequence, for he called the colorless cells of the Coelenterate retina, sense cells, and similar elements of the retina of Molluscs and Worms, secreting cells! But, so far as I could find, he gave no reason for regarding them as morphologically different elements. In such simple eyes as those of *Nereis cultrifera*, the optic vesicle has been described as being filled with a vitreous body, but we may be sure that a part of it is, in reality, composed of a layer of rods, just as in the Molluscan eye. Indeed, in *Alciope*, the rods are very highly developed, and do not differ essentially from those of *Pecten*, or of the Cephalopods.

The same modification of the ommatidia has taken place in Alciopidae as in the Cephalopods. The retinulae have been reduced to a narrow collar of rodless pigment cells which surround the neck of each retinophora. The double rod of the latter is very highly developed and contains an axial nerve fibre, which can be traced into the body of the retinophora. These facts render it almost certain that the retinophorae are double, as in Mollusca, and therefore we should expect to find two nuclei. GRABER claims to have found three nuclei in the »Retinalschläuchen«, as he calls the retinophorae, but it must be understood that I do not lay any stress on this fact, for there appears to be no doubt that the extra nuclei he saw did not belong to the retinophorae, but to the surrounding pigment cells. The second nuclei of the retinophorae, that I have shown to be present in *Arca*, *Pecten*, and *Haliotis*, are bodies very difficult to observe, even in the most carefully prepared sections. The cells must be isolated by maceration, in order to demonstrate, with certainty, the presence of the second nucleus.

The open ends of the rods in the Alciopidae are very interesting, for they offer a further confirmation of the supposition that they are double; they may be compared with the rods found in *Pecten*, where we have evidence of a former opening, now completely closed, in the fact that the central nerve issues from the end of the rod to form the »loops of the axial nerve«. It is very probable that the axial nerve of Alciopidae, and also that of other highly developed forms, extends through the opening of the rods to form »axial loops« similar to those in *Pecten*.

The slightly modified ommatidia, found even in the highly developed eyes of some Worms, render it very probable that the isolated ommatidia are present in the scattered pigment areas so often found there. This is still more probable when we consider the frequency with which eye-like pigment spots occur. I have examined superficially, without sections or maceration, the segmentally arranged pigment spots in *Asterope candida* and *Tomopteris* (sp. ?), and found that they resembled so strongly the ommatidial areas in the Lamellibranchiata, that there can be little doubt that they represent aggregations of simple ommatidia. Although the cuticular covering is thin, the ommatidia are very sharply defined and regular, consisting of rather large, colorless retinophorae surrounded by a complete ring of pigment cells. To settle the question beyond doubt, it would be necessary to show that the colorless cells end inwardly in points, have axial nerve fibres, and contain two nuclei, at least one of which is nucleolated. When irritated, *Asterope* gives off, apparently from the colorless cells, a beautiful, emerald green secretion. This fact militates against supposing the organs in question to be eyes. But it is not improbable that the secretion may be a pathological result of the violent contractions, similar to what CHUN has described for the Ctenophorae, where a strong irritation causes the Chromatophores to burst; the contents in this case, however, being forced inwards.

In the Vertebrates, there seems to be little evidence for supposing that isolated ommatidia are present. The structure of the so-called luminous organs of the Scopelidae is too imperfectly known to allow any conclusion as to whether they are composed of ommatidia, or not. If they should prove to be eyes instead of luminous organs, we would have good reason for supposing that ommatidia are present in the general epithelial covering of the body. Sense hair cells may be found in all parts of the body, and it is only necessary to bring any part of the sensitive epithelium into constant relation with certain agents to develop at that point a special organ of touch, taste, or hearing, as the case may be. GRABER has shown by experiment upon blinded Reptiles that the skin has, to a certain extent, the power of distinguishing light from darkness. This would lead us to suppose that scattered ommatidia were present in the skin. Now if animals provided with scattered ommatidia lived in dark places, as at great depth in the sea, then, in order to see in the dim light, their visual organs would undergo changes by which a diminution in the amount of light would be accompanied by a corresponding increase in the area and complexity of the sensitive surface, and would probably result in the appearance of numerous eyes at various parts of the body. But we have seen, in those cases when it was necessary for a great amount of light to be used, or to make an economic use of very little light, that reflecting surfaces are developed, either in each retinophora, behind the rod (*Haliotis*, *Arca* etc.), or as a continuous membrane behind the inner layer of rods (the argentea in

Cardium, *Pecten*, and nocturnal, or deep sea Vertebrates). Therefore under these conditions, the accessory eyes would also develop to a high degree such reflecting surfaces. These reflecting bodies are usually combined with highly refractive condensing lenses, and both together give the organs thus provided a very brilliant sparkle or glow, which may be mistaken for independent luminosity. The lateral eyes of *Euphausia* are provided with a remarkably well developed argentea and lens.

It is extremely probable that the retina of the Vertebrates consists of highly modified ommatidia, whose retinulae have lost their pigment and become transformed into ganglionic cells. Some of these ganglia. — Landolt'sche Keule and their homologues, — retain their primitive position around the base of the retinophorae, or rod cells, and constitute, with the nuclei of the latter, the nucleated layer between the rods and the basal plexus. The fibres of the latter layer may, like the basal branch of the optic nerve in *Pecten*, consist only of axial fibres, and like them enter the retinophorae and extend through the centre of the rods as axial nerves. The ganglionic layer of the retina is produced by the modification of retinulae into ganglionic cells which, instead of wandering away from the retina to form an isolated optic ganglion, remain in close proximity to the sensitive rod cells. An axial nerve of the rods has already been described by several authors, and, as the statements have been received with more or less doubt, it may be worth while to say that I have been able to confirm the statement by observation made upon the macerated retina of the dog-fish. The basket-work of fibres on the surface of the rods is too well known to require any confirmation. Max Schultze (Stricker's Handbuch der Histologie) considers these fibres, which have been isolated toward the base of the rods, as forming a part of the connective tissue skeleton of the retina. Judging entirely from the facts obtained by a study of the rods in the Invertebrates, we consider the external fibres in the Vertebrate rods to be exactly similar to those found on the surface of the rods in *Pecten*, i. e. ganglionic nerve fibres. The nerve fibres in the centre of the rods in both groups, Vertebrates and Mollusca, would be axial nerves. To carry out the comparison to its full extent, the lamellae of the Vertebrate rods must be produced by the successive etages of fibrillae which radiate from the axial nerve toward the periphery of the rod, there uniting with fibrillae from the external fibres. In other words, a rod of the Vertebrate retina contains a retinidium exactly similar to that found in the rods of the Mollusca and Arthropods.

The axial nerve and the external fibres of the rods in Vertebrates are so strikingly like those found in the Invertebrates, that our supposition that the retina is formed of modified ommatidia receives some confirmation. But, if we would compare the rod cells with their axial nerves, to the double retinophorae of the Mollusca, we must carry out the comparison still further, and suppose that the rod cells are double and contain two nuclei, otherwise we cannot explain the presence of the axial nerve in the centre of the cell. Now in the rod cells of the Vertebrates, we actually do find two bodies, one of which is an undoubted nucleus with a nucleolus, and the other a refractive, unnuclear-like body. We find exactly the same bodies in the double retinophorae of *Arca*, *Pecten* and *Haliotis*, and in these cases they are undoubtedly nuclei, by the fusion of whose cells an external nerve fibre came to lie in the centre. Now in the Vertebrates we have the two nuclei, one of which is nucleolated and the other aborted, and the axial fibre, and we can explain this condition only on the supposition that the rod cells, like the retinophorae of Mollusca, are formed by the fusion of two cells. They then have all the essential characteristics of retinophorae, and consequently we are justified in supposing that the retina of Vertebrates is formed by the modification of ommatidia.

There is a striking similarity between the structure of the retina in *Pecten* and that of Vertebrates, due solely to the similarity in conditions. If we should shorten the retinophorae of *Pecten*, so that the nuclei came to lie more in the centre of the retina, above the rods, then we would have the same conditions found in the simple forms of the Vertebrate retina. For instance, beginning at the inner surfaces of the retinae there would be in both cases: (1) a layer of rods; (2) a fibrous layer or membrane (pseudo-membrane of *Pecten*) separating the rods from the overlying cells; (3) the retinophorae with their nuclei, and the inner layer of ganglionic cells (*Pecten*), or Landolt'sche Keule (Vertebrates); (4) a layer of axial nerve fibres (*Pecten*), or basal plexus (Vertebrates); (5) the outer layer of ganglionic cells (*Pecten*, or ganglionic layer (Vertebrates), and (6) the nerve fibres of the ganglionic branch of the optic nerve (*Pecten*), or the inner layer of optic nerve fibres (Vertebrates).

In *Pecten*, the fifth layer, or the outer ganglionic cells, shows the same tendency as in the similar layer of the Vertebrate retina to break up into etages of bipolar and multipolar ganglionic cells.

I do not consider that the frequently present, double rod cells of Vertebrates have anything in common with the double retinophorae of Invertebrates.

Chapter VI[1]. Theoretical Remarks Concerning the Origin and Function of Sense Organs and of Animal Pigment.

Living bodies are distinguished by their power to absorb matter and energy, and from them produce high compounds, by whose disintegration force is liberated as motion. This sequence of events is vitality. It consists of four processes: (1) absorption of matter; (2) absorption of energy; (3) production of high compounds; (4) the fall of these compounds, producing motion. An inseparable result of vitality, but not a vital process, is excretion, or the discharge of disenergized matter. We have only to deal with the second of these processes, the absorption of energy, or dynamophagy, and more especially with the absorption of solar energy, or heliophagy.

The most primitive and universal method of dynamophagy is the absorption of solar energy by chlorophyll; but in animals we have good reason to believe that various forms of energy are absorbed in several ways: (1) solar energy, by means of pigment or by nerve fibres; (2) energy of sound vibrations, by auditory hairs; (3) energy of coarser vibrations, of pressure, contact, or movement, by tactile hairs; and (4) that of gases, solutions, or chemical compounds, by means of so-called taste cells. All these processes in their higher stages suppose the presence of a nervous system, and, since the development of nerves and sense organs go hand in hand, we must have some idea of how a nervous system could have originated, if we would follow the development of sense organs.

Let us suppose that we have before us the simplest form of a multicellular animal, then all the cells will be alike, each performing for itself all the functions necessary for its existence; each cell would absorb its own matter and the energy, or stimuli, necessary for its conversion into living compounds. The relation between the matter and energy absorbed is a constant one. The cells would tend to vary in two directions: (1) towards the absorption of more energy, or (2) of more matter.

---

[1] The following chapter is not so much an attempt to discuss the evidence for, or against any conclusion, as to make clear my own opinion upon the subject. With this object in view, I have omitted the discussion of several doubtful questions, and I have also made preparatory suppositions, which it is neither the place nor my intention to discuss here. My statements have been made positive for the sake of brevity and clearness, but they must be regarded as suggestions, for which I can, as yet, bring no proof, rather than as positive assertions.

But if a cell absorbs more matter than it has energy to transform, the matter will remain stationary unless the necessary stimulus is brought from those cells which receive an excess of energy, or stimuli. But the excess of energy in the one cell would not be lost, but transferred to others near it, by mere contact. This would be the first step in the transformation of indifferent cells, or those in which the entire sequence of events called vitality is fulfilled, into those which perform only a part of this process. As soon as an indifferent cell absorbs more energy than is necessary for its own vital processes, it becomes a dynamophagous, or sense cell. Those which absorb more matter than is necessary for themselves become hylophagous. The origin of the latter is not so simple as that of the former, since it was the result of two distinct processes: (1) the direct absorption of matter by certain cells; and (2) the deposition in them, by the generating body, of matter, before they were capable of independent motion. To follow these two processes is not at present our object, only in so far as they have to do with the origin of the sense cells. We have said that the transfer of energy from a dynamophagous cell to a hylophagous one was, at first, by simple contact, and it follows that the two cells must be developed side by side. Our supposition of an independent group of indifferent cells was only to make our meaning clear, for it is very probable that no such condition ever existed. We see in many Protozoa a constant differentiation of one pole from the other, so that the so-called animal functions are confined to one end, and the vegetative to the other. According to the laws of division, or of segmentation, such a bipolar cell would never give rise to a group of indifferent ones, but to a bipolar body, the relation of the poles in the single cell, and in the group of cells, remaining the same. Therefore, in the simplest, multi-cellular animal, the cells are already differentiated, the vegetative ones being confined to one pole, around which the energizing, or sense cells, would form a ring. This condition is realized in the simplest Coelenterates. In the simplest condition, the distance between the organs receiving stimuli and those giving them, or sense organs, is not great, so that the latter perform a double function: (1) receive the stimuli from without, and (2) conduct them to the necessary centres. Such organs are very commonly found in the Coelenterates and Molluscs, and consist of slender cells with large, basal, and nucleolated nuclei, ending externally in sensory hairs and internally in long, sensitive fibres (in Mollusca, usually a single one) whose exact method of termination is unknown, but from theoretical reasons there can be but little doubt that they terminate either in contractile, or digestive cells, within the body (Pl. 32, fig. 153, c. d. e.).

After, or coincident with, the production of digestive and sensitive cells, certain of the still indifferent, and probably ciliated ones, developed internal, amoeboid processes which were capable of contractions caused by stimuli received from without. The contractile powers of a single cell can only increase at the expense of the sensitive ones. It is not unreasonable to suppose that two cells situated close together would possess, in unequal degrees, the power of sensitiveness and contractility: but the more one cell became contractile, the more it would lose its power of receiving direct stimuli, and would tend to absorb them from that cell which had the sensitiveness to an unusual degree; two such cells would then become dependent upon each other, the one increasing in contractility, and losing its power of receiving direct stimuli, while the other would lose its contractility and gain in sensibility in the same proportion. The sum of the labor performed by both cells in the indifferent condition would exactly equal that performed by the two specialized ones. The communication between the two cells would be at first one of ordinary contact. But in proportion as the contractile cell became more contractile, those parts devoted to this purpose, i. e. the inwardly directed processes, would be more developed, while there would be a corresponding diminution of the outwardly directed part, or that necessary for receiving impressions. In its companion cell, the sensitive one, the reverse would be the case. As the contractile cell moved more toward the interior, it could retain its contractility only as long as it received stimuli from without: it could therefore never separate itself from its partner, the sense cell, to whose aid it owes its contractile powers. The contractile cell would, therefore, draw with it a part of the sensitive one, which, since it must necessarily remain in contact with the outer world, would be drawn out into a long fibre, its line of communication with its cell partner. The two cells have now reached an unequal degree of differentiation, since the contractile one is entirely adapted to contractility, while the sense cell has not only to receive direct stimuli, but transmit them to its partner. This is an obvious disadvantage, and steps are soon taken to avoid it. In the Mollusca, as well as in the Coelenterates, we have seen that the more highly sensitive the sense cells are, the thinner they become, until they finally communicate with the outer world by a very fine bunch of sense hairs, while the cell body is reduced almost to a fibre. We have also seen how the fine prolongations of the sense cells in the retina of *Pecten* produce very fine lateral branches, which become attached to neighboring sense cells. The same process takes place upon the epidermis, so that one of the slender sense cells (Pl. 32, fig. 153, d), which still retains its sense hairs, becomes united to a neighboring sense cell (e) by fine fibres. The advantage thus gained is too great to be left undeveloped, therefore the cell (f) assumes more and more the sensitive roll, while (f^1—^{2}) gradually losing its sense hairs, and therefore the power of receiving direct stimuli, only transmits the stimuli received from (f_1. We have now reached the last change in the development of these cells; all are reduced to the same level, since each is subservient to a single function. The most highly developed sensory, nervous, and contractile systems are only modifications of the condition represented by these three cells. The cell (f) is the sense organ (s)[1], the muscular system, and (f^1—^{2}) the nervous centre, which is connected on the one hand with the receptive centre for energy, or the sense organs, and on the other, with the contractile centre, or organs of motion. The specialization, or growth of all three systems must go hand in hand; increase of one is life to the other, the loss of one, death to the other.

Sensory, muscular, and nervous systems must primarily have originated from the same areas, and the growth of one in a given direction is followed by that of the other.

As the origin of purely sensitive, and of conducting cells, took place after the origin of purely contractile ones, so we find, even in highly developed forms, a more intimate connection maintained between sense organs and nervous centres, than between the contractile centre and either of the other two. The above described differentiation gave rise to four sets of cells, which may be divided into two similar groups: A[1], the hylophagous cells, situated at the vegetative pole of a spherical, or ovoid, multicellular animal; A[2], contractile cells forming a ring around the vegetable pole: and a third ring, outside of, and concentric with the other two, consisting of (B[1]) sense, and (B[2]) nervous cells. The remaining part of the body would be composed of nearly indifferent cells.

The continual transformation of sense cells into conducting, or ganglionic ones, with deeply situated nuclei, gave rise to a ring of ganglionic cells whose union with each other and with the contractile cells became more and more complicated.

A sense organ is a collection of cells for the reception

---

[1] Unfortunately, not represented in the figure.

of energy. The sensitiveness of the organ depends upon the number of sense cells which have at that point been converted into nerve fibres, or ganglionic cells, and may be approximately estimated by the size of the group of ganglionic cells thus formed by the modification of sensory ones.

We have spoken of the cells modified for the reception of the energy absorbed. We consider that dynamophagous organs are of two natures; those formed by the modification of ciliated, and those formed by the modification of pigmented, or chlorophyll cells. The former receive energy in the shape of coarse movements of the surrounding medium, or of fine vibrations like sound; and the latter, the still more subtle vibrations of light.

First, let us make a proposition, which we advance simply on the grounds of its plausibility and the difficulty we have found in explaining certain facts in any other way, viz.: Animal pigment, especially that of colorless plastids contained in the living protoplasm of external, epithelial cells, is not a waste product formed by the solar decomposition of protoplasm, nor is it a protective covering, but a living substance with a physiological activity necessary for the animal, and dependent for this activity upon the presence of the sunlight.

These pigment granules are modified chlorophyll granules, and like them have the power of absorbing solar energy.

There is little reason for supposing that pigment is a product of decomposition. In plants, where it is well known that, under the influence of the sunlight, a constant decomposition is in progress, there are no pigmented waste products; neither is there any color produced by the decomposition of dead animal matter in the sun, while all other well known waste products, such as carbonic acid gas, sulphides, ammoniates, and ureates, are formed in abundance. The supposition that pigment is a waste product of solar energy is not so different from my own, as the supposition that pigment is simply a dead protective covering; for it is of little consequence, for the present, whether we regard the pigment as a waste product of solar energy, or as the receptive agent for the solar energy, so long as we admit that the sunlight has an important beneficial effect upon animal protoplasm. Most epithelial pigments, not modified for special purposes, are very unstable, and therefore cannot be regarded as waste products. In some cases they are extremely resistant, but they then have a simple, protective function, as we hope to show later.

The pigment found deposited in the cells of the lower animals, such as Protozoa, Cœlenterates and Crustacea, cannot be a merely protective coloring, for in innumerable cases it has just the reverse effect. Among pelagic animals, otherwise perfectly transparent, regularly distributed chromatophores containing red, brown, or black pigment are widely present. These chromatophores, according to the theory that pelagic animals are transparent in order to escape notice, must be a decided disadvantage. They are highly sensitive to changes in the amount of light. Mayer (83) has shown that the chromatophores of Crustacea are not only sensitive to the amount of light, but are under the control of the will. This fact is of interest, since we must suppose that, originally, the action of the chromatophores was involuntary and dependent upon irritation from without. I have myself observed the slow modifications in the shape of the beautifully starshaped chromatophores of *Beroe ovata*, produced by changes in the intensity of the light.

It is well known that pigment, like chlorophyll, is dependent for its existence upon the sunlight; animals living in absolute darkness, as in caves, being colorless. It is very probable that the color of animals depends upon the color of the light they receive, those receiving sunlight directly, without reflection, showing a tendency to have dark, or black pigment, or to be transparent, as in pelagic animals; those living upon green objects being green, etc. That this coloration is not due primarily to natural selection is shown by the remarkable modification in color undergone by those animals kept in confinement, the change being due without doubt to the change in color of surroundings, and hence the color of light received, rather than to changes in the amount or quality of nourishment. The absence of color in those animals which live in absolute darkness, as in deep caves, is very significant. It would be of great value to show whether any colorless cave animals regain to any extent their pigment when brought into the light. That cave animals are colorless and blind is in direct contrast with the fact that animals from the deep sea, where there is, presumably, no light, are often provided with large visual organs, and are almost invariably intensely colored with red and purple pigments. If then this color of the pigment depends upon the nature of the light received, and there seems to be very good reason for believing it, then we must suppose that certain rays of light, the red, purple and ultra-violet ones, really do penetrate to the bottom of the deep seas, causing the brilliant coloration of the animals inhabiting those places. This supposition would also account for the enormous development of the eyes, or of the so-called »luminous organs« of deep sea-fishes.

Protozoa are highly colored and contain pigment of all shades from green and red to black. But this coloration cannot be regarded as protective in the sense of making them less easily seen, since they are so small as to be invisible, in most cases, to their enemies. Their number does not depend hardly at all on their animal enemies, but upon the amount of food and their power to withstand great changes in the amount of heat and moisture. But we know that these animals, as well as nearly all others, are greatly influenced by, or dependent upon the amount of sunlight; the effect it has upon the highest Vertebrate animals is too well known to require any confirmation. We cannot suppose that the light affects all parts alike, there must be some organs, or substances, particularly affected by it. Of all living organisms, plants are most dependent upon the sunlight for their energy, and their pigment, or chlorophyll, is without doubt the substance affected by sunlight. We know that animal pigment like that of plants is dependent upon the sunlight for its existence, that it is extremely sensitive to changes in the quality and quantity of light, and since animal pigment cannot be regarded as a waste product, or as a protective covering, except in special cases, the only rational supposition is that pigment is the substance in animals directly affected by the sunlight. But what is this effect of the sunlight? It must be either injurious, or beneficial to the animal. The almost universal dependency of animals upon the sunlight makes it absurd to suppose this effect to be an injurious one. The experiments of ROMANES and GRABER (81) show that many Coelenterates and Echinoderms are heliotropic i. e. they select those places best provided with light. I have myself noticed the same property in certain species of Starfish, *Asterias glacialis*, which always occupy the side of an aquarium next the window. A species of Ascidian, *Clavellina*, that I have often observed, almost always has its free extremity directed towards the light. *Pecten Jacobaeus* and *P. opercularis*, nearly always has its open side directed towards the light; I believe that the same is true of *Cardium*, *Pectunculus* and *Avicula*, although my observations upon these three genera were too scanty to be of much importance. It is well known that very many Copepods and Cladocera show a decided preference for the best illuminated side of a jar. The same is true of innumerable larvae and Protozoa. Moreover we know that light is of the utmost importance for the continuation of plant life. These considerations, together with innumerable others, render it almost certain that the effect of sunlight upon the animal organism is a beneficial one. We have, therefore, arrived at the conclusion that pigment is the receptacle of the beneficial effects of the sunlight upon animal organisms.

The most modified form of pigment is probably black; between this color and the brown, yellow, and green, there is a complete gradation. We find the yellow and green colors most abundant in the lower animals, while the black and brown are less common.

In the development of the higher animals, as in Mollusca, the pigment first appears as colorless granules, or plastids, which become yellow, yellowish green, brown, and finally black.

In the Protozoa and even in some worms, a green pigment resembling chlorophyll, and probably having a similar function, is found. These facts: (1) the tendency of pigment granules to form many intermediate stages between undoubted animal pigment and plant pigment, and consequently the difficulty in many cases of distinguishing between the two; (2) the greater resemblance, in its early stages of development, of highly developed animal pigment to chlorophyll; and (3) the almost complete identity in function between animal, and plant pigment, lead us to conclude that animal pigment and chlorophyll, are extreme modifications of the same structures. We can therefore say that chlorophyll absorbs from the sunlight the energy necessary for the transformation of inorganic into organic matter; without this supposition vegetable matter would be a living contradiction to the theory of conservation of energy, for we would have to suppose that vegetable protoplasm itself could create the force necessary for the conversion of inorganic salts into organic matter. But the same reasoning will apply equally well to animal protoplasm; it, also, must absorb, in some way, the force necessary for the conversion of matter into higher compounds, and one way of doing this is by the absorption, not merely of heat, but of chemical rays, or more simply, of energy from the sunlight. In plants, this sun energy is used in the chlorophyll grains, for in them the production of organic matter takes place. But in animals it is probable that the pigment granules are only the receivers of the energy, the heliophags as we shall call them, while this energy is transmitted by nerve fibres to centres where it is consumed in the production of protoplasmic compounds. When a sufficient amount of energy has been accumulated in this manner. it is suddenly discharged, in large or small quantities. in the shape of motion. In all except the very lowest animals, the energy liberated as motion more than equals that absorbed directly from the light; for this motion is the sum of the energy absorbed by the animal from the sun, and that which was absorbed by plants in the production of suitable food for the animal. We can say that vegetable protoplasm times sun energy and inorganic matter, to the nth power. equals x organic matter. Animal protoplasm times organic matter and energy, to the nth power, equals motion and inorganic matter.

Plants store energy; animals convert it into motion.

Heliophags, or sun consumers, are found in animals as well as plants. In the latter instance, they are usually present as chlorophyll granules, which, in some zoospores of the lower plants, are specially modified to form red pigment spots, usually situated near the ciliated pole of the spore. They probably represent modifications of chlorophyll adapted for the consumption of especially large quantities of sun energy. Such spores are extremely active and heliotropic. In Protozoa. we also find special modifications of the pigment, or of the chlorophyll, to form »red eye spots«. They likewise have a tendency to be formed at the animal pole, where the vital processes are presumably most active. In the Coelenterates and Echinoderms, we have pigment spots which, without doubt, are homologous with, and have the same functions. whatever they may be, as those seen in Protozoa, and in the zoospores of certain plants. The pigment, always red but occasionally containing black, is here deposited in special cells in such a manner, however, that their relation with the simpler eyes of the Mollusca and Worms is placed beyond doubt.

Now we have already come to the conclusion that pigment and chlorophyll are different phases of the same substance, and have essentially the same function, i. e. absorption of the chemical rays, or of the energy of the sun. But we can show, by a comparison of the lowest forms of ocelli, such as those formed in Protozoa, Coelenterates and Echinoderms, with those of still higher forms, that the ocelli are the bodies of all others which stand in most intimate and dependent relation with the sunlight; but they are especially characterised by the high form of pigment that they contain; therefore we are led to suppose that the red and black pigment, but principally the former, have in the highest degree the power of absorbing energy from sunlight. If this be true, then the accumulations of pigment cells, called ocelli, are organs especially adapted for the absorption of sun energy. This supposition of course rests entirely upon our former conclusion that animal pigment in general performs a physiological function, and like chlorophyll, absorbs energy from the sunlight.

This conclusion appears more reasonable to us on account of the many difficulties which may thus be accounted for, as well as the impossibility of explaining these difficulties in any other manner known to us. In the first place. I believe that no explanation of the function of the ocelli in Coelenterates, Echinoderms, and in such Mollusca as *Chiton*, *Onchidium*, and *Arca*, will be of any value, which does not include the ocelli or pigment spots of Protozoa and plant zoospores. Now to suppose that these ocelli simply distinguish light from darkness is absurd, for we cannot in any case suggest any reasonable necessity for such a power. No one can fail to be impressed by the interesting experiments of Romanes, who has shown that Medusae will collect with great avidity around a ray of sun-light entering a darkened jar. No one would suppose that they enter the light in order to see it! But on the contrary because they receive some benefit from it. But how can this benefit be any other than that received by plants from the sunlight, i.e. energy? Surely no Medusa could escape its enemies or obtain its food any easier with ocelli than without them. But it is possible that it might be able to distinguish with them whether it is at the surface or at a considerable depth, and could then sink to avoid storms, or rise to obtain food. But if we apply this reasoning to *Arca* or *Pectunculus*, it will not work, since both are incapable of motion, while *Arca* is permanently attached by its byssus. Neither can it be shown that *Onchidium* uses its innumerable eyes to escape its enemies — in spite of the reasoning of SEMPER — or to obtain its food. The same difficulties apply to *Chiton*, which is also provided with innumerable eyes in all stages of development; and there can be no doubt that there are many more animals, as yet imperfectly known, which possess so-called eyes as numerous and as anomalous as those found in *Chiton*, *Onchidium*, *Arca*, *Pectunculus*, *Cardium* and *Pecten*, as well as those of many Echinoderms and Coelenterates.

A supposed explanation of these eyes, widely current and apparently generally accepted, is that they are organs for the perception of heat, and that by gradual changes they developed into organs for the perception of light. But I believe it would be perfectly safe to challenge any one to show what advantage it would be for a Protozoan, Coelenterate, or Mollusc, to perceive heat! This theory arose from the frequent presence of black pigment in many less complicated eyes, and consequently it required no great effort of the imagination to suppose that the black surface absorbed the heat, and produced an impression upon the animal. But this supposition was founded upon ignorance, or blindness to the fact that by far the majority of the simplest eyes contain only red pigment, which, as far as we know, has no special power to absorb heat.

Even if we grant that the ocelli distinguish the amount of heat, or even light from darkness, neither supposition would furnish any adequate explanation of the hundreds, and, in some cases, thousands of eyes present in certain Coelenterates and Molluscs. If, according to the existing suppositions, it is difficult to ascribe any function to these numerous ocelli, and therefore any necessity for their existence, it is infinitely more difficult to imagine any sufficient cause for their creation! But I think that it will be generally admitted that all these difficulties are removed, or at least rendered comparatively easy to explain, if we accept the suppositions we have advanced in these pages.

We have offered some reasons for supposing that (1) animal pigment has a physiological activity beneficial to the animal; (2) the activity, and existence of the pigment, depends upon the presence of sunlight; (3) that animal, and plant pigment, or chlorophyll, represent two phases of the same substance, and have essentially the same function, i. e. the absorption from the sunlight of the energy necessary for the maintainance of vital processes; (4) that the highly modified plant or animal pigment, or the red pigment which we shall call ommerythrine, has this property to a special degree. According to these suppositions we have no difficulty in ascribing a necessary function to the simplest ocelli, neither is there any difficulty in tracing an uninterrupted series of changes from collections of pigment or chlorophyll granules, to an undoubted ocellus, and these changes necessitate a corresponding increase of advantages to the animal. We may also follow the development of the simplest ocellus from a red pigment spot of the plant zoospores, to the most perfect Vertebrate eye, without a break in the functional activity of the organ, or in the advantage gained from it by the animal. We can also trace a complete series of changes from the absorption of light energy by means of pigment, or by nerves, up to the perception of light. We are also enabled to account for the increase in the number of the organs in various groups of animals and their subsequent diminution in numbers. It also furnishes us with the only adequate explanation of the number of highly developed eyes in *Pecten*. For instance, in ascending from the Protozoa to the Coelenterates and lower Molluscs, a gradual increase in the number and complexity of these organs is very easily understood, since the more there are, the better it is for the animal. This process would go on until by a very gradual series of changes they were converted into organs capable of perceiving objects, or fine differences in the gradation of light. There would be a tendency for all of the organs to be modified in the same direction, until finally they are converted into many structural eyes (as in *Pecten* and *Arca*). But under general circumstances, the number of eyes necessary for an animal is very small, so that a degeneration would set in by which the organs would be reduced in number. Such appears to be the case with *Pecten* and *Arca*. But in many instances it is supposable that the degeneration would not be rapid, for both functions would be held at once; there would be too many eyes for seeing, but not too many for the absorption of energy. For instance the amount of energy absorbed would depend upon the most perfect condensation of light upon a given area: as we shall see later, this energy is absorbed in the higher forms, directly, by especially modified nerve fibres. Thus it happens that an organ most perfectly adapted for the condensation and absorption of the greatest amount of energy, is likewise perfectly constructed for the perception of objects. The formation of an inverted image in a visual organ is an incidental result of the most advantageous concentration of light; but this is just the condition essential for the most perfect heliophagous organ. Therefore we have an organ that can perform to great advantage two functions at once; this is the essential, and only possible condition, upon which we are able to explain the change of function in organs. However perfect the conditions might be for the perception of objects, no true visual organs would be produced, and therefore no perception of objects, until the various systems of organs were sufficiently developed for the performance of this highly complex process. The construction of the eye of *Charybdaea*, is sufficiently perfect for the perception of objects. But if we imagine the most perfect Vertebrate eye attached to a Coelenterate, there could never be any perception until other faculties were developed in the highest degree. There is a greater difference between the most simple and most complex Vertebrate retina, than between the most simple Invertebrate one and that of *Pecten*. In fact, the latter excels in complexity that of the lower fishes, or of certain reptiles: it also possesses an advantage over the retina of all Vertebrates in the absence of a blind spot.

A simple form of heliophag is a red pigment spot usually situated near the animal pole of a single cell (zoospores and Protozoa). In such cases, no nerve fibres(?) are present, and therefore these receptacles of energy are situated near, or in the centre, of animal activity, that is in the centre of the greatest consumption of energy. In the Coelenterates they are necessarily situated near the nervous system, for the latter is simply an accumulation of ganglionic cells arising from the ocelli and other sense organs to be spoken of later. The ocelli consist of colorless and pigmented cells. The latter are, in nearly all cases, pigmented at their outer ends, and if we suppose, as we have good reason to, that the same method of nerve endings prevails here as in the Mollusca, then there will be the retia terminalia of nerve fibres over the outer ends of the pigmented cells, and therefore exactly in the position necessary to receive the light stimuli given to the pigment, and carry them to the necessary centres.

We often hear it said of any pigmented spot that it is not an eye, but simply a meaningless collection of pigment. No good reason can be given why this should be called a mere pigment spot, and that an eye. We cannot say that one is a pigment spot on account of the absence of nerves, and the other is an eye spot because it is supplied with nerves, because it is to be presumed that nerve fibres of some kind are everywhere present in the skin; and moreover the instances in which actual nerve endings have been proved to be present or absent in pigmented areas of doubtful meaning are extremely few. For instance, one of the pigmented cells in the skin of *Beroe* or of *Phronima* would be considered as pigment spots, but an exactly similar spot on the head of a worm or of a larval Mollusc would be an ocellus! I think it would puzzle those who believe that pigment is a waste product to attempt to define the difference in the function of a pigment spot like that found in the skin of *Phronima*, or in the velum of a larval *Polygordius*, and a simple eye spot or ocellus like that in some Protozoa, or in larval Worms, Molluscs, etc.

In the development of ganglionic, from sense hair cells, we have said that the former were sense cells too delicate for the direct reception of the coarser vibrations, and therefore they were modified for conducting sensations, and other sense cells, for the direct reception of them. This process is somewhat modified for the reception of the most delicate of all vibrations, that of light, in that in the higher forms it is probable that the nerve fibres alone receive the light vibrations.

In the simplest heliophags, the red pigments play the most prominent role.

With the accession of more nerve fibres, an increase in their sensibility, and a more advantageous arrangement, they are enabled to receive the light vibrations directly, without the intervention of pigment. It then becomes difficult to distinguish between pigment destined for the reception of energy, and that for secondary, protective purposes. What might, perhaps, furnish a rather uncertain criterion as to the nature of the pigment, would be its solubility. Chlorophyll, as is well known, is extremely unstable, and soluble in many fluids, even in water, but more especially in alcohol. The pigment of the lower animals is very often soluble in alcohol, the red pigment, almost without exception. The red pigment in the eyes of starfish is entirely dissolved by alcohol (CARRIÈRE). In *Cardium* this is also the case as well as in *Pecten* (at least sections of *Pecten* eyes, killed only with alcohol, were colorless). Sections of the red pigmented eyes of *Euphausia*, treated only with alcohol, are also colorless. The red coloring matter in the rods of the Vertebrates, is destroyed even by a short exposure to the sunlight. But it is well known that the pigment in certain compound eyes is extraordinarily difficult to dissolve. Such pigment is undoubtedly of a protective nature, as we have various reasons for believing. The pigment spots of *Phronima* are dissolved with sublimate, so is also the brownish red pigment on the wart-like papillae in the skin of *Pterotrachea*, as well as the black pigment of the eye. It can be no mere accident that the eye-spots of zoospores and of almost all Protozoa, Coelenterates, and Echinoderms, should be red as well as the tapetum of the eyes of *Pecten*, *Alciopa*, and *Euphausia*. Wherever the eyes appear to be entirely black, they will probably be found to contain a mixture of red and black pigment, producing brown, or the red pigment will be found in the rods alone. It also appears that the red color, like the reflecting surfaces, is best developed in the eyes of nocturnal, or deep sea animals.

The appearance of retinophorae, and the arrangement around them of pigment cells, is an extremely primitive and universal arrangement. In the Coelenterates, the retinophorae seem, from their shape and general appearance, to be true sense cells. It seems to be a general law that all sense cells are colorless.

The most economic distribution of a given number of pigmented, and sense cells upon a given area, so that each pigment cell should touch a nervous one, would be the arrangement of the pigmented cells in a single circle around each colorless or nervous one: then, since the nerve fibrillae are distributed over the walls of the colorless cells, they would come in contact at all points with the pigment of the surrounding cells. This might possibly account for the first appearance of the ommatidia; but I am inclined to regard the subsequent, progressive development of the retia terminalia overying the colorless cells, as being due, as already remarked, to the appearance of the refractive granules, in consequence of which the overlying nerve fibrillae, or the retinidium of the retinophora, became doubly irritated, by the incident rays, as well as by the same when reflected by the refractive plates or globules beneath. The rods of the retinophorae owe their predominant development not only to the underlying reflectors, but also to the presence of the axial nerve, which reached its position by the union of two adjacent cells, and the disappearance, partial (Insects, Crustacea etc.) or complete (*Pecten*, Cephalopods, etc.), of the apposed cell walls. **This axial nerve permits the most economic arrangement in etages of radiating fibrillae, which are always at right angles to the direction of the rays of light.** By the concentration of the latter at varying levels, perfectly distinct impressions would be produced, a result that could not be obtained by simple and vertical axial fibres.

The retinophorae, without exception, seem to be double in the Mollusca, and probably in the Worms as well. In the Coelenterates, they appear to be single, but it is not improbable that a closer examination would in some cases show them to be double also. That the retinophorae are double in the Vertebrates we have the very best reason to believe, owing to the presence of the axial nerve fibre and the two nuclei.

A moments consideration will show that »rudimentary« eyes are not the only dynamophagous organs of the lower animals. The numerous otolithic sacs found in certain Coelenterates have been regarded as rudimentary hearing organs; but I think it would puzzle any one to explain why it is necessary for a Medusa to hear. It is absurd to suppose that these organs enable them to escape their enemies better, or to obtain more food. If it is difficult to ascribe any adequate function to these organs, which have, even in the Coelenterates, reached a high stage of development, how much more difficult is it to discover any sufficient explanation of how, and by what agency they reached their present development, or how they were first brought into existence. For although an organ for the transmission of sound vibrations into corresponding nerve sensations is very useful to the higher animals, which are able to distinguish between the different kinds, it would be absurd to suppose that a Coelenterate, with its simple organization, could make a similar use of such an organ.

Surely, then, these otolithic sacs cannot function as auditory organs, in the ordinary sense of the term; but that they are homologous with them, or have an analogous function, i. e. the reception of vibrations, is beyond doubt. We are therefore compelled to assume that they, like the eyes, are structures which have, or may have, two different functions; that construction most advantageous for the performance of the first being likewise most favorable for the performance of the second. When the structure of the organ reached this condition, equally favorable for the performance of either function, then the transfer of function took place.

The difficulty of accounting for these organs according to the generally accepted, or prevalent views has led me to explain their existence by supposing that they are not organs by which the animal becomes cognizant of certain vibrations, but organs for the reception, and for the conversion, of these vibrations into nerve stimuli. Upon these stimuli, together with those received by other organs, depends the entire activity of the animal. There is no such thing as voluntary muscular contraction in these simple organisms. All the contractions depend upon stimuli received from without, and which are carried by the nerves to the contractile organs; however slight these irritations are, still they are forms of energy and just the energy, or force, necessary to liberate that potential energy contained in complex protoplasmic compounds, in the shape of motion. The stimuli may also be used for the concentration of the energy contained in comparatively large quantities of matter into a much smaller volume. Additional stimuli liberate the energy as motion. It is very probable that all sense hair cells convert the energy of movement, or coarser vibrations, into nervous stimuli.

The amount of work done by these stimuli depends upon the amount lost in receiving and transmitting them, or, in other words, upon the delicacy of the sense cells and nerve fibres. Therefore the isolated and unprotected sense cells tend to accumulate in groups, sheltered in pits or sacs. Accessory bodies in favorable positions, as otoliths, are added to incorporate the vibrations, so to speak. Now a Medusa may possess an otolithic sac capable of recording to perfection the finer vibrations, and converting them into corresponding nerve sensations;

but little more could be said of any auditory organ; yet, in spite of this fact the Medusa would be infinitely removed from hearing. But such a structure could at once become a true auditory organ as soon as the animal was sufficiently organized to distinguish, by association, certain vibrations from others, so that some would cause contractions, and others, equally strong, would not. This definition is an arbitrary one, but it appears probable that some such change must have taken place in all auditory organs, at one time or another, just as in the eye. It would be, however, extremely difficult to decide, in innumerable cases, whether a certain animal with an otolithic sac simply received a constant current of stimuli through it, or whether it was able to associate certain kinds of vibration with certain conditions, so that different muscular contractions would follow. This, however, carries us away from our subject into the uncertain domain of the origin of the will.

Physiologists consider that the constant semi-contracted condition of the muscles in the human body, is due to a constant stream of impressions, however minute, received from the skin and sense organs. It is a well known fact that the otoliths of a great many Mollusca and Worms are in a constant state of vibration, so that a stream of energy must be transmitted, by the sense hairs receiving the blows of the otoliths, through the nerves, to the various centres where the consumption of energy takes place.

Another form of sense hair cells is that which records the impressions produced by various changes in the chemical composition of fluids or gases, giving rise to the perception of taste or smell. These processes are much more obscure than those of hearing. Smell and taste cells are, undoubtedly, modifications of the same elements, for functioning under different conditions: the distinction between them is without doubt, wanting in the Invertebrates, and possibly in many Vertebrates.

It is possible that the so-called olfactory pits of the Coelenterates, Mollusca, and Worms arose as modifications of ciliated respiratory cells. Let us suppose a patch of ciliated cells, either used for locomotion or respiration; now it is known that in some way or other carbonic acid gas acts as a stimulus, and causes, for a certain time, renewed activity; it is not improbable that other noxious substances would produce the same effect. It is also probable that some of the cells would be more affected by certain compounds than others. Such cells, from being at first simply stimulated by certain fluids or compounds, would, by a series of changes exactly similar to those undergone by the auditory and visual cells, be converted into cells especially sensitive to these changes.

We have already seen how constant the two kinds of cells are in the lower forms of eyes, and how a single or compound sense cell is surrounded by pigmented ones. A remarkable similarity maybe found in the arrangement of those sense cells supposed to have the function of testing the chemical composition of the water.

Over a year ago, before the present paper was thought of, I made some studies upon the sense papillae of Mollusca, especially of *Pecten* and *Haliotis*, and, in looking over the drawings then made, I find that they confirm, in general, my conclusion concerning the structure and innervation of the sense cells, and their gradual transformation into ganglionic ones. There are several points which I desire to examine once more before publication, but one or two facts will be of interest to us here. In *Haliotis*, each papilla contains a central core of twelve sense cells ending inwardly in as many single fibrous prolongations, while their distal extremities, just beneath the tip of the papilla, are fused into a single, protoplasmic mass. The tip of the papilla is surrounded by a perfect circle of numerous, stiff sense hairs, each of which is connected with the fused ends of the sense cells by a minute fibre. The wall of the papilla is clothed with trumpet-shaped sense cells ending in single fibres. Each papilla also contains 8 very large, club-shaped and gland-like cells filled with innumerable, but distinct, refractive bodies, and extending the whole length of the papilla, terminating at the outer extremity in a bent end. They form a not very compactly arranged circle around the central core of sense cells.

In *Pecten*, the papillae are essentially of the same structure, but smaller. The bunch of sense cells is reduced to eight, while there is only one large gland-like cell.

In *Lima*, there are no sense papillae, but the long tentacles contain rings of sensory and gland cells, with smooth intervening spaces, which cause a jointed appearance. Some of the gland-like cells are enormous, and are usually arranged in twos: between their outer ends is a minute sense cell ending, externally, in a tuft of stiff hairs, and inwardly in a long fibre. The sense cell is therefore enclosed in a circle of two, large gland cells.

In the organs of taste, and in the sense organs of the lateral line, the sense hair cells are usually arranged in groups, surrounded by circles of large gland-like cells, often called support cells. The almost constant, if not universal association of these gland cells, with sensory ones renders it certain that they have an important physiological function to perform.

The gland cells in Mollusca contain a transparent substance which expands enormously when brought in contact with water: — I believe that they also possess the power to absorb to a great degree gases or other substances held in solution. It has been suggested that the slime cells are closely united with sense hairs so that the slightest irritation would cause the immediate secretion of the slime, which might have a poisonous property. This explanation sounds fairly reasonable when applied to the Mollusca; but it loses its force when applied to the sense organs of the lateral line, or to the organs of taste in the Vertebrates. Whatever effects this absorption has upon the gland cells, causing contraction or expansion, or concentration of the foreign gases or fluids, — could then be transmitted to the adjacent sense cells. It is difficult to imagine just how an odor, a gas, or any foreign substance held in solution, would affect a sense cell, but they surely do affect them in some way, causing distinct sensations. If we had certain cells placed around the sensory one, for the absorption of these gases or fluids, then the effect would be intensified, or much smaller quantities of foreign matter would cause sensations. If this be true, then one of the sense papillae of *Haliotis*, or groups of cells in *Lima*, might be compared with an ommatidium. In both there are central sense cells surrounded by pigmented, or glandular ones, for the absorption, and therefore intensification, of that particular form of vibration for which the organ is developed.

It is extremely difficult to express in words the difference between a respiratory, or locomotive cell, which is simply irritated to renewed activity by the presence of irritating substances in the water, and one which is a pure sense cell, or destined simply for the reception of such stimuli, which are then transferred to other cells. But we may say that, in general, all cells are susceptible to stimuli from without. Each one may receive directly only stimuli enough to sustain its own vital processes; when, however, it receives more stimuli than are necessary, the surplus being transmitted to other cells, it becomes a sense cell, or a cell specially adapted for the reception of stimuli.

Animals receive stimuli, or energy, in various forms: from the sun, sound, movements and chemical compounds, and they have various forms of organs for the reception of each form of energy. Plants, however, have but one kind of dynamophagous organ, i. e. chlorophyll, which absorbs only solar energy.

The fully developed eyes of the Vertebrates, and higher Invertebrates, bear the same relation to the isolated ommatidia that the highly developed organs of smell and hearing do to the isolated tactile and olfactory hairs of the lower Invertebrates. In both cases the functional perfection of the fully developed organ depends, primarily, upon the accumulation of the constituent elements at definite localities and their coincident, progressive development; and secondarily, upon the addition of organs for the accumulation or intensification of the vibrations to be transmitted to the seat of perception. In the lower forms, as in the Coelenterates, the sense organs, ocelli, otolithic sacs, olfactory pits, and sense hair papillae, or tentacles, are mainly confined to a narrow ring surrounding the digestive tract. As we have said, the acquirement of certain properties by certain cells of a colony necessitates the loss in a corresponding degree of other faculties. But this loss is, on the other hand, made good by the special development in neighboring cells of those properties lost by the other, and a loss of those it had gained. The dynamophagous, and hylophagous faculties were the first to be specialized. The latter cells were, by the laws governing segmentation, confined to the so-called vegetative pole, while, immediately around them, was formed a ring of sensory cells, increasing in sensitiveness according as the vegetative cells lost this faculty. As this sensory ring was more specialized, its cells became modified in different directions for the reception of various forms of energy, or irritants, giving rise, in close proximity to each other, to ocelli, otolithic sacs, olfactory pits, and sense hair cells.

The almost universal presence, in all kinds of eyes, of some reflecting body showing the greatest variety in structure and origin, indicates that it must have some very important function to perform in the process of vision. Just as pigment, the reflecting body or argentea, may be found in two different localities, where the part it has to play must be essentially different. For instance, reflecting membranes may be found outside the eye, as in Fishes, Cephalopods, Worms etc. or within the eye, behind the retinidia. In the first instance they serve, instead of pigment, for the exclusion of lateral rays of light. The latter they have another purpose, that of reflecting the light so that it passes a second time through the nerve fibrillae of the retinidia; in other words the argentea, instead of absorbing, like pigment. the rays of light, reflects them, so that the intensity of the light irritation is doubled. The argentea has, then, a function not necessary for the perception of light and it may be absent or present according to the habits of the animal. Nocturnal ones, which must make the most of the little light at their disposal, are consequently well provided with the reflecting surfaces. Those fishes which are best provided with reflectors are either nocturnal, or live in deep water where there is little light.

Many animals, as *Cardium*, *Arca* and *Pecten*, are provided with numerous eyes, rather for the reception of great quantities of light than for fine destinctions of its gradation. Such animals are likewise provided with reflecting surfaces for collecting and economizing the light.

In the very simple, isolated ommatidia, the central cell is colorless, and beneath the retinidium is a layer of refractive granules which, as we may easily see upon a superficial examination, act as minute reflectors to the rays of light which have passed the overlying retinidia. We have here the explanation of the almost universal absence of pigment in the retinophorae, and the predominance which their retinophorae have acquired over those of the pigment cells.

The brilliant sparkle of the faceted eyes of *Arca* is due to the layer of refractive globules at the base of the retinophorae. In *Pecten* the rods are reversed, and it is therefore impossible for the retinophorae to act as reflectors; therefore a single but large, cellular reflector, the argentea, is formed back of the rods. In this case, the argentea has become so perfectly developed in its reflective powers and curvature that rays of light, forming inverted images upon the rods, are perfectly reflected by the argentea, and again brought to a focus so as to form a second image upon the first (Pl. 32, fig. 119). It is extremely probable that the argentea of the Vertebrate eye fulfils the same function as that of *Pecten*.

Just as the formation of inverted images upon the retina is an incidental result of the best concentration of light upon a given surface, so is the formation of a second image by the argentea an incidental result of the most perfect reflection of the light. It is also worthy of notice that both the reflected and incident rays are approximately parallel with the rods through which they pass, and therefore parallel with the axial fibres. but at right angles to the fibrillae of the retinidia.

In the Insecta and Crustacea, the frequent presence of the swelling at the base of the retinophorae, or the pedicel, composed of alternating layers of differently refractive plates, the arrangement of whose surfaces is so admirably adapted for reflecting light, indicates that they may have a function similar to that of the argentea. This supposition is strengthened by the fact that such structures are often found in nocturnal Insects.

The views expressed concerning the function of the argentea were the result of the direct observation of a second image in the retina of *Pecten*. I inspected all the more probable sources in hopes of finding some hint as to the function of the argentea in other animals, but without success. Even in the large Physiology of HERMANN, in WIEDERSHEIM's Comparative Anatomy of the Vertebrates, and in the Histological text-books, I could find no hint or reference to the subject. After my notes upon the argentea were completed, Prof. DOHRN very kindly called my attention to LEUCKART's summary in the Handbuch der Augenheilkunde of GRAEFE and SAEMISCH, p. 218, where he speaks of the argentea as intensifying the light effect, in that it causes the same ray to pass twice through the same rod. Although there is an agreement between these views, which appear to have been neglected by later writers, and those expressed above, concerning the ultimate effect produced by the argentea, i. e. to intensify the light irritation, there is a radical difference in the manner in which we believe such an effect is produced. According to the view elucidated by LEUCKART, first expressed by BRÜCKE 52a) and subsequently repeated by HELMHOLTZ (52b) a ray of light once entering a rod could not leave it on account of the different refractive indices of the cortical layer of the rod and the axial portion; each rod would be acted upon by an incident and reflected ray, both following approximately the longitudinal axis of the rod. According to this view, then, since the rods are parallel with each other, all the incident and reflected rays would also be parallel, and neither an incident nor a reflected image could be formed! That such an effect does not obtain is evident from the fact that a second image is actually formed by the argentea of *Pecten*, proving that the rays of light do not become parallel owing to the reflection caused by the sheath of the rod. In *Pecten*, at least, the rods form a perfectly continuous layer: the difference between the refractive index of the axial core and that of the rod sheath is, in all probability, produced by the differentiating effect of the reagents. That these changes are probably artificial and post-mortem is shown by examining the fresh retina, or lens, when it will be seen that the difference between the refractive indices of the nuclei, cell walls, and protoplasm, is so slight as to produce no disturbing optical effect.

The difference between the refractive index of the nuclei and that of the surrounding bodies is greater than that between the sheaths of the rods and their axial cores; but the light passes without any disturbing effect through several layers of large nuclei and thick cell walls, so that it is not probable that the rods, which are much more homogeneous, would cause any breaking up of the rays of light.

As we construe the facts, the result would be that the rays of light from any external object are brought to a focus upon a definite niveau in the layer of rods, and there act upon a certain layer of cross. retinidial fibrillae, producing at that point an impression of an image; the divergent rays then impinge upon the concave argentea, and, by reflection, come again to a focus in exactly the same place as before, and therefore upon exactly the same set of cross fibrillae. In all parts of the rod layer, except at the common points where both incident and reflected images are formed, no distinct impression will be produced except that of light.

Chapter VII. Remarks upon the Classification of Eyes.

The facts and deductions stated in the foregoing pages tend to show that all eyes consist of ommatidia, upon the construction and arrangement of which depends the perfection of the eye. Therefore any classification of eyes should be founded upon the modification of the ommatidia. But it is certain that many complex eyes have originated independently, in very limited groups of animals. Therefore we can classify eyes, (1) as organs which attain essentially the same ends by various means. Such a classification would entirely ignore the genetic relation of the animals possessing the various types of organs. (2) We may classify eyes — having principally in view the genetic relationship of their possessors. On account of the frequent, independent development of eyes in closely related forms, the latter method cannot be logically applied except in restricted groups, and even then with considerable uncertainty.

GRENACHER (39) is inclined to lay great stress upon the fact that the retina in Cephalopods and Heteropods is single layered. His arguments in favor of his opinion are remarkable ones. He says, p. 216: »Am prägnantesten gebe ich vielleicht dem scharfen Gegensatz, in dem ich mich darin zu meinen Vorgängern finde, dadurch Ausdruck, dass ich überhaupt eine »Schichtung« der uns hier beschäftigenden Retina nicht anerkennen kann, und den Gebrauch dieses Wortes als inadäquat dem wirklichen Sachverhalte verwerfen muss. Der Ausdruck ist ein Überbleibsel einer irrigen Auffassung und Deutung der Beobachtungen, daher bei der Einführung einer neuen, besseren, zweckmäßig völlig zu cassiren; mag er für die Wirbelthierretina auch noch so gut am Platze sein, hier, wie überhaupt bei Evertebraten, ist er es nicht. Man halte es nicht für bloße Wortklauberei, wenn ich ihn beseitigt wünsche; die Worte des wissenschaftlichen Sprachgebrauches sollen doch ein möglichst richtiges Bild, nicht aber falsche Vorstellungen von den Dingen, die sie zu bezeichnen haben, geben. — Ein Beispiel wird wohl am besten zeigen, aus welchen Gründen ich den Ausdruck beanstande. Sicht man einer aufgestellten Reihe Menschen, etwa Soldaten, entlang, spricht man da von einer »Schicht« Köpfe, einer Brust-, Bauch-, Bein-»Schicht«? Genau so, wie hier Kopf, Brust, Bauch und Beine integrirende Bestandtheile derjenigen Individualitäten sind, aus denen sich die ganze Reihe zusammensetzt, genau so sind auch die Zellenschicht, Pigmentschicht, Stäbchenschicht nur gebildet aus Differenzirungsproducten derjenigen Einheiten, aus denen sich die Retina aufbaut: der Retinazellen.«

He has made a most excellent comparison, but unfortunately for him it proves just the opposite of what he desired! According to this comparison, the different zones are formed by the different parts of exactly similar cells: that is if there is a rod layer, a pigmented layer, etc., there should be a corresponding part in each and every cell. That is, every cell should have a rod, a pigmented band, a colorless portion etc. This he knows is absurd and cannot be true, for in the Arthropods there are several rows of pigment cells: some secrete rods and some do not, and again some are colorless and give rise to the crystalline cones. In *Limulus* and *Scorpio*, LANKESTER has proven that there are two or three layers of pigment cells which secrete no rods, while there are colorless cells which do. In the Cephalopods and Heteropods he has just taken especial pains to demonstrate that there are two destinct and widely different kinds of cells present, some producing the rods, and the others, according to him, secreting the limiting membrane. If he will take the pains to refer to HENSEN's excellent work (12), he will find that the retina of *Pecten* consists of two distinct parts, an outer layer of ganglionic cells, and an inner one consisting of the retinophorae bearing the rods. These facts are sufficient to show that GRENACHER's stand on the subject has been poorly chosen. I cannot agree with him, for my own observations tend to show that in all Molluscan eyes, except the faceted ones of *Arca*, there is a tendency for the retinulae, or pigmented cells to lose their rods, and become transformed into ganglionic ones. According as this process is more or less complete, we have a greater or less tendency to form layers of retinulae, ganglionic cells, and retinophorae.

It is difficult to give any satisfactory definition, covering all cases, of a single or double layer of cells. Compound layers may obviously arise in two ways; by folding, or by delamination. He who would regard the retina of Cephalopods, Heteropods, and *Pecten*, for instance, as a single layer, must do the same for the retina of the Vertebrates (not including the choroidea). If we regard the retina of Vertebrates as single layered, because it originated from a single embryonic layer, then we would have the same right to say that the brain consists of a single layer of cells. We would also have to regard the entire ommateum of the compound Arthropod eye, together with its underlying optic ganglion, as forming a single layer, since both have originated from a single row of hypodermic cells. But both of these extremes lead to an evident absurdity. The retina of the Cephalopods or Heteropods is no more formed of a single layer of cells than the optic ganglion and ommateum of the Arthropod eyes: the latter represent an extreme condition of the same kind of change that is going on in the eyes of Cephalopods, *Pecten*, or Vertebrates. In all sensitive layers, a delamination of the single row of embryonic, hypodermic cells, into sense and ganglionic ones, takes place. In Cephalopods for instance, the delamination has resulted in the production of the optic ganglion and the retina, both of which are never entirely separated from each other. The retina then undergoes still further delamination, in that some of its cells become ganglionic, but without being separated any distance from the true sense cells. The retina in Vertebrates has undergone an exactly similar process. The separation of the retina from the optic ganglion (the thalamencephalon) takes place very early, and is modified by secondary changes. A further delamination of the primitive retina into several layers gives rise to numerous strata of ganglionic cells, which only differ from those of the brain in that they are not so far removed from the true sense cells. The same process has occurred in *Pecten*, as well as in *Haliotis*, except that in the latter case the number of ganglionic cells closely united to sensitive ones is very small. In Arthropods, the delamination of the single row of primitive, hypodermic cells early gives rise to the optic ganglion and ommateum, all the ganglionic cells being removed from the ommateum to the optic ganglion. An ommateum therefore consists entirely of sense cells and protective ones, or retinulae: the arrangement of the cells is necessarily such that there is no room for ganglionic ones. This applies to the compound eyes of *Area* as well as those of Crustacea and Insects. In the ommateum, there is a very marked effort to from a single layer, since each of the retinulae and retinophorae, although greatly enlarged at varying levels, invariably extend from the inner to the outer surface of the ommateum. But still in the strictest sense it cannot be regarded as a single layer, since it contains also the nerve fibres, which must be considered as the outer ends of ganglionic cells originally situated between the ommateal cells.

We shall attempt to follow the ommatidia in their various phases of modification.

Among those heliophagous organs less specialized than the ommatidia, may be mentioned chlorophyll, the red eye spots of zoospores and of Protozoa; the ill-defined red, yellowish or black pigment spots found upon the general epithelium, or upon the tentacle tips of larval Echinoderms, Worms etc.; the red, orange, or black, star-shaped chromatophores of many Crustacea and Coelenterates: the chromatophores of Cephalopods, and the beautifully radiating pigment cells so commonly found in the larvae of pelagic fishes. Although the highly complicated Cephalopod chromatophores, the development of which shows that they have several points of resemblance to the ommatidia, may be useful as protective organs, it does not follow that this is their only function, neither could it have been their principal, or original one, for on this supposition we can give no satisfactory explanation of their origin. It is more than probable that they still act as heliophags, and that their protective function is an incidental and secondary one.

There are often very extensive deposits of pigment at the outer ends of epithelial cells in Molluscs, and therefore in just those places where the retia terminalia are most abundant. When the pigment serves a purely protective purpose, it is deposited at the inner ends of the cells, as in the iris of *Pecten*. A still farther differentiation is produced by the development, at certain, limited areas, of a clear space beneath the very outer layer of the cuticula; this space contains the greater part of the retia terminalia, while just beneath is the stratum of pigment.

Beginning with a simple pigmented layer, ommatidia arise by the formation of pigmented cells around a central colorless one provided with a nucleolated nucleus. Such organs undergo the following changes: (1) they collect at certain points to form ommateal tracts; (2) the colorless cells, or retinophorae, become double, and acquire axial nerve fibres; (3) the retinidial cuticula becomes thickened, and over each cell divides into segments, the rods, containing specialized parts of the retia terminalia; and (4) the retinophorae develop argentinulae. Groups of such ommatidia may remain upon an even surface, or become invaginated; in either case they form a retineum (e.g. pseudo-lenticulate eyes of *Arca* or *Haliotis*). If both the retinulae and retinophorae retain their rods, which form a continuous layer, a primitive retineum is produced (e. g. *Haliotis*). If the retinulae still retain their pigment, but lose their rods, a secondary retineum is formed (Heteropods and Alciopidae); this is a condition prior to the formation of a retina. If the ommatidial tract becomes convex, the retinulae lose their rods and form a protective ring around the highly developed rods of the retinophorae. The rods, therefore, no longer form a continuous layer, and an ommateum is produced (compound eyes of *Arca*).

In all Molluscs the rods retain their primitive, terminal position. Arthropods are characterized by the frequent presence of axial rods, the terminal ones being found only in the simplest ocelli. In the latter case the ommatidia form invaginate retinea which may without other change be gradually converted into an invaginate ommateum, by the development of axial rods in the retinophorae (Spiders, Scorpions and *Limulus*). In the latter genera, the retinophorae increase to five or ten in number. By the evagination of the cup-like ommateum, this form reaches its highest perfection, giving rise to the compound eyes of Insects and Crustacea; during this process, the retinophorae of each ommatidium increase to four in number.

By the great development of the retinophorae and their rods, and the conversion of the retinulae into colorless, ganglionic cells, a retina is formed (*Pecten* and Vertebrates). The latter always contains a great many ganglionic cells in intimate association with the retinophorae. In a retineum, there are very few ganglionic cells; in the ommateum there are none.

In a retina, the inverted position of the rods is due to the development of the outer wall of the optic vesicle, instead of the inner.

Some of the more important groups of ommatidia may be arranged in the following manner:

Ommatidia.

I. ommatidia diffuse.	(A') chromatophores; (modified ommatidia)		
	(B) isolated ommatidia:	Coelenterates. (?) Molluscs. Crustacea. (?) Worms. (?) (Universal. (?))
II. ommatidia aggregate.	(A) ommatidial tracts:	retinidial cuticula, thin; no rods developed.	(Mollusca.)
	(B) pseudo-lenticulate:	ommatidial tracts, non-invaginate, or but slightly so; rods form a lens shaped, unprotected protuberance.	pseudo lenticulate eyes of Arca and of Coelenterates.
	(C) invaginate: (a') retineum:	(1) primary: optic cups. or vesicles; corneal cuticula forms a vitreous body ± a primary lens.	Coelenterata, Mollusca, Worms.
		(2) secondary: optic vesicles; tripoblastic: vitreous body ± primary¹ or secondary lenses.	Arthropod ocelli. Stemma.
	(b) retina:	optic vesicle: anterior wall forms the retina: tripoblastic: cellular lens.	Pecten and Vertebrates.
	(c) ommateum:	optic vesicles: cuticula lens. single and secondary.	Spiders. Scorpio. Limulus.
	(D) evaginate: ommateum.	(1) monoblastic: corneal cuticula present, but no lens is formed.	Arca, Pertunculus.
		(2) dipoblastic: a modified optic vesicle: corneal cuticula present forming no lens. or many.	Compound Eye of Insects and Crustacea.

---

¹ A primary cuticular lens is one formed by the corneal cuticular within the optic vesicle; a secondary one is formed by the cuticula of the hypodermis overlying the optic vesicle.

Technique.

Notwithstanding the fact that a considerable number of workers have given their attention to the study of the eyes of *Pecten* and related genera, no progress in our knowledge of these interesting organs has been made since HENSEN published his studies upon the eyes of the Cephalopods; indeed many points, clearly demonstrated by him, were by later writers entirely overlooked.

If we have made any addition to the knowledge of this subject, it is only because the treatment to which the tissues are now subjected allows us to demonstrate with ease what, twenty years ago, would have been impossible. As it required much time and patience to find a reagent with which the eyes could be properly preserved, it will, perhaps, not be amiss if I should describe the methods by which the results given above have been obtained.

In the study of the various components of these complicated organs, it was necessary to resort to different methods for the study of different parts; no one treatment was found by which all the facts given could be observed. Almost any of the ordinary reagents would preserve sufficiently well the cells of the cornea, iris and lens. More care in the choice of fixing reagents was necessary for a proper treatment of the outer ganglionic layer and the retinal cells, while it was only after repeated trials of all the reagents at my command, with their various combinations and methods of application, that I was, at last, enabled to obtain the rods, with their complex network of ganglionic fibres, in a tolerable state of preservation.

The eyes of *Pecten* have been studied fresh, as well as by means of sections and maceration. The principle underlying my whole method of treatment, when sections have not been used, has been to harden the tissues a very little, and then macerate. After staining in picro-carmine, which I consider in such cases to be better than alcoholic solutions, the isolated cells are examined in a medium with a very low index of refraction; either distilled water or the macerating fluid. When I desired to keep the preparations for further study, I was obliged to use acetate of potash, a good preserving medium with a low index of refraction, but for soft macerated cells, it must be used with great care, for it often causes considerable shrinkage.

The young *Pectens*, from 1 to 3 mm long, were thrown into a mixture of equal parts of concentrated sublimate and picro-sulphuric acid, and, after being fixed, were washed in 35, and 70% alcohol. The shells are then opened and the edges of the mantle dissected out with needles. In this manner, the shape of the mantle is retained, whereas if removed before hardening it becomes very much coiled and twisted by the reagent. If now one tries to cut the curved mantle edge, it will be a mere chance if accurate cross sections are obtained. Moreover, one is never sure of getting sections of eyes in the desired stages. To save time, I cut each mantle edge, according to its size and curvature, into three or four pieces, which are then tolerably straight. As many as 20 or 30 of these pieces, after being stained etc., are transferred to a watch-glass full of melted paraffine. With a little care, 10 or 12 pieces, with their long axes parallel, may be arranged in a bundle on the bottom of the watch-glass. After cooling, the bundle may be cut out and sectioned »in toto«.

Weak solutions of sulphuric acid in sea water (15 drops to 30 grams) have been used with good results: the only drawback to this reagent is the difficulty of getting a sharp stain. KLEINENBERG's alcoholic haematoxylin seems to give the best results. There are difficulties in using sulphuric acid: for it is necessary to fix the mantle while still attached to the shell, so that crystals, seriously interfering with the sectioning, are precipitated upon the tissues. Some of the sections were examined in balsam, others in glycerine or acetate of potash. A large number of sections both of young and adult eyes were mounted in Sandarack dissolved in absolute alcohol. For fibrous structures and very fine nerves, it gave good results on account of its low index of refraction, but at the end of two or three weeks the sections were absolutely worthless.

In order to study the very complex structure of the adult eye, it was found necessary to resort to a different reagent for almost every component of the eye. A great deal of time was spent in trying to discover some method by which good sections could be obtained, showing, at the same time, all the various structures.

One of the most useful reagents was chromic acid[1]; the most varied results were obtained by different methods of application as regards strength, time of action, and temperature of the solution, or by various combinations of all three. For instance chromic acid of $1/20$ to $1/5$ %, for 30 to 40 hours, utterly failed to give any conception of the

---

[1] All solutions of chromic acid were made from a 1% solution in distilled water, subsequently diluted with sea water.

structure of the rods, while other parts of the retina, and of the eye itself, were well preserved: but when allowed to act for half an hour, at a temperature of from 50 to 55° C., the most perfectly preserved rods with their nervous networks were obtained, while, on the other hand, the remaining tissues became so granular and homogeneous as to be unfit for study. Chromic acid, $1/10\%$, when allowed to act from one to three or four days, did not give good results, whereas, if the eyes were placed in $1/10\%$ for half an hour, in order to kill them, and then left for twenty-four hours in $1/20\%$ chromic acid, and twenty-four hours more in $1/10\%$, and finally for forty-eight to sixty hours in $1/5\%$, the best results, as regards a good fixation of all the parts of the eye, were obtained.

For the cornea and general epithelium, picro-chromic acid gave the best results. In such preparations, the teeth of the cornea and of the pigmented epithelium may be most easily seen.

The lens is best prepared for sections by either sulphuric, or picro-sulphuric acid; by the first reagent, the shape is best retained, and the lens itself is less liable to be drawn away from the surrounding tissue; the latter reagent, however, brings out more sharply the configuration of the cells, and allows a better stain of the nuclei to take place.

Treatment with chromic acid, $1/5\%$ for twenty-four hours, gives the best result for the layer of nervous fibres just below the septum, and also for the outer layer of ganglionic cells and their fibrous prolongations. In order, however, to study to the greatest advantage the arrangement of these fibres, the retinophorae should be somewhat shrunken; this can be done by treating the eyes for two or three days with $1/5\%$ chromic acid.

The retinophorae are well preserved by nearly all the reagents; but either in sublimate, or in picric acid, or in their combinations, they become slightly granular, and remain so closely packed that it is difficult to distinguish the cell boundaries. Chromic acid, by which the cells are somewhat shrunken, gives preparations in which the boundaries and general arrangement of the retinophorae may be most easily studied.

The rods with their retinidia, and the subjacent vitreous network, are best prepared by treatment with $1/5\%$ chromic acid at 50° C., for $1/2$ an hour. The wall of the rod remains clear and glassy, but slightly tinged with yellow. The central core is less refractive, and with good light the nervous network may be easily seen. I was for a long time greatly puzzled to understand certain structures observed in retinas macerated in weak sulphuric acid. This treatment usually cuts off the ends of the rods, which first become longitudinally striated, or fibrous, leaving the basal ends attached to the retinophorae. Between the remnants of each rod, could then be seen a short, conical projection, attached to the pseudo-membrane. For a long time I regarded these structures, which showed great regularity in shape and position, as a set of cones similar to those of the Vertebrate eye, and belonging to the long and slender retinophorae. But by treatment with hot chromic acid the cones had disappeared, and I finally discovered that they were produced by the sulphuric acid, which coagulated the external nerve fibres of the rods, causing them to adhere to the pseudo-membrane in the shape of the conical projections referred to above. All reagents, applied in whatever manner, caused a disarrangement of the rods, so that, in most cases, the whole retina was drawn away from the sclerotica toward the centre of the eye, leaving a larger or smaller space between the bases of the rods and the argentea. When hot chromic acid of $60^°$ C., or picro-sulphuric acid of the same temperature, was used, the effect was nearly obviated, but on the other hand, the relations of the retina, lens etc., to each other were greatly disturbed. In order to obtain the best preparations, with all the parts in the most natural position, it is necessary to kill the eyes first with $1/10\%$ chromic acid for $1/2$ hour, then allow them to remain in chromic acid, $1/2\%$ for 24 hours; $1/10\%$ for 24 hours; and finally $1/5\%$ for 48 hours or more[1]. Next to this method, I think that solutions of sulphuric acid (20 drops to 50 grams) give the best preparations for every thing except the rods.

The double layer of the sclerotica, and the fibres penetrating it, can be seen in sections of eyes treated for 24 hours in $1/5\%$ chromic acid. Besides these methods almost all the other reagents have been tried, in different combinations and at different temperatures, but with poor results.

Maceration and dissection.

For isolation of the pigmented epithelial cells, and the cells of the cornea, weak solutions of MÜLLER's fluid, or bichromate of potash, gave excellent results. For the maceration of all other elements, I have used

---

[1] The smaller eyes of other species of *Pecten* are much more easily prepared, but, on account of their small size, are not so good for study.

either weak chromic. or sulphuric acid. For the outer ganglionic cells, which are very difficult to isolate, maceration in $1/50\%$ chromic acid gave excellent results, after previously fixing the tissue in $1/5\%$ for a few minutes.

For the retinophorae, $1/20\%$ chromic acid for 4 or 5 days proved very useful.

Treatment with sulphuric acid, 5 drops to 30 grams of sea water, gave the very best results for the nerve endings in the retinophorae, — not in the rods — and for the nervous, inner prolongations of the outer ganglionic cells. It was only by prolonged maceration, twenty days or more, that the inner ganglionic cells could be separated from the retinophorae.

In order to isolate pieces of the cornea with the subjacent pseudocornea and the circular fibres on the outer surface of the lens, it is better to macerate the eyes in sulphuric acid. In the same way, the lens, which, by this treatment, retains to perfection its natural shape, may be dissected out and studied to advantage.

It is necessary for the study of the circular retinal membrane, the septum, and the retina itself, to isolate the latter intact. Maceration in chromic acid either makes the retina too brittle, or too inconsistent, while the nerve fibres of the axial nerve branch remain so firmly attached to the retina that it is difficult to isolate it without injury. But this may be easily and successfully done by maceration, for 1 or 2 days, in a weak solution of sulphuric acid. By this treatment, the retina, together with the septum and circular retinal membrane, remains intact, while its connections with the wall of the eye are so weakened that there is little difficulty in detaching the retina entire.

The color of the red pigment layer is destroyed by all reagents except sublimate: but after it is once fixed in this manner, it is not altered by any subsequent treatment.

In *Pecten Jacobaeus*, it is only possible to isolate the retinophorae by maceration: by treating with hot chromic acid, their rods may be isolated without the cells.

By macerating the small eyes of *Pecten opercularis* in rather strong sulphuric acid, the entire retinophorae together with the rods may be isolated, giving very instructive preparations.

The peripheral, outer ganglionic cells may be seen by macerating the eyes for 24 or 48 hours in sulphuric acid, and then studying the outer surface of the isolated retina.

The argentea may be very easily separated in large sheets, by macerating for 4 or 5 days in bichromate of potash.

Sulphuric acid has proved to be a most valuable macerating, as well as preservative reagent. In weak solutions (40 drops to 50 grams entire Molluscs, without the shell, have been kept in a perfect state of preservation for more than six months. For cilia and nerve endings, it is exceptionally good. Besides preserving the lens, which may subsequently be isolated in perfect condition, it has been of great value in isolating the entire retina, the different layers of which may then be studied »in toto«.

In the study of the eyes of *Arca* as well as those of *Pectunculus*, I have had special recourse to maceration of the eyes either in MÜLLER's fluid or chromic acid. I find that the use of undiluted MÜLLER's fluid for 24 hours gives more satisfactory preparations than a weak solution for a longer period. Chromic acid ($1/5 \%$) for 10 or 12 days gave most of the preparations from which my drawings of the nerve endings were made. I have found that a few drops of acetic and osmic acid added to distilled water give a very energetic macerating fluid for the epithelium of marine Mollusca. It was in preparations made in this way that I first observed, in the compound eyes of *Arca*, the very delicate continuations of the inner ends of the pigmented cover cells to the outer surface. My studies upon this subject have convinced me of the very great importance of a thorough control over a good method of isolating the cells. I have not found any method by which all the structures of the cells could be equally well preserved: it was, therefore, necessary to use several different macerating fluids in order to discover the effects of each fluid upon the individual elements, so that by comparison we might distinguish between the pathological and normal characters. Besides preparations of isolated cells, I have studied sections of the mantle edge fixed in picro-chromic-osmic (FOL), and chromo-acetic-osmic acid, as well as in picro-sulphuric acid.

Die Redaction erlaubt sich zu pag. 687 eine Anmerkung. Während des Druckes der PATTEN'schen Arbeit hatten die Herren PAUL MAYER und WILH. GIESBRECHT die hier seltene Gelegenheit, 3 große lebende Exemplare von *Euphausia* (⚥ mit Embryonen) zu untersuchen. Isolirte und während der Beobachtung mit dem zusammengesetzten Mikroskope unter dem Deckglase zerquetschte Brustaugen leuchteten stark; das Licht strahlte höchst wahrscheinlich vom Stäbchenbündel aus. Ein unverletztes Thier wurde in der Rückenlage mit Ammoniaklösung gereizt; sofort traten sämmtliche sog. Augen als eben so viele leuchtende Punkte hervor, während der Rest des Körpers dunkel blieb. Etwa $^1/_2$ Minute lang leuchteten die Brust- und Bauchorgane lebhaft, die Organe in den Stielen der zusammengesetzten Augen schwächer; selbst im Halbdunkel waren die blaugrünen Lichtpunkte mit bloßem Auge deutlich sichtbar. Die Angaben von SARS erfahren hierdurch eine Bestätigung.

Literature.

Pecten.

1. Poli, Xaverio Josepho, Testacea utrisque Siciliae, etc. T. II. 1795. *Spondylus Gaideropus:* pl. XX fig. 1, 2, 4 and 5, p. 107. *Pecten Jacobaeus:* pl. XXVII fig. 5, 14 and 15, p. 153.
2. Garner, Robert, On the Nervous System of Molluscous Animals. in: Trans. Linn. Soc. London 1837, p. 488. Figures are given in: On the Anatomy of the Lamellibranchiata Conchiferous Animals. in. Trans. Zool. Soc. London. Vol. II., 1841. Pl. 19 fig. 1 and 3.
3. Krohn, A., Über augenähnliche Organe bei *Pecten* und *Spondylus*. in: Arch. Anat. Phys. 1840. p. 381—386. Taf. 11.
4. Grube, E., Über Augen bei Muscheln. in: Arch. Anat. Phys. 1840. p. 24—35, Taf. 3 Fig. 1—3.
5. Will, Fr., Über die Augen der Bivalven und der Ascidien. in: Froriep, Neue Notizen aus dem Gebiete d. Nat. u. Heilkunde. Bd. 29, 1844. p. 81—87 und 99—103.
6. Chiaje, St. delle, Miscellanea Anatomico Patologica etc. Tomo II. Napoli 1847. Spiegaz. delle fig: Tav. 70 fig. 16, 17 and 18.
7. Siebold, C. Th. v., Lehrbuch der vergleichenden Anatomie der wirbellosen Thiere. Berlin 1848. p. 261.
8. Duvernoy, G. L., Mémoire sur le système nerveux des Acéphales. in: Mém. Acad. Sc. Tome 24. 1852.
9. Leydig, Franz, Lehrbuch der Histol. des Menschen u. der Thiere. Frankfurt a. M. 1857. p. 261.
10. Bronn, Classen und Ordnungen etc. Bd. 3. Abth. I. 1862.
11. Keferstein, Wilhelm, Untersuchungen über niedere Seethiere. IX. Über den Bau der Augen von *Pecten*. in: Zeit. f. w. Zool. 12. Bd. 1862. p. 133—136. Taf. 7.
12. Hensen, V., Über das Auge einiger Cephalopoden. Zeit. f. w. Zool. 15. Bd. 1865.
13. Chatin, J., Bulletin de la Société Philomatique. Paris 1877.
14. Gegenbaur, C., Grundriss der vergl. Anat. 2. Aufl. 1878.
15. Hickson, Sidney J., The Eye of *Pecten*. in: Quart. Journ. Micr. Sc. Vol. 20 1880. p. 443—455. Pl. 24 and 25.
16. —— The Eye of *Spondylus*. ibid. Vol. 22. 1882. p. 361—363.
17. Schmidt, E. O., Handbuch der vergl. Anatomie. 8. Aufl. Jena 1882.

18. Sharp, Benj., On the visual Organs in Lamellibranchiata. in: Mitth. Z. Stat. Neapel 5. Bd. 1883.
19. Carrière, J., Die Sehorgane der Thiere. 1885.

Other Molluscs.

20. Babuchin, A., Vergleichende histologische Studien. I. Über den Bau der Cephalopoden-Retina. Würzburger Naturwiss. Zeitschr. 5. Bd. 1864.
21. —— Über den Bau der Netzhaut einiger Lungenschnecken. Sitzungsber. der k. Akademie der Wiss. in Wien. 52. Bd. Abth. 1. 1866. p. 16—27.
22. Hensen, V., Über den Bau des Schneckenauges. in: Arch. f. Mikr. Anatomie 2. Bd. 1866. Pl. 21. p. 399—430.
23. Schultze, M., Die Stäbchen in der Retina der Cephalopoden und Heteropoden. Arch. f. Mikr. Anat. 5. Bd. 1869. Taf. I u. II. p. 1—24.
24. Bonnet, Ch., Collection complète des oeuvres de Ch. Bonnet. Tome. V. 1. 1871.
25. Hoffmann, K., Über die Pars ciliaris Retinae und das Corpus epitheliale lentis des Cephalopodenauges. Über die Stäbchen in der Retina des *Nautilus*. Niederl. Arch. Z. 1. Bd. 1872.
26. Huguenin, Neurologische Untersuchungen. I. Über das Auge von *Helix pomatia*. Zeit. f. w. Zool. 22. Bd. 1872.
27. Grenacher, H., Zur Entwicklungsgeschichte der Cephalopoden. Zeit. f. w. Zool. 24. Bd. 1874.
28. Lankester, E. Ray, Observations on the development of the Cephalopoda. in: Quart. Journ. micr. Sc. Vol. 15. 1875.
29. Rabl, C., Die Ontogenie der Süßwasserpulmonaten. Jena. Zeit. Naturw. 9. Bd. 1875.
30. Simroth, H., Über die Sinneswerkzeuge unserer einheimischen Weichthiere. Zeit. f. w. Zool. 26. Bd. 1876, p. 227—349. Taf. 15—21.
31. Bobretzky, A., Untersuchungen über die Entwickelung der Cephalopoden. Moskau 1877.
32. Semper, C., Über Sehorgane vom Typus der Wirbelthieraugen. Wiesbaden 1877.
33. Rabl, C., Über die Entwicklung der Tellerschnecke. Morph. Jahrbuch. 5. Bd. 1879.
34. Bergh, R., Die Doriopsen des Mittelmeeres. Jahrb. D. Mal. Ges. 12. Jahrg. 1880.
35. Carrière, J., Studien über die Generationserscheinungen bei den Wirbellosen. Würzburg 1880.
36. Fraisse, Paul, Über Molluskenaugen mit embryonalem Typus. Zeit. f. w. Zool. 35. Bd. 1881.
37. Trinchese, S., Per la fauna maritima italiana. Aeolididae e famiglie affini. in: Atti Accad. Lincei (3). Mem. Vol. II. 3—142. 1881.
38. Ryder, J. A., Primitive visual Organs. Science. Vol. II. p. 739. 1883.
39. Grenacher, H., Abhandlungen zur vergleichenden Anatomie des Auges. I. Die Retina der Cephalopoden. Abh. Nat. Ges. Halle. 16. Bd. 1884.
40. Hilger, C., Beiträge zur Kenntnis des Gastropodenauges. Morph. Jahrb. 10. Bd. 1885.
41. Bütschli, O., Nachschrift zu vorstehender Arbeit.
42. Carrière, J., On the Eyes of some Invertebrata. Quart. Journ. Micr. Sc. Vol. 24. 1884. p. 673—681.

43. Grenacher, H., Abhandlungen zur vergleichenden Anatomie des Auges. II. Das Auge der Heteropoden. in: Abh. Halle. 1886.
44. Moseley, H. N., On the presence of Eyes in the Shells of certain Chitonidae etc. in: Quart. Journ. Micr. Sc. Vol. 25. 1885.

Arthropods.

45. Müller, J., Zur Physiologie des Gesichtssinnes. Leipzig 1826.
46. Gottsche, C. M., Beitrag zur Anatomie und Physiol. des Auges der Fliegen und Krebse. Müller's Arch. f. Anat. u. Phys. 1852. p. 483—492.
47. Claparède, E., Morphologie des zusammengesetzten Auges bei den Arthropoden. Zeit. f. w. Zool. 10. Bd. 1860.
48. Leydig, Fr., Lehrbuch der Histologie. 1857. Das Auge der Gliederthiere. Tübingen 1864. Tafeln zur vergleichenden Anatomie. Tübingen 1864.
49. Weismann, A., Die nachembryonale Entwicklung der Musciden. Zeit. f. w. Zool. 14. Bd. 1864.
50. Schultze, M., Untersuchungen über die zusammengesetzten Augen der Krebse und Insecten. Bonn 1868.
51. Exner, S., Über das Sehen von Bewegungen und die Theorie des zusammengesetzten Auges. in: Sitzungsber. Wien. Akad. 72. Bd. 3. Abth. 1875.
52. Leuckart, R., Organologie des Auges. in: Graefe u. Saemisch, Handbuch der gesammten Augenheilkunde. 2. Bd. 1874. 1. Abth. p. 290.
52 a. Brücke, Arch. f. Anat. u. Physiol. 1844. p. 445—451.
52 b Helmholtz, Physiol. Optik. 1867. p. 167—189.
53. Schmidt, O., Die Form der Krystallkegel im Arthropodenauge. in: Zeit. f. w. Zool. 30. Bd. Suppl. 1878. p. 1—12.
54. Grenacher, H., Untersuchungen über das Sehorgan der Arthropoden. Göttingen 1879.
55. Grobben, C., Die Entwicklungsgeschichte von *Moina rectirostris*. Arb. d. Zool. Inst. Wien 1879. 1. Bd.
56. Graber, V., Über das unicorneale Tracheaten- und speciell das Arachnoiden- und Myriapoden-Auge. in: Arch. Mikr. Anat. 17. Bd. 1879. p. 58—94. with 3 Pls.
57. Sograff, N., Vorläufige Mittheilung über die Organisation der Myriapoden. in: Zool. Anz. 2. Jahrg. 1879. p. 16.
58. —— Anatomie von *Lithobius forficatus*. Moskau 1880. 4°. 3 Pl.
59. Grenacher, H., Über die Augen einiger Myriapoden. in: Arch. Mikr. Anat. 18. Bd. 1880. p. 415—467. With 2 Pls.
60. Notthaft, Jul., Über die Gesichtswahrnehmungen mittels des Facettenauges. in: Abh. Senckenberg. Naturf. Ges. 12. Bd. 1880. p. 35—124. T. 1—3.
61. Exner, S., Die Frage der Functionsweise der Facettenaugen. in: Biol. Centralblatt. 1. Bd. 1881—82. p. 272.
62. Lankester, E. Ray and Bourne, A. G., The minute Structure of the Lateral and the Central Eyes of *Scorpio* and of *Limulus*. in: Quart. Journ. Micr. Sc. Vol. 23. 1883.
63. Viallanes, H., Etudes histologiques et organologiques sur les centres nerveux et les organes des sens des animaux articulés. I. Le ganglion optique de la langouste (*Palinurus vulgaris*). Bibliothèque de l'école des Hautes Etudes sect. des Sc. nat. Tome 29. 1884.

II. Le ganglion optique de la Libellule (*Aeschna maculatissima*). Ann. Sc. N. 6) Tome 18. No. 4—6.
64. Ciaccio, V. G., Figure dichiarative della minuta fabbrica degli occhi de'Ditteri. Bologna 1884.
65. Lowne, B. Thompson, On the Compound Vision and the Morphol. of the Eye in Insects. Trans. of Linn. Soc. of London. Vol. 2. Part 11. 1884.
66. Hickson, Sidney, J., The Eye and Optic Tract of Insects. Quart. Journ. Micr. Sc. Vol. 25. 1885.
67. Carrière, J., Einiges über die Sehapparate von Arthropoden. Biol. Centralblatt. 5. Bd. 1885.
68. Exner, S., Über Cylinder, welche optische Bilder entwerfen. in: Arch. Phys. Pflüger. 38. Bd. 1886.
69. Carrière, J., Kurze Mittheilungen aus fortgesetzten Untersuchungen über die Sehorgane. Zool. Anz. 9. Jahrg. No. 217. 1886.

General Works.

70. Blanchard, R., Sur les Chromatophores des Céphalopodes. in: Compt. Rend. Tome 96. p. 655—657.
71. Carrière, J., Die Augen von *Planaria polychroa* etc. Arch. Mikr. Anat. 20. Bd.
72. Claus, C., Über *Charybdea marsupialis*. Arb. Zool. Inst. Wien. 1878. 1. Bd.
73. —— Studien über Polypen und Quallen der Adria. Wien 1877.
74. Haeckel, E., Über die Augen und Nerven der Seesterne. Zeit. f. w. Zool. 10. Bd. 1860.
75. Hamann, O., Nervensystem und Sinnesorgane der Echinodermen. Zeit. f. w. Zool. 39. Bd. 1883.
76. Hertwig, O. u. R., Das Nervensystem und die Sinnesorgane der Medusen. Leipzig 1878.
77. Girod, P., Recherches sur la peau des Cephalopodes. in: Arch. Zool. Expér. (2). Vol. 1. p. 225—266.
78. Greeff, R., Über die pelagische Fauna an den Küsten der Guinea-Inseln. Zeit. f. w. Zool. 42. Bd. 3. Hft. 1885.
79. —— Untersuchungen über die Alciopiden. Nova acta Acad. Leopold. Carol. Vol. 39. 1876.
80. —— Über pelagische Anneliden von der Küste der canarischen Inseln. Zeit. f. w. Zool. 32. Bd.
81. Graber, V., Über die Helligkeits- und Farbenempfindlichkeit einiger Meerthiere. Sitzungs-Ber. Akad. Wien. 91. Bd. 1885.
82. —— Morphologische Untersuchungen über die Augen der freilebenden marinen Borstenwürmer. Arch. f. mikr. Anat. 17. Bd. 1880.
83. Mayer, Paul, Über Farbenwechsel bei Isopoden. in: Mittheil. Zool. Stat. Neapel. 1 Bd. 1879. p. 521—522.
84. Meyer, Ed., Zur Anatomie und Histologie von *Polyophthalmus pictus*. in: Arch. f. mikr. Anat. 21. Bd.
85. Leydig, Fr., Die augenähnlichen Organe der Fische.
86. Sarasin, C. F. und P. B., Über einen mit zusammengesetzten Augen bedeckten Seeigel. in: Zool. Anz. 8. Jahrg. No. 211. 1885.

Explanation of the Plates.

Plate 28.

On the Development of the Eyes of *Pecten opercularis* and *Pecten pusio*.

ag^1.	outer layer of argentea.	l.b.	lateral, or ganglionic, branch of the optic nerve.
ag^2.	inner " " "		
b.b.	basal, or axial, branch of optic nerve.	n.f.	nerve fibres.
		n.r.f.	nuclei of the retinophorae.
b.s.	blood sinus.	o.f.	ophthalmic fold.
c.	cornea.	op.n.	optic nerve.
c.g.	cuticular gland.	pg.	pigment.
c.op.v.	cavity of optic vesicle.	ps.c.	pseudo-cornea.
cp.n.	circumpallial nerve.	r.	retina.
c.t.c.	connective tissue capsule of the eye.	rh.	rods.
		r.m.	rector muscles of the eye.
cu.	cuticular covering of the shell.	r.v.	rete vitrosum.
d.c.c.	inner row of ganglionic cells.	s.	septum.
d.m.	depressor muscles of the eye.	sc.	sclerotica.
		s.c c.	outer layer of ganglionic cells.
E.	Eye.	sh.f.	shell fold of the mantle.
g.c.	ganglionic cells.	s.l.	suspensory ligament.
hy.	hypodermis.	s.pa.	sensory papilla.
hy.c.	hypodermis core of young eye.	t.	tentacle.
i.	iris.	ta.	tapetum.
l.	lens.	v.	velum or velar fold of the mantle.

Fig. 1. Section through the mantle edge of a young *Pecten opercularis* (2 mm long) in the neighborhood of the hinge. The ophthalmic fold is not developed in this region; on the side next the branchial cavity, the wall is thrown into several ciliated folds, *a*, of which the outer is characterized by peculiar tufts of cilia over each cell.

Fig. 2. Section through the median part of the mantle edge of *P. opercularis* (5 mm long). At the summit of the ophthalmic fold is a problematical cell *x*; at *y*, is one of the minute transitional and invaginate eyes.

Fig. 3. Section through the mantle edge, near the hinge, of *P. opercularis* (2 mm long), showing the thickened folds, *a*, on the branchial side of the mantle, and the bilobed ophthalmic fold, *o.f.*

Fig. 4. Section through a young eye of *P. opercularis*, showing the first stages in the development of the optic vesicle, already surrounded by the connective tissue capsule, into the retina, argentea and tapetum. Cam. Hart. obj. 7, oc. IV. tube out.

Fig. 5. Section through a more advanced eye of *P. opercularis*, in which are shown the first traces of the lens, *l*, the thickened retinal layer, *r*, the inner and outer layers of the argentea, ag^1 and ag^2, and the tapetum, *ta*. The iris has made its first appearance as a ring of pigment granules, *i*. Cam. obj. XX. Leitz, oc. III.

Fig. 6. Section through the mantle of *P. varius*, showing a young sensory tentacle, *s.pa*, with the rudiments of the tentacular nerve formed by the proliferation of the hypodermic cells, *x*; at the summit of the papilla is a specially large tuft of sense hairs. The cuticula over the summit of the ophthalmic fold was unusually thick. Cam. Hart. obj. 7, oc. II.

Fig. 7. Section through the mantle edge of *P. opercularis*, showing the development of a tentacle, *t*, between the ophthalmic fold and the eye; *s.pa.*, is a pigmented sense hair papilla which occupies the usual position of the young eyes; *x*, one of the problematical cells which occur at regular intervals along the summit of the ophthalmic fold.

Fig. 8. A pigmented sense hair papilla whose sense cells, *g.c.* are being transformed into ganglionic ones.

Fig. 9. Section through the mantle edge, near the hinge, of a young *P. opercularis*. The ciliated ophthalmic fold has been divided by the tentacle, *t*, into two parts; *a*, thickened ciliated folds on the branchial wall of the mantle.

Fig. 10. Section, at right angles to the edge of the mantle, through an almost complete eye of *P. pusio*. The vitreous network is much thicker than in the adult, and the two layers of the argentea still contain a few flattened nuclei. At *x*, are many remarkable fibres, the remnants of the primitive nerve fibres, fig. 4 *n.f.*, which penetrate the sclerotica and pass up to the rods. Cam. Hart. obj. 5, oc. IV.; tube out 1 in.

Fig. 11. Section through the ophthalmic fold and eye papilla of a young *P. opercularis*. At *hy.* the hypodermis, by proliferation, has given rise to the hypodermic core, which, later, will give rise to the optic vesicle; some of the cells, *g.c.* are separating themselves from the others to form ganglionic cells, which always remain connected with the core by means of nerve fibres. Cam. H. obj. 7, oc. IV.

Fig. 12. Section through the ophthalmic fold of *P. pusio*; the proliferation of the hypodermic cells has given rise to a solid core of cells; mesodermic cells have grown round the core forming the connective tissue capsule, *c.t.c.* Some of the cells of the core have wandered into the underlying tissues to form ganglionic cells, one of which is represented, *g.c.* Cam. H. obj. 7, oc. IV.

Fig. 13. Section, near the hinge, of the mantle edge of a young *P. opercularis*, showing the remarkable modification of the ophthalmic fold into a thick-walled ridge, the cilia having disappeared. Cam. H. obj. 5, oc. IV.

Fig. 14. Section of the ophthalmic fold of a very young *P. opercularis* (1 mm long); the summit of the fold is imperfectly forked and is covered with unusually long cilia; at the base, is a very young optic papilla. The nuclei are scanty at *y*, while at *hy.c.* they are two or three deep, showing the first stages in the formation of an hypodermic core. Cam. H. obj. 7, oc. IV.

Fig. 15. Section through a highly developed fold, similar to those marked *a* in figs. 1, 3 and 9, from the branchial wall of the mantle of a young (2 mm) *P. opercularis*. The cilia are extraordinarily long and their proximal ends are continued as fine lines a long way into the protoplasm. Cam. H. obj. 5, oc. IV.

Fig. 15a A more magnified section of the peripheral part of the thickening, showing the thick and beaded cuticula, containing the pores for the passage of the cilia.

Fig. 16. Section through the ophthalmic fold of a young *P. opercularis*. Showing an optic papilla with a half formed hypodermic core from which some cells are separating themselves to form ganglionic cells, *g.c.* The young eye lies in a pigmented furrow at the base of the fold. Cam. II. obj. 7, oc. IV.

Fig. 17. Section through a nearly perfected eye of *P. opercularis*. All the parts, except the rete vitrosum, are formed; the scattered nerve fibres, which had not united to form an optic nerve, are not represented; at *y* are the small dark bodies found in the fibrous layer at this period, and which ,later' disappear.

Fig. 18. Section through the ophthalmic fold of a very young *P. pusio*, 1 mm long, showing the double-lobed fold, *o.f.*, and the slight thickening, *x*, of the hypodermis to form the first rudiment of the eye; a ganglionic cell, *g.c.* is already separating itself from the hypodermis.

Plate 29.

The Anatomy of the Eye of *Pecten Jacobaeus* and *Pecten varius*.

ag.	argentea.	*l.b.*	lateral branch of the optic nerve.
ag¹.	» outer layer.	*m.b.*	terminal membrane of the retino-
ag².	» inner »		phorae.
ax.f.	axial nerve fibre.	*m.t.*	median teeth of the corneal cells.
b.c.	blood corpuscles.	*n.f.*	nerve fibres.
b.b.	basal branch of optic nerve.	*n.rf.*¹	nuclei of the rod-bearing retino-
b.s.	blood sinus.		phorae.
c.	cornea.	*n.rf.*²	nuclei of the short, pseudo-retin-
c.f.l.	circular fibres of the lens.		ophorae.
cl.	ciliaris.	*op.n.*	optic nerve.
c.m.	circular membrane of the retina.	*ps.c.*	pseudo-cornea.
c.n.f.	circular nerve fibres of the rods.	*ps.rf.*	pseudo-retinophorae.
c.t.c.	connective tissue capsule of the eye.	*S.*	septum.
		rf.	retinophorae.
cu.	cuticula.	*rf.*¹	pseudo-retinophorae.
d.c.c.	inner row of ganglionic cells.	*r.fl.*	radiating nerve fibrillae of the
ex.f.	external nerve fibres of the rods.		rods.
f.rf.	fibrous prolongations of the retinophorae.	*rh.*	rods.
		r.c.	rete vitrosum.
g.c.	ganglionic cells.	*sc.*	sclerotica.
i.	iris.	*s.c.c.*	outer layer of ganglionic cells.
i.t.	inner teeth of the corneal cells.	*s.l.*	suspensory ligament of the lens.
*l.ax.f*¹.	loop of the axial nerve.	*ta.*	tapetum.
*l.ax.f.*²	nerve loop connecting two axial nerves.		

Fig. 19. Section of a fully developed eye of *P. Jacobaeus*, perpendicular to the edge of the mantle.

Fig. 20. A constructed drawing of two rods, from the retina of *P. Jacobaeus*, together with the distal ends of the retinophorae, showing the two inner ganglionic cells, *d.c.c.*, and their fibrous prolongations, *ex.f*, to form the external nerve fibres of the rods; *ax.f.* is the axial nerve fibre of the retinophorae, giving rise, in the rods, to many cross fibrillae. Many of the fibrillae unite to form, in the rod, circular fibrillae around the core; from the circular fibrillae arise other minute fibres, continued outwards to the surface of the rod, where they unite with the smaller branches of the external fibres. The axial fibres are continued through the end of the rod, dividing into the two axial loops, $l.ax.f.^1$ and $l.ax.f.^2$ One loop unites two axial fibres, while the other extends along the external wall of the rod. At x. is a clear vesicle, often present at that point. At the distal ends of the rods the branches of the external nerve fibres unite with each other to form the loops of the external nerve fibres.

Fig. 21. A fragment of the rete vitrosum of *P. Jacobaeus*, treated with hot chromic acid, 55° C. The hexagonal meshes form a kind of crown for each rod; at the confluence of the bars there is a spike, d, which projects a short distance between the rods; b is one of the spikes seen from above; a is a portion of the network beneath the pseudo-retinophorae.

Fig. 22. A flake of rods from the retina of *P. Jacobaeus*, seen from their inner ends; treated with hot chromic acid for one half an hour, at 55° C. One sees the two loops of the axial nerve fibres, and many smaller fibrillae. Cam. homog. ims. obj. 20. Leitz, oc. III.

Fig. 23. Isolated lens from the eye of *P. rarius*, treated for 24 hours in weak sulphuric acid; at a^1 and a^2, one sees two specially well defined rows of circular fibres, and at $s.l.$, the collection of fibres to form the suspensory ligament. The lens is attached to the septal membrane by a nucleated mass of fibres, $l.l.$ and $y.$, many of which extend over the surface of the lens, x; at y are radiating and circular fibres of the outer surface.

Fig. 24. A cross section of a rod from the retina of *P. Jacobaeus*, showing the axial nerve, the radiating and circular fibrillae of the retinidium and the external nerve fibres.

Fig. 25. Cross section through the distal ends of the retinophorae with their axial fibres $ax.f.$ and showing two for the inner ganglionic cells $d.c.c.$ with several nerve fibres on the surface for the retinophorae; $rf.^1$ is one of the very slender, fibre-like retinophorae often found in the retina of *P. Jacobaeus*.

Fig. 26. Cross section through the proximal ends of the rods of *P. Jacobaeus*, showing the axial fibres with the radiating retinidial fibrillae; at x, is a section through the thin, structureless septum, separating the retinophora from its rod.

Fig. 27. A median, cross section through the rods of *P. Jacobaeus*.

Fig. 28. A still deeper cross section, belonging to the same series as that of figs. 26 and 27, through the distal ends of the rods. At $ex.f.$ one sees sections of the loops of the external nerve fibres.

Fig. 29. Section through the outer layer of the argentea, showing the thin membranes composed of minute, square plates with bevelled edges.

Fig. 30. Surface view of a portion of a membrane composing the argentea.

Fig. 31. An isolated, corneal cell of *P. Jacobaeus* with the median teeth $m.t.$, and the inner ones $v.t.$, some of which are drawn out into fibres, x.

Fig. 32. A portion of a retina of *P. Jacobaeus*, isolated entire and seen from the under side; a—d represent successive layers of cells seen by varying the focus; a, the inner layer for the retina; the fibres, with their node-like swellings on the periphery, representing the membrana circularis: the nuclei, circularly arranged, lie just beneath the circular membrane. At b, are the swellings of the pseudo-retinophorae, fig. 38, $n.rf.^2$, containing a nucleus surrounded by a clear space; at c, one sees the two sets of nuclei belonging to the retinophorae. At *d*, the large, circularly arranged peripheral cells of the ganglionic layer, together with the circular fibres of the septum.

Fig. 33. Two isolated cells from the outer ganglionic layer. The end of one is drawn out into many nerve fibres *c.r.* which formed a part of the fibrous layer of the retina; *x* is a ganglionic cell with two fibrous prolongations, *a*, extending towards the rods; the end, *b*, was connected with the ganglionic nerve branch; it gives off two lateral branches which divide into minute fibrillae spread out over, and attached to, the wall of the neighboring cell; *n.f.* is a single nerve fibre, extending from the ganglionic nerve branch to the rods.

Fig. 34. An entire retinophora, from the median part of the retina of *P. Jacobaeus*, with its two nuclei, *a* and *b*, and axial nerve fibres, *ax.f.*

Fig. 35. A short and thin retinophora, from the periphery of the retina of *P. Jacobaeus*.

Fig. 36. Two retinophorae, with nerve fibres from the ganglionic layer, *y*. One of the nerve fibres *n.f.* terminates on the wall of a large retinophora in several fine branches surrounded by a circular one; *b*, is the second nucleus of a very slender retinophora from the median part of the retina. (Macerated in weak sulphuric acid.)

Fig. 37. A detached flake of corneal cells seen from their inner ends, showing the serrated walls, and the circular fibres underlying the cornea. *P. Jacobaeus*.

Fig. 38. Section through the peripheral portion of the retina of *P. Jacobaeus*, showing the continuation of the outer ganglionic layer, beneath the outer edge of the nucleated septum with its circular fibres, to the very edge of the retina; one sees the continuation of the retinophorae with the fibres of the axial nerve branch; the membrana circularis, *c.m.*, the ganglionic cells *g.f.*[1] and *g.f.*[2] with their fibrous prolongation towards the rods, and the rete vitrosum *r.v.*; one also sees the double layered sclerotica, continuous with the septum; and the tapetum and double argentea, continuous with the retina. Through carelessness, the two layers of the sclerotica have been reversed; see Pl. 30, fig. 39.)

Plate 30.

ax.f.
ax.n. } axial nerve fibre.
ag. argentinula of a retinophora.
ag.[1] outer argentea of *Pecten*.
ag.[2] inner »   »   »
bc. bacillus.
b.m. basal membrane.
b.s. blood sinus.
c.c. corneal cuticula of general hypodermis.
c.c.[1] corneal cuticula of the eye.
c.c.c. nerveless cuticular cap of retinula.
cp.n. circumpallial nerve.
cu. cuticular membrane of the shell.
E. eye.

ex.n. external nerve fibres.
in.e. invaginate eye.
fc.e. faceted eye.
gc. ganglionic cell.
l. lens.
nf. nerve fibres.
n.rf. nucleus of retinophora.
n.rf.[1] nucleolated nucleus of the retinophorae.
n.rf.[2] aborted nucleus of the retinophorae.
o.f. ophthalmic fold.
om. ommatidium.
omt. ommateum.
op.n. optic nerve.

r.c.	retinidial cuticula of the general hypodermis.	rt.s.	retinidial sheath.
		r.v.	vitrosum.
r.c.[1]	retinidial cuticula of the eye.	sc.	sclerotica.
rh.	rods.	sc.[1]	outer layer of sclerotica.
rh.[1] and rh.[2],	halves of the rod.	sc.[2]	inner » » »
rf.	retinophorae.	sh.f.	shell fold of the mantle.
rt.	retinulae.	sl.c.	slime cells.
rt.[1]	outer retinula.	ta.	tapetum.
rt.[2]	inner retinula.	v.	velum.
r.t.	retia terminalia.	v.b.	vitreous body.

Fig. 39. Section through the tapetum, argentea and double layered sclerotica of *P. Jacobaeus*; one sees the problematical fibres (degenerate nerve fibres?) with the spindle-shaped swelling in the sclerotica. The inner layer of the argentea contains a degenerate nucleus.

Fig. 40. A detached, peripheral piece of the septum of *P. Jacobaeus*, showing the fibrous-like projections upon its inner surface, a.

Fig. 41. A portion of the anterior mantle edge of *Arca barbata*, showing the compound eyes situated in the triangular, pigmented areas; the latter also contain a number of isolated ommatidia. Four of the eyes are united to form two pairs. The single, as well as the double, eyes are situated in slight depressions, represented by the light rings, upon the summits of gentle elevations.

Fig. 42. Section through an invaginate eye of *Arca barbata*. The double-layered cuticula c.c. and r.c. is continued over the retineum, where the retinidial layer, r. c., becomes greatly thickened to form the retinidial layer, r.c.[1] of the eye. This layer, r.c.[1], is not distinctly divided into segments, or rods, for each cell. One may follow the nerve fibres of the retinidial layer between the cells, and through the basal membrane, b.m. Below the retineum are several slime cells, sl.c.

Fig. 43. Section through the ophthalmic fold of *Arca barbata*, showing a facetted eye, omt., and immediately below it, an invaginated one.

Fig. 44. A highly magnified eye of *Arca Noae*. The dark circles represent the colorless retinophorae, through which one sees the black pigment of the inner row of cover cells. The refractive, lens-like bodies seen on the periphery, are the protuberant rods of the retinophorae.

Fig. 45. Section through the ophthalmic fold and eye of *Pectunculus*. One sees the nuclei of the inner and outer row of retinulae, or cover cells, and the nucleolated ones of the retinophorae, n.rf. The double rods of the retinophorae, rh, are also seen, somewhat shrunken by the reagents, with their inner faces represented either as simple, or double concavities. In this instance some of the fibres had united to form a distinct optic nerve op.n. Blood cavities are specially numerous in those parts of the ophthalmic fold where there are many eyes.

Fig. 46. Surface view of an invaginated eye, in.e., and of isolated ommatidia, om., from the median portion of the mantle edge of *Arca barbata*. The invaginate eye is open and one sees several points of white light issuing from the refractive and colorless globules in the retinophorae. At x. is a group of three or four intensely black pigment cells, which, apparently, do not contain a retinophora. One often finds such clusters of cells in sections, where they are particularly striking; they are often sunken below the surface to form minute pits.

Fig. 47. Represents a nearly colorless portion of the mantle edge of *Arca barbata*, containing two faceted eyes and a nearly closed invaginate one. Around the eyes one sees numerous colorless cells, some of which are double, surrounded by pigment. They represent incipient ommatidia.

Fig. 48. A detached, double rod from the compound eye of *Arca Noae* (macerated in chromic acid $1/50$ %). The division between the two halves of the rod, $rh.^1$ and $rh.^2$, is well marked. To the sides of the rod are attached numerous nerve fibres from which are given off many lateral branches that cling very tenaceously to the surface; the free portions of the fibres are covered with innumerable fibrillae. In this example the loops of the external nerve fibres were not visible.

Fig. 49. A detached pigment cell, with its rod, showing the large, basally situated nucleus, the root-like prolongations of the cells, and the external nerve fibres, $e.x.n.$

Fig. 50. A colorless sense cell (incipient retinophora?) from the epithelium of *Pectunculus*. The cuticula is very slightly developed and can hardly be said to form a rod; the nucleus is nucleolated and the base of the cell is drawn out into a single, long fibre. A nerve fibre, $n.f.$, extends along the wall of the cell, and is free everywhere except at its outer end where it is firmly attached to the cell wall.

Fig. 51. A peculiar, hyaline structure, which I have observed several times among the isolated cells from the eyes and ophthalmic fold of *Arca Noae*; I cannot offer any suggestion as to its nature or origin.

Fig. 52. A nearly fresh retinophora (macerated for twenty four hours in MÜLLER's fluid) from the compound eye of *Arca Noae*. It is a very instructive example, in that it shows with great clearness that the retinophora is composed of two cells, the outer ends of which remain ununited; the rods belonging to the halves are likewise perfectly distinct; in each half of the cell is a nucleus, that marked $n.rf.^2$ is the smaller, and more difficult to stain.

Fig. 53. An isolated pigment cell from the general epithelium of *Pectunculus*; two long and comparatively large, nerve fibres are attached to the outer end of the cell.

Fig. 54. A section through one of the pseudo-lenticulate eyes of *Arca Noae*. In this example the retineum is quite deeply invaginated; in other cases it is perfectly flat or nearly so.

Fig. 55. Section through the mantle edge of *Pectunculus*.

Fig. 56. Section through the mantle edge of *Arca Noae*, showing the prominent ophthalmic fold, $o.f.$, upon the summit of which is situated a compound eye.

Fig. 57. A section of the mantle edge of *Arca barbata*, showing a portion of the epithelium, highly magnified, with the retia terminalia of hypodermic nerve fibres.

Fig. 58. Section through the eye of *Haliotis*. The double layered cuticula has, over the retineum, divided into two very distinct layers; an inner one, $rh.$, divided into distinct segments, or rods, containing a highly developed part of the retia terminalia; and a second, outer layer, formed by the thickened corneal cuticula; the corneal layer is divided into two secondary parts, a semi-fluid inner portion, the vitreous body, $c.b.$, and a harder, outer portion, or lens, *l*. At *x*. one sees a layer of minute, lightly stained bodies which may represent the swollen outer ends of the retinophorae (fig. 67).

Fig. 59. A constructed drawing of an ommatidium from the faceted eye of *Arca Noae*. One sees the double retinophora, containing two nuclei, and bearing two rods provided with a network of external nerve fibres, some of which form distinct, external loops, *ex.f.*, as in *Pecten*. At the base of the cell are the refractive globules, *ag.*, forming an argentinula; within the cell, the axial nerve fibres, *ax.f.* The retinulae of the inner row are continued outwards as hyaline membranes, *rt.s.*, to form a retinidial sheath. The retinulae of the outer row are continued inwards as colorless stalks or bacilli, *bc*.

Fig. 60. An isolated retinula from the inner row, showing its colorless prolongation, *rt.s.*, and the system of external nerve fibres, *n.f.*, with which it is covered. The system of lateral fibrillae, similar to those seen on fig. 63, has not been represented by the lithographer.

Fig. 61. A fragment of the retinidium, fig. 63, *x.*, more highly magnified, and showing the continuity of the ultimate fibrillae.

Fig. 62. An isolated retinula from the retinenum of *Haliotis*. Cam. II. obj. 7, oc. III.

Fig. 63. The outer end of a retinula of *Haliotis*; the cuticular substance of the rod has been dissolved by treatment with glycerine and bichromate of potash, leaving the entire system of nerve fibrillae intact, *x.*; the fibrillae of the remaining nerve branches have not been represented. The length of the unbranched nerve stalks has been, for convenience, reduced to one half.

Fig. 64. A portion of the epithelium from the mantle edge of *Arca barbata*, showing the extension of some of the larger nerve branches *n.f.* to the very outer surface of the cuticula; the lateral fibrillae of these nerves may also be seen. Cam. obj. 20, Leitz, oc. III.

Fig. 65. The inner end of a bacillus, belonging to a retinula of *Haliotis* (compare fig. 68 *bc.*), surrounded by several nerve branches, *n.f.*, all of which are not represented in the figure.

Fig. 66. An isolated retinophora (*Haliotis*) with the two nuclei *n.rf.*[1] and *n.rf.*[2]; a remarkably instructive preparation since in this instance the outer end of the cells is divided into two stalks, *x.*, which represent the unfused ends of the two primitive cells, by the union of which the retinophora was formed; the body of the cell contains many refractive globules, *ag.*, similar to those which form the argentinula in *Arca*. Cam. obj. 20, Leitz, oc. III.

Fig. 67. The most common form of retinophora, from *Haliotis*, containing two nuclei, but with the outer end of the cell single instead of double. Cam. obj. 20, Leitz, oc. III.

Fig. 68. Two retinulae from the retina of *Haliotis*; only a part of the rod, *rh.*, with its constricted neck, is represented. At *ge.* is a retinula partly transformed into a ganglionic cell, but still retaining some of its pigment.

Plate 31.

ag.	argentea.	*c.c.*	crystalline cone.
ax.b.	axial nerve bundle.	*bc.*[1]—*bc.*[2]	bacilli of pigment cells *pg.*[1]—[2].
ax.f.	» » fibre.	*b.m.*	basal membrane.

$b.pg.^{1-2}$	bacilli of pigment cells $pg.^{1-2}$.	$n.rt.$	nuclei of the retinulae.
$c.^{1}$	outer layer of corneal cuticula.	$o.pg.^{1}-o.pg.^{2}$	hyaline, outer continuations of pigment cells $pg.^{1-2}$.
$c.^{2}$	inner » » » »		
$c.h.$	corneal hypodermis.	$pg.$	pigment.
$c.ax.f.$	canal of axial nerve fibre.	$pg.^{1-3}$	three circles of pigment cells.
$c.f.$	circular fibres around the openings in the basal membrane.	$pg.c.$	pigmented collar of the calyx.
		$pd.$	pedicel.
$c.t.f.$	connective tissue fibres.	$p.pl.$	primary plates of the pedicel.
$d.$	median division in corneal facet.	$r.m.^{1-2}$	retractor muscles.
$d.b.$	diagonal bar of basal membrane.	$rm.$	retinidial nerve fibrillae.
$d.f.$	divisions between corneal facets.	$rt.$	retinulae.
$ex.n.f.$	external nerve fibres.	$rt.s.$	retinidial sheath.
$g.c.$	ganglionic cells.	$s.^{1-7}$	hyaline, outer ends of cells $^{1, 2, 3, 4, 5, 6}$ and ^{7}.
$l.$	lens.		
$n.c.$	neck of the calyx.	$st.$	style of the retinophorae.
$n c.h.$	nuclei of corneal hypodermis cells.	$se.pl.$	secondary plates of the pedicel.
		$st.pl.$	stalk of the pedicel.
$n.f.$	nerve fibres.	$tr.$	tracheal branch.
$n.rf.$	nuclei of retinophorae (SEMPER's nuclei).	$w.rf.$	cell wall of the retinophorae.
		$1-7$	seven retinulae of *Penaeus*.

Fig. 69. Outer end of an ommatidium of *Penaeus*; $x.$, is a peculiar shaped accumulation of thickened cell substance in which are imbedded the nuclei of the retinophorae; $y.$ clear, refractive bodies often found in the outer row of pigment cells.

Fig. 70. A piece of the style of the retinophorae, containing the axial nerve fibre (*Penaeus*).

Fig. 71. The same with the external fibres.

Fig. 72. Longitudinal section through the pedicel of the retinophorae, showing the alternating plates with the fibres at right angles to each other; the pedicel rests upon the basal membrane by a delicate stalk which divides into four legs, representing the inner ends of the retinophorae. Only the scalloped and median retinula, 1, is represented (*Penaeus*).

Fig. 73. Two entire ommatidia from the eye of *Penaeus*, showing the proportion of the different parts; especially the small size of the pedicel and enormous dimensions of the crystalline cone. At $x.$ is a zone of coagulated semi-fluid substance.

Fig. 74. The inner end of a pedicel showing, in a semi-diagrammatic way, the positions of the seven retinulae.

Fig. 75. Inner surface of the corneal cuticula, treated with boiling caustic potash, showing the divisions between, and the markings upon, the corneal facets; y probably represent the fibrous ends of or the markings produced by, the circle of cells surrounding the inner ends of the ommatidia (fig. 73, $y.$; $x.$ is a peculiar indentation always present in the centre of the facet; $d.$ is a very faint line of division always corresponding with the line of division between the two corneal cells of each facet.

Fig. 76. Represents a portion of the inner face of the cornea to which the outer ends of the ommatidial cells are attached. In the area above, I, are seen the two nuclei of the corneal cells, $c.h.$, and the ends of the four retinophorae with their nuclei, $n.rf.$; below III, only the two corneal cells with their nuclei are represented; the four armed figures, $rt.s.$, represent various views of the hyaline, outer ends of the inner circle of retinulae, 1—7.

Fig. 77. Is an enlarged drawing of the outer ends of the retinulae $1-7$; at I, the membranous sheath is seen projected upon the figure, $s.^2-s.^4$; at II. the tube is beginning to break up into its component parts; at II'. this process is completed and we see only the seven outer, and isolated ends of the seven pigment cells which help constitute one of the membranous tubes (compare $rt.s.$ fig. 79 etc.); $s.^1-^7$ represent the outer ends of the inner circle of retinulae, fig. 74 etc. $1-7$; $s.^1-s.^2$ represents a single (?) piece the outer end of the large median retinula 1.

Fig. 78. A section through the pigmented collar of four ommatidia. At the corner $III.$, $II'.$ and $I'.$ representing a section through the inner portion of the collar, only the two cells $pg.^1$ and $pg.^2$ have pigment, while only the colorless bacilli $bc.^1-^2$ of the other two are seen; at II. the section is supposed to pass through the middle of the collar, where both circles of cells are well pigmented.

Fig. 79. Section of an ommatidium of *Penaeus* just below the collar, showing the pigmented prolongations of the two inner pigment cells $pg.^2$. Each ommatidium is surrounded by sixteen of these bacilli, but only four belong to one ommatidium, e. g., 1, 2, 3 and 4. Each bundle of bacilli is surrounded by a membranous sheath, $rt.s.$

Fig. 80. Cross section of the ommatidia (*Penaeus*), towards the inner ends of the rods, showing the two sickle-shaped thickenings of the walls of the retinophorae $x.$; these thickenings are striated, and contain horizontal nerve fibrillae.

Fig. 81. Cross section of ommatidia (*Penaeus*) below the rods.

Fig. 82—88. Represent a series of cross sections taken at intervals from the inner end of the calyx fig. 82, to the inner end of the style fig. 88, all the sections are placed in the same direction.

Fig. 89—92. Represent four successive sections through the swollen ends of the seven retinulae: all the sections are placed in the same direction, and the cells are numbered like those of fig. 74.

Fig. 93. Cross section through the middle of the pedicel, showing the arrangement of the seven retinulae, and the markings of the two systems of plates.

Fig. 94. Cross section through the inner end of a pedicel, passing through one of the primary plates; at this end of the pedicel one sees the axial nerve fibre exceptionally well.

Fig. 95. Still deeper section of the pedicel, passing through a secondary plate, as is shown by the direction of the fibres. The dotted area around the retinulae in figs. 95—101, is occupied by a circle of cells, fig. 74 $y.$, which are completely filled with fat-like crystals, not represented in the drawing.

Fig. 96—100. Represent successive sections through the retinulae surrounding the the stalk of the pedicel; one sees that the two pairs of bacilli, $bc.^1$ and $bc.^2$, gradually move from the opposite sides of the ommatidia towards each other, one also sees, with especial clearness, the nerve fibres which surround each section of the bacilli.

Fig. 101. A section of an ommatidium, just above the basal membrane; the retinulae have separated themselves from the stalk of the pedicel, but their general arrangement is the same as before. One sees a few fibres, near $bc.^1$ and $bc.^2$, belonging to the outer part of the diagonal bar of the basal membrane.

Fig. 102. A diagrammatic representation of an imaginary primary and secondary plate of the pedicel, by a modification of which, the actual plates, as they exist in *Penaeus*, could have arisen; the dotted line, *a*, represents the change necessary to transform the flat plates into ones like those seen in figs. 103 and 104.

Fig. 103. A diagram of a primary plate; the fibres extend from *a*. to *b*.; at *a*. should be an indentation to receive a fold of the pigment cell, *1*. (compare figs. 72 and 93).

Fig. 104. A diagram of a secondary plate; the fibres extend from *c*. to *d*., therefore at right angles to those of fig.103; each plate is divided into two parts by four planes which form an angle, the apex of which lies in the middle of each side of the plate, but is directed in one way on one side, and in the opposite direction upon the other; each piece (not strictly a half) then consists of four smaller and equivalent, but not identical pieces, for the two upper ones are i m a g e s of the two lower, while the two right hand pieces are bevelled on one side, and the two left hand pieces on the opposite. Therefore of the eight pieces composing such a plate only two of any of the four kinds are identical.

Fig. 105. Diagram of two primary and two secondary plates of the pedicel of *Penaeus*.

Fig. 106. Diagram of the basal membrane of *Penaeus*, seen from the upper surface. Each cross is a thickening in the membrane, and lies directly beneath an ommatidium; the axial nerve of each ommatidium penetrates the centre of each cross. Each cross, and therefore each ommatidium, has a capital letter while the ends of the seven retinulae are marked with small letters similar to the large letter of the cross to which they belong. At *E*. and *H*. the unseparated retinulae are projected upon the cross to which they belong (compare figs. 97—100'; in all other cases the retinulae have taken their respective positions in the corners of the square spaces or holes separating the crosses.

Fig. 107. Four crosses of the basal membrane of *Penaeus*, seen from the under side; to the centre of each cross are attached several connective tissue fibres *c.t.c.* In one corner of each cross is a shallow pit, into the bottom of which opens the canal for the axial nerve, *c.a.c.f.*

Fig. 108. Diagrammatic representation of the retinulae, the bacilli, and the nerve fibres, of each ommatidium; the continuation of the cells below the basal membrane represents the bundle of nerve fibres which goes to the base of each cell. The drawing represents an imaginary section of the diagram fig. 106, through the points *x*. and *y*. The cells and their nerve fibres are lettered to correspond with fig. 106.

Fig. 109. A diagrammatic section of the nerve bundle going to the openings II. and III. of the basal membrane represented in fig. 106. (Compare the letters of these two nerve bundles with those of figs. 108 and 106, II. and III.

Fig. 110. Highly magnified and partly diagrammatic view of a basal membrane cross with the ends of the retinulae and bacilli upon it.

Fig. 111. Inner end of an isolated bacillus with the surrounding nerve fibres.

Fig. 112. Longitudinal section through the tentacle-tip of *Cardium edule*.

Fig. 113. Less highly magnified tentacle of *C. edule*, showing the pigmented cap at the tip, and the lateral fold *x*.

Fig. 114. Corneal facets of *Galathea*, to one of which are attached the corneal cells which constitute a kind of iris; the centrally situated nuclei are surrounded by a fold, which can probably be modified in shape by the radiating fibres; the latter are attached to a thickened ring, x., at the periphery of the cells; at a., is a simple facet with a median division; the corneal cells have been removed (fresh).

Fig. 115. Corneal facets of *Palaemon*, seen from inner surface (maceration in MÜLLER's fluid). The outer ends of the four retinophorae and their nuclei are seen at $n.rf.$; in each facet are two small nuclei belonging to the corneal cells; the light colored bars probably represent the thickened, outer ends of the inner row of retinulae. (Compare figs. 76 and 77 s. and $r.ts$.)

Fig. 116. Seven corneal facets of *Galathea*; the middle one is remarkable on account of the distinctness with which it is divided into two halves, the line corresponding to the division between the two corneal cells.

Fig. 117. Strongly macerated pedicel of *Palaemon*, showing its continuity with the inner end of the style which has separated into four pieces.

Fig. 118. Two ommatidia from the eye of *Mantis*, the right hand one is seen in section, and the other in surface view.

Fig. 119. Cross section through the middle of the calyx of *Mantis*; the axial walls of the four cells are seen at x.; within each cell is a bundle of large nerve fibres from which arise innumerable lateral fibrillae which undoubtedly stand in direct continuity with the longitudinal fibres upon the outer surface of the calyx, $w.rf.$; the four retinophorae are surrounded by a delicate membranous sheath, $rt.s.$

Fig. 120. Cross section of the calyx of *Mantis*, just above the pigment cell, pg^3, fig. 118.

Fig. 121. Section through the calyx of *Mantis* at the level of the pigment cell, $pg.^3$ fig. 118. One sees six nuclei of the yellowish brown cells, $pg.^2$, fig. 118; the axial walls of the four retinophorae are reduced to a single, median one.

Fig. 122. Section through the neck of the calyx of three ommatidia from *Mantis*. One sees with distinctness that the style contains a bundle of f o u r a x i a l nerves.

Fig. 123. Section of three ommatidia (*Mantis*) just below $pg.^3$ fig. 118, and through the outer ends of the three longest retinulae. (Compare fig. 89.)

Fig. 124. Section through an ommatidium, showing the seven retinulae surrounding the style which contains an axial nerve bundle of four fibres; the outer wall of the style is surrounded by six nerve fibres.

Fig. 125. Section through the inner end of an ommatidium; the cell wall of the retinulae cannot be distinguished; the pigment is only confined to a narrow circle around the style. Around the retinulae are sections of seven or eight bacilli belonging to the pigment cell, $pg.^1, ^{2-3}$ fig. 118. One cannot distinguish at this point the division of the axial bundle into four fibres; around the bundle are six nerve fibres.

Fig. 126. Cross section through the outer part of the basal membrane of *Mantis*, showing the nucleated connective-tissue walls surrounding the canals, through which passes a nerve bundle to each ommatidium.

Fig. 127. Longitudinal section through the basal membrane of *Mantis*; the inner boundary of the membrane is much denser than the remaining parts, and might easily be mistaken for a basal membrane, while the outer canallated portion might be mistaken for a part of the ommateum.

Fig. 128. Highly magnified section through the outer end of the style and neck of the calyx, showing the sheath, $rt.s.$ and the axial nerve bundle from which arise numerous lateral fibrillae.

Eyes of Molluscs and Arthropods. 755

Fig. 129. Outer end of one of the crystalline cone cells (retinophora), isolated by maceration, showing the system of external nerve fibres (*Palaemon*).
Fig. 130. The same seen from the abaxial surface.
Fig. 131. Style of *Palaemon* (macerated), with the external nerve fibres.
Fig. 132. Same seen in optical section, showing axial nerve with lateral fibrillae.

Plate 32.

ax.n.	axial nerve.	$pg.^{1,2,3}$	first, second and third circle of pigment cells.
bc.	bacillus.		
b.m.	basal membrane.	*rf.*	retinophorae.
c.c.	corneal cuticula.	$rf.^{1}$	innermost ends of crystalline cone cells, or retinophorae.
c.c.c.	crystalline cone cells.		
c.hy.	corneal hypodermis.	*rh.*	rod, or crystalline cone.
ex.n.	external nerve fibres.	*rt.*	retinula.
g.c.	ganglionic cells.	$rt.^{1,2,3}$	hyaline continuation of the retinulae.
n.f.	nerve fibres.		
n.rf.	nuclei of retinophorae.	*st.*	style of the retinophorae, or crystalline cone cells.
$n.rf.^{1}$	nucleolated nucleus of retinophorae.		
		v.l.	vitreous cell layer.
$n.rf.^{2}$	aborted nucleus of retinophorae.	*v.b.*	vitreous body.
pd.	pedicel.	*v.*	crystalline cone, or vitrella.
pg.	pigment cells.		

These diagrams show, among other things, ommatidia and ocelli in various stages of modification. They are drawn partly according to the observations of GRENACHER, LANKESTER, GRABER and CARRIÈRE, and partly according to my own. Where direct observations were wanting, the ommatidia and ocelli were constructed according to deductions from my own observations.

Fig. 128. Diagram of an ommatidium, with the corneal facet and its cells, from a compound Arthropod eye. The pedicel, walls of the retinophorae and the style have been drawn in red for the sake of clearness, in all other cases the red indicates nerve fibres; *x.* is the refractive division between adjacent facets; *a.* that between the halves of each facet; *y.* thickening of abaxial wall of calyx, often, but not always, present; the crystalline cone may be present or absent, but it can never fuse with the facet, as is supposed to be the case in *Lampyris*.

Fig. 128a and 128b are cross sections through the calyx and middle of the style, respectively.

Fig. 129. An ommatidium from a compound eye, constructed according to GRENACHER's statements; he does not recognize the corneal hypodermis, and separates the eye into two layers at $bm.^{1}$; the dotted line, *y.*, shows the position of the crystalline cone when it appears to be absent. 129a is a cross section of the retinulae, showing the seven (or four) rods which they are supposed to secrete.

Fig. 130. One of the isolated ommatidia from the general hypodermis of a Mollusc.
Fig. 131. Two ommatidia from a vertebrate retina (without the outer ganglionic layers). 131a, is a cross section of the rods.
Fig. 132. Ommatidium from a Molluscan retineum.
Fig. 133. Ommatidium from the compound eye of *Arca* or *Pectunculus*; the retinulae $pg.^{1-2}$ have lost their rods, as is the case in all the succeeding diagrams, and serve only to protect the rod of the retinophorae or become transformed into ganglionic cells.
Fig. 134. Ommatidium, with an overlying portion of the vitreous layer, corneal hypodermis and corneal lens, from a larval insect ocellus.

50*

Fig. 135. Same, with cross section, from the anterior ocellus of a spider.
Fig. 136. The same, from ocellus of *Scorpio*.
Fig. 137. The same, from posterior ocellus of a Spider.
Fig. 138. The same, from the compound eye of Insects and Crustacea.
Fig. 139. Two retinophorae from the retina of Cephalopods, with the ganglionic cell $g.c.$, producing the external fibres of the rods, and the axial nerve fibres, $ax.n.$; the body of the retinophora (or retinal cell of GRENACHER), contains two nuclei.
Fig. 140. Two retinophorae with their ganglionic cells, from the retina of *Pecten*, showing the loops of the axial, and external, nerves of the rods, the two nuclei of the retinophorae, and five characteristic forms of ganglionic cells; $b.m.$ basal membrane or septum of the eye; $x.$ a nerve fibre terminating on the small ganglionic cell $g.c.^5$; $z.$ and $y.$ two methods of nerve endings upon the cell wall of the retinophorae.
Fig. 141. Ancestral Arthropod eye.
Fig. 142. Eye of *Peripatus*. (Modified from CARRIÈRE.)
Fig. 143. Ocellus of Myriapod.
Fig. 144. Same of larval Insect.
Fig. 145. Ocellus of *Scorpio*; only one ommatidium is represented.
Fig. 146. Posterior ocellus of Spiders.
Fig. 147. Diagram of compound eye, constructed according to GRENACHER.
Fig. 148. Diagram of compound eye to illustrate its origin at a modified single ocellus (compare fig. 146).
Fig. 149. Diagram of the eye of *Pecten* to show the formation of a second image over the first; the rays of light from $a.b.$ form a curved, inverted image upon the layer of rods, $x.y.$; but the rays of light diverging from $x.y.$ are reflected by the curved mirror $ag.$ (the argentea), and come again to a focus at $x.y.$; with the microscope one sees the less distinct, second image at $x.y.^1$.
Fig. 150—152. Three drawings to show the supposed method by which the eyes of *Pecten* originated; fig. 150 an open cup, the retineum of which consists of rodless retinulae, arranged in two layers, $pg.^1{-}^2$, and of colorless and double retinophorae. Fig. 152, the cup has closed, and the anterior wall of the vesicle has become most highly developed, while the rods of the posterior wall, $rh.^1$, nearly disappear; the basal membrane, fig. 150, $b.m.^1$ forms the septum. Fig. 152, some of the nerve fibres have united to form two branches, those which supplied the floor of the primitive cup remain isolated $n.f.^1$ and probably give rise to the fibres, with spindle-shaped swellings, which penetrate the sclerotica, and tapetum; Pl. 30, fig. 39, $x.$; the rods of the posterior wall of the optic vesicle form the vitreous network of the adult, $v.r.$
Fig. 153. Diagram representing the transformation of a neuro-epithel cell, $b.$, with its nervous prolongation, $x.$, into a bipolar ganglionic one, $e.$, and finally into a multipolar ganglionic one $f.^1$ and $f.^2$; $a.$, is a myo-epithel cell with its root-like and radiating fibres which unite to form a basal membrane; $c.c.$ is the corneal cuticula, and $r.c.$ the retinidial cuticula, containing the retia terminalia of the hypodermic nerves; $g.$, and $h.$, represent modifications of hypodermic cells, with their retia terminalia, to form the ommatidia of an invaginate and compound Molluscan eye.

www.ingramcontent.com/pod-product-compliance
Lightning Source LLC
Chambersburg PA
CBHW020823230426
43666CB00007B/1084